Defining Statesmanship

Defining Statesmanship

A Comparative Political Theory Analysis

Clyde Ray

LEXINGTON BOOKS
Lanham • Boulder • New York • London

Published by Lexington Books
An imprint of The Rowman & Littlefield Publishing Group, Inc.
4501 Forbes Boulevard, Suite 200, Lanham, Maryland 20706
www.rowman.com

6 Tinworth Street, London SE11 5AL

British Library Cataloguing in Publication Information Available

Library of Congress Control Number: 2019953038

ISBN: 978-1-7936-0374-6 (cloth)
ISBN: 978-1-7936-0376-0 (pbk)
ISBN: 978-1-7936-0375-3 (electronic)

For my parents,
Clyde and Doris Ray

Contents

Introduction

The Enduring Importance of Statesmanship

Tuesday, November 8, 2016: Election Day in the United States. With sighs of relief and exasperation, citizens across the nation dutifully stream into voting booths to cast their votes after a presidential campaign that proved to be in equal measures acrimonious and dispiriting. Presented with the choice of either Republican candidate Donald J. Trump or Democratic candidate Hillary Clinton, many Americans fell back on the familiar refrain of being forced to choose between the lesser of two evils among the contenders for the highest office in the nation. Indeed, for many of those jaded with American politics as usual, the motives of the major parties' nominees were written off as inauthentic at best and deceitful at worst.[1] Nonetheless, an anxious public watched as the results rolled in: the electoral votes of the states of Ohio, Florida, then dramatically those of Pennsylvania, Wisconsin, and Michigan all fell to Trump, assuring his surprise victory. Amid the shocked anguish and lusty cheers, however, any unity of purpose directed toward the common welfare seemed to be drowned out. And since that fateful evening, the volume of the cacophony has only been turned up. Little during the Trump Presidency has transpired to mend partisan divisions in the country, nor have subsequent government shutdowns, battles over Supreme Court nominees, and congressional investigations diminished the widespread belief that public servants just aren't built like they once were.

Beyond this point agreement usually ends. Indeed, the political heroes many Americans long for are often as sharply polarized as their political beliefs. Today, most Democrats yearn for the halcyon days of President Barack Obama and his administration's promise of hope, change, and transformational leadership. In contrast, many Trump-supporting Republicans believe that strong leadership is finally on the scene, while a smaller number of conservatives pine after the principled conservatism of Ronald Reagan or even George W. Bush, longing for a return to standards of moral decency or smaller government. Setting aside the revisionist history implicit in most objects of nostalgia, however, what brings together these groups is a shared concern for a kind of leadership that now appears to be in short supply from any political vantage point. We are united in our wistfulness for a mythic bygone era when partisanship and self-dealing took a backseat to far-sighted leadership that appealed, in the famous words of Abraham Lincoln, "to the better angels of our nature."

Rest assured, our attraction to great (or even adequate) political leadership is not new. From ancient Greece and Rome to the present, civilizations have always looked up to the example or possibility of individuals that, through their exceptional abilities and vision alone, have the power to ameliorate if not cure many social ills. This is not altogether surprising: the past usually exerts a powerful pull on the human as well as political imagination, as Trump's successful promotion of his promise to make America great "again" indicates. Call it a collective messiah complex, our streak of utopianism, a cry of desperation in moments of political crises: whatever its provenance, the concept of statesmanship seems embedded deep inside our political DNA.

What is statesmanship? Invisible as time, it is an idea as old as politics itself. Yet as much as the idea has been invoked, its definition is not very easy to pin down. There is no generally accepted set of terms that go beneath the label. As Wilfred McClay has recently put it, "the skill of statesmanship is always a tricky, elusive matter—hard to come by, hard to measure, and hard even to define or describe."[2] In this respect, it is not unlike most concepts political theorists work with—liberty, virtue, sovereignty—whose meanings shift over the course of history. For the moment, we may posit that statesmanship is a particular excellence in political leadership that relates to cultivating and promoting the public good, broadly conceived.[3] This is a reasonable definition, but by itself cries out for the kind of elaboration indulged by political writers since time immemorial. Thinkers such as Plato, Aristotle, and Xenophon idealized statesmanship as a political leader's ability to mold the character of a people along the lines of the classical virtues, guiding them through life's contingencies using a mixture of persuasion and force.[4] The ultimate object of such leadership was not left open-ended, however, but rather sought to promote both the ideal citizen and person by inspiring individuals to transcend their immediate material desires.[5] Just as a physician uses his or her expert knowledge to promote the health of his or her patient, so the analogy goes in Plato's *Statesman*, the statesman's art is concerned with supervising and nurturing the health of the city and its members.[6] Relocating these ideas from Athens to Rome, orators such as Cicero took a more restrained but not markedly different approach to statesmanship, typically grounding ideas of good leadership in the more severe virtues of temperance and fortitude while taking seriously the leader's role as caretaker of Roman laws, customs, and morality.[7]

Ancient Greece and Rome were arguably statesmanship's high-water mark. In the Middle Ages, the importance of virtuous leadership continued to be defended primarily by religious thinkers such as Thomas Aquinas,[8] John of Salisbury,[9] and Desiderius Erasmus,[10] even as traditional preconceptions regarding statesmanship were soon challenged and undermined by the daring interventions of thinkers such as Marsilius of Padua and Niccolò Machiavelli. Thanks to the religious controversies of the era, the ethical dimension of statesmanship, its formative influence over citizen character, was eclipsed by more practical considerations. With stops and starts along the way, the loosening of the political leader's grip on authority continued into the modern era, with the rise of institutional checks and balances, equality, privacy, and the rule of law conspiring to render leadership concerned with either the moral or civic development of citizens obsolete.[11] By the early eighteenth century, the Dutch philosopher Bernard Mandeville spoke for many in declaring that "[a]s to consummate Statesmen, I don't believe that there ever were three Persons upon Earth, at the same time, that deserv'd that Name. There is not a quarter of the Wisdom, solid Knowledge, or intrinsick Worth, in the world, that men talk of, and compliment one another with."[12] His skeptical view was shared by many other leading intellectual lights of the time, including the drafters of the American Constitution. Justifying the document's ability to adjust "clashing interests" through an almost mechanical system of divided authority and shared powers, the chief architect of the Constitution, James Madison, was famously unequivocal in his defense of the framers' work: "Enlightened statesmen will not always be at the helm."[13]

In the contemporary era, the tide of statesmanship has continued to recede. To be sure, we can name many exemplars of transformative political leadership in recent memory, such as Winston Churchill,[14] Charles De-Gaulle,[15] Margaret Thatcher,[16] or Nelson Mandela.[17] But the truth is that such figures are glaring exceptions to the rule, bright stars made all the more lustrous by their rarity in our otherwise gloomy political firmament. Traditional understandings and responsibilities belonging to statesmanship have long been stripped away, and consequently clear definitions applicable to the present day are hard to come by. This scarcity has resulted in a curious phenomenon: a term once rich in meaning has now become rather impressionistic, resulting in detailed analyses of theories of administrative statesmanship, judicial statesmanship, and even international statesmanship.[18] In light of such wide variation, perhaps it is best to pause abstract definitions— we have too much of that in our politics anyway—and see what concrete examples may be able to teach us about this popular but also fugitive idea.

But if historical examples allow a better grip on this old and elusive idea, is such rehabilitation actually desirable? Whether in its ancient, modern, or contemporary formulations, political theorists have mostly assigned statesmanship to the dustbin of history.[19] Democratic theorists have denied it any role in their defenses of liberal democratic government, arguing that political leadership is best left to the people themselves. Rather than extolling individual leadership, many such authors find it more fulfilling to seek the will of the people through ever more byzantine democratic procedures and institutions.[20] For the quintessential liberal philosopher John Rawls, all persons in a liberal democracy should be treated as reasonable agents with political offices open to mostly everyone, a commitment that seems to foreclose the possibility of citizens in possession of a superior political acumen worthy of acknowledgment, let alone reverence.[21] Or, in the political theorist Robert Dahl's imagery, statesmanship intimates a form of quasi-Platonic guardianship whose tutelage jars with commitments to equality and popular sovereignty.[22] For their part, postmodern theorists such as Richard Rorty have denied the possibility of any sublime idea of the good society that a political leader might promote.[23] More recently, Benjamin Barber has summed up the consensus, arguing that statesmanship embodies a form of "aristocratic rationalism" that has had a negative influence on democratic politics: "strong leaders," he concludes, "have on the whole made Americans weak citizens."[24]

Such critiques are not entirely unwarranted. Writing in the aftermath of the dire consequences of autocratic rule during the twentieth century, polemics against statesmanship dispense a salutary tonic to any cult of personality associated with political leadership. Certainly, citizens must be vigilant about the facile but always dangerous temptation to transfer or lay down civic obligations, a caution that today should be all the more keenly felt as we cast about for individuals who might solve intractable global problems through the sheer exertion of willpower alone. Ultimately, vigilance continues to be the price of liberty. But if we simply belittle or ignore the admittedly old-fashioned topic of statesmanship, will that make the concept disappear?[25]

My answer is no. Indeed, disavowing the importance of good political leadership is not without particular dangers for republican governments, including our own.[26] It is true that, following Madison's caveat, the constitutional government the framers designed was created to make the need for individual leadership less important than it had been in the past. But neither was the Constitution intended to eliminate concern for the character of citizens and democratic leadership. Many of those same framers also believed that the nation required role models conveyed through educational institutions, voluntary associations, and as we will see, political biographies and histories.[27] The goal was not simply to maximize the possibilities of future leaders in the mold of the founding generation, but to inspire and teach both citizens as well as their representatives about the bases of their roles as keepers of the republic. The importance ascribed to such outlets reflects the political scientist Joseph Schlesinger's Cold War–era observation that "a political system unable to kindle ambitions for office is as much in danger of breaking down as one unable to restrain ambitions."[28] Thus in spite of even the most smartly devised political institutions, our current discontent with American political leadership may have something to do with the civic harms flowing from insufficient attention to the subject of political leadership in liberal democracies—a topic that begins with discussion of its preconditions, purpose, and character.[29]

There is also a less controversial and more practical reason to care about the theme of statesmanship. For better or worse, individuals have mattered and will continue to matter on the world stage.[30] The history of Calcutta, India would in all likelihood have been worse had individuals of less steel than Mahatma Gandhi or Mother Teresa been present. Conversely, the personal influence, grandiose rhetoric, and barbaric power wielded by leaders such as Stalin, Hitler, and Mao Zedong were major if not the only causes leading to the death of millions, altering the course of world history forever.[31] Their example illustrates that not all leaders—or citizens—are saviors that will articulate a political vision that appeals to the best in human nature.[32] Whether employing political power for good or ill, however, the individual who claims to be this or the next generation's great statesman or stateswoman is an element we will have to account for in the political realm. It is certainly a factor that it would behoove Americans to take more seriously in our current political milieu. Politics, like nature itself, abhors a vacuum; it is the responsibility of citizens to determine who fills it.

At the very least a historical estimate of statesmanship provides a contextualized vocabulary and portfolio of illustrations to aid in our discussions of political leadership, with accounts that reach beyond the partial and vague use of the term in our current political parlance. Some of the exemplars considered in the following pages, such as George Washington, will be recognizable to most readers. Other figures, such as the theologian Saint Augustine, are seldom thought of as having anything to do with the concept. Still other illustrations, such as Jane Addams, would appear at first glance to have little direct bearing on political affairs at all. Yet whether familiar or obscure, each of these individuals left a mark on his or her time through the deeds they accomplished on behalf of their commonwealth. As well, each one helps stimulate our understanding of the identifiers of good political leadership today.

The departure point for this analysis is Rome *circa* the first century, and our first spokesperson on behalf of statesmanship is the Greek biographer Plutarch. One might plausibly argue that his massive *Lives of the Noble Greeks and Romans* is one big volume on statesmanship in its own right, but here we focus our attention on two of his most memorable exemplars. Chap-

ter 1 examines Plutarch's "Life of Alcibiades," the Greek military commander and orator whose public service to Athens (and several other city-states)
exemplifies the civic-mindedness we might hope for if not expect from a
political leader. His outsized ambition helped him to accomplish many
achievements on behalf of his fellow countrymen, while his consummate
flexibility helped him escape from more than one difficult situation dealt out
by fortune. Yet the fate he suffered also points to the danger posed by the
political leader's overreliance on ambition and flexibility to the exclusion of
any other moderating qualities or abilities.

A stark contrast to Alcibiades is presented in Plutarch's "Life of Cato the
Younger." On the heels of Alcibiades' itinerant and unpredictable nature,
Cato's steady devotion to republican virtue is a breath of fresh air. Cato
embodies many of the virtues we hope to find in politics but that today seem
altogether absent: self-restraint, thrift, and the ability to sniff out demagogues
loyal to their own self-interest. Above all, Cato was a defender of the Roman
republic and its constitution at a time when internal enemies threatened its
very survival. He stood by his civic principles and spurned any iota of political corruption, even when all seemed lost to the forces of imperial rule.
Plutarch's portrayal of his life illustrates how conviction, resistance to
change, and courage are all important qualities within the political leader's
repertoire. Yet in his refusal to allow any considerable room for flexibility
and change in response to the heady political events of his day, Cato's demise suggests the limits of an approach to statecraft that lacks any play in its
joints.

From Plutarch's *Lives*, we turn to St. Augustine and his masterwork, *The
City of God*. Writing in the immediate aftermath of the sack of Rome by the
Visigoth tribes, Augustine was keenly aware of the ramifications of failed
leadership. To the degree that Plutarch's *Lives* celebrates the figures that
established Greece and Rome as the leading political powers of their time,
Augustine calls attention to the follies and errors committed by public officials that contributed to the decline of the Empire that Plutarch so admired.
For all his depreciation of Rome's supposed greatness, however, Augustine's
Civitas Dei reveals that he was not unconcerned with matters of statecraft. In
place of civic glory and ambition, Augustine counseled humility and care as
constitutive of his ideal political leader. While his appeals may have fallen on
deaf ears in his own time, his political counsels are worth hearing in the
realm of modern politics, where qualities of pride, anger, and moral certainty
reign. Like his political theory in general, Augustine's Christianized theory
of political leadership portrays a different kind of model, one less romantic
and more realistic. His outlook on statesmanship is fixed somewhere south of
heaven but north of hell, mindful of the past but with a fixed eye on the
kingdom to come. He offers a praiseworthy if incomplete account of statesmanship for the here and now.

Leaving Augustine and the Middle Ages behind, we move forward in time to scenes and persons more recognizable. When Americans think of the most prominent statesman during the American Revolution and the republic's early years, George Washington's name springs readily to mind. Washington's renown as the foremost statesman of the United States needs no defense, nor does his career and accomplishments cry out for further scholarly reconstruction. Yet his leadership is rarely viewed through the writing of his fellow Federalist and the nation's fourth Chief Justice of the United States, John Marshall. In his largely unheralded biography, *The Life of George Washington*, Marshall's articulation of Washington's blend of expedient and circumspect leadership during both war and peacetime is held up for Americans who, then as now, were embroiled in partisan conflict. In Marshall's eyes, the *Life* was intended to be a heuristic rather than a hagiography, a work he hoped might inspire future generations of readers to perpetuate the achievement of the founding era. By turning to Marshall's depiction of Washington, we can better appreciate the role of discretion in political leadership, and the tightrope the modern political leader must walk between action and deference.

Not all citizens can be George Washington, however. This book concludes with a more everyday form of political leadership. The Progressive social reformer Jane Addams is an unlikely heroine in the canon of political leaders, for she was not at the forefront of politics in the same overt manner as Plutarch's heroes, Augustine's emperors, or Marshall's Washington. On the contrary, most of the civic deeds she performed were done outside the formal political domain, notably at the settlement house she helped found in Chicago, Illinois. In her *Twenty Years at Hull-House* (1910), Addams recounts the tireless planning and efforts that went into making Hull House a success in relieving urban plight and poverty. Despite facing long odds, Addams and her fellow volunteers succeeded in educating and mobilizing some of the city's most downtrodden. The feat was made all the more remarkable by the manifold obstacles that were set before Addams and her fellow reformers: social indifference, entrenched and parochial power centers, and their own self-doubts about Hull House's mission. Yet Addams remained steadfast in her commitment to making the settlement a refuge for all visitors as a place that provided not simply the necessities of survival but also nourished individuals intellectually, socially, and civically. In her example of democratic statesmanship, Addams underscores the value of the concept for citizens today.

Together, the figures examined here confronted enduring tensions such as those between personal ambition and citizenship, God and man, war and peace, the hardscrabble existence of the poor and the opulent life of the wealthy. In doing so, their successes and shortcomings point the way toward a better vocabulary for speaking about political leadership today. And I daresay that not the least beneficiaries of a more robust and clear lexicon of statesmanship are political theorists. Justified or not, and whether one likes it or not, scholars of political theory are feeling ever-mounting pressure to focus less on abstract philosophy and turn their attention to the practical challenges confronting ordinary citizens in liberal governments.[33] Yet this reified focus need not abandon close analysis of the major political stalwarts among the mighty dead. While the scope and variety of our political challenges differ in kind from those facing our forbears, as inheritors of their civic history the models of the recent and not-so-recent past remain useful heuristics for conceiving leadership today. Thus, this *tour d'horizon* of statesmanship shows that the concept is of enduring importance not only for thoughtful citizens disenchanted by the uninspired conduct of the ship of state, but for political theorists interested in charting a way out of our current political morass.

That said, the narrative that follows illustrates the clashes that inevitably transpire for us all when personal principle meets with collective life, and thus is not one of unbroken political success and triumph. On the contrary, several of the articulators of the concept examined here suffered failures even while embodying some of the characteristics of statesmanship we seek. But the bug is in fact a feature. If we are to appreciate the character and difficulties of political leadership, the lessons conveyed by the setbacks, defeats, and personal foibles of its representatives are as deeply significant as their victories and good fortune. While not the most celebratory way to parse the concept, we tend to learn more through failures than we do through great success. Moreover, the shortcomings of even the most formidable political leaders gesture toward a more general teaching: operating in the pell-mell world of politics, success will always be uncertain and subject to the forces of constraint and contingency, whether doled out by forces outside one's control or by those within the human heart. Statesmen, like all the rest of us, are to some extent at the mercy of chance, born to fight and struggle in an ever-changing context beyond their choosing. Luck as well as skill dictates the arc of the political leader's career.

Although this analysis proceeds chronologically, my hope is that the aspects of statesmanship we move through in the writing of Plutarch, Augustine, Washington, and Addams complement each other, with one author compensating for the weaknesses or insufficiencies of another. By way of a final orientation, think of what follows as a dinner menu, presented to the modern reader hungry for a more elevated form of political leadership. The meal begins with Alcibiades, an *amuse-bouche* whose brief yet sharp life of political ambition prepares the palate for heavier fare. Following Cato's sumptuous yet somewhat recognizable civic mindedness is St. Augustine, whose bracing counsels on behalf of personal virtue and humility prepare the stomach for the rich and satisfyingly familiar narrative of Washington's embodiment of expedience and sober thinking. Following the elaborate main course is the sweet but not cloying hope for a theory of statesmanship, found in the work of Jane Addams, that reinforces liberal democratic principles. On the whole, the authors here make for a harmonious experience that is more than the sum of its parts, and I hope we rise from the meal refreshed but not sated by a new appreciation for this old concept.

Bon Appétit.

NOTES

1. As John Schaar once noted, "our skepticism toward all notions of disinterested, public-regarding behavior is so thoroughgoing that the patriot can hardly appear. We are inclined to regard all professions of disinterested and altruistic motive as the blandishments of a charlatan or the intrigues of a schemer—and we are largely right, for over time, a people gets the politics it expects and asks for." See his "The Case for Patriotism," in *Legitimacy in the Modern State* (New Brunswick, NJ: Transaction Publishers, 1989), 285–311: 294.

2. Wilfred M. McClay, "Response to Papers by Major, Baldwin, and Bailey: Democratic Statesmanship and the Blue Guitar," *Perspectives on Political Science* 41, no. 2 (2012), 90–92: 90. Ralph Lerner has pointed out that "the accolade, 'statesman,' is usually applied in retrospect, as in 'elder statesman' when speaking of someone still living, or from a historian's perspective when speaking of someone long dead." See his *Naïve Readings: Reveilles Political and Philosophic* (Chicago: University of Chicago Press, 2016), 57.

3. On the fine distinction between statesmanship and leadership, see David R. Weaver, "Leadership, Locke, and The Federalist," *American Journal of Political Science* 41, no. 2 (1997), 420–46: 428–29; Jeffrey K. Tulis, "The Possibility of Constitutional Statesmanship," in *The Limits of Constitutional Democracy*, eds. Jeffrey K. Tulis and Stephen Macedo (Princeton, NJ: Princeton University Press, 2010), 112–23; Terry Newell, *Statesmanship, Character, and Leadership in America* (New York: Palgrave Macmillan, 2012), 186–87, 206; and Jordan Barkalow, "American *Paideia*: Public and Private Leadership and the Cultivation of Civic Virtue," *Expositions* 8, no. 2 (2014), 131–54.

4. John Wendell Coats, Jr., *Statesmanship: Six Modern Illustrations of a Modified Ancient Ideal* (Selinsgrove, PA: Susquehanna University Press, 1995).

5. See James McGregor Burns, *Leadership* (New York: Harper and Rowe, 1978), 4–5, 19.

6. Plato, *Statesman*, trans. Christopher J. Rowe (Indianapolis, IN: Hackett, 1999), 64–65.

7. See Daniel J. Kapust, *Republicanism, Rhetoric, and Roman Political Thought: Sallust, Livy, and Tacitus* (New York: Cambridge University Press, 2011), 62; Jed W. Atkins, *Cicero on Politics and the Limits of Reason* (New York: Cambridge University Press, 2013); and Benjamin Straumann, *Crisis and Constitutionalism: Roman Political Thought from the Fall of the Republic to the Age of Revolution* (New York: Oxford University Press, 2016), 149–90.

8. Thomas Aquinas, "On Kingship, to the King of Cyprus," in *On Law, Morality, and Politics*, second ed., trans. Richard J. Regan (Indianapolis, IN: Hackett, 2002), 203–10.

9. John of Salisbury, *Policraticus*, ed. and trans. Cary J. Nederman (New York: Cambridge University Press, 1990).

10. Erasmus, *The Education of a Christian Prince*, ed. and trans. Lisa Jardine (New York: Cambridge University Press, 1997).

11. This transition is famously described in Benjamin Constant's "The Liberty of the Ancients compared with that of the Moderns," in *Constant: Political Writings*, ed. and trans. Biancamaria Fontana (New York: Cambridge University Press, 1988), 308–28.

12. Bernard Mandeville, "Sixth Dialogue," in *The Fable of the Bees, or Private Vices, Publick Benefits*, ed. F. B. Kaye (Indianapolis, IN: Liberty Fund, 1988) II, 266–357: 341.

13. James Madison, "Federalist No. 10," in Alexander Hamilton, John Jay, and James Madison, *The Federalist*, eds. George W. Carey and James McClellan (Indianapolis, IN: Liberty Fund, 2001), 42–48: 45.

14. Harry V. Jaffa (ed.), *Statesmanship: Essays in Honor of Sir Winston Spencer Churchill* (Durham, NC: Carolina Academic Press, 1981).

15. Daniel J. Mahoney, *De Gaulle: Statesmanship, Grandeur, and Modern Democracy* (New York: Routledge, 2017).

16. Jonathan Aitken, *Margaret Thatcher: Power and Personality* (London: Bloomsbury, 2013).

17. Richard Stengel, *Mandela's Way: Lessons for an Uncertain Age* (New York: Random House, 2018).

18. A good overview of the secondary literature arguing on behalf of a less state-centric approach to political leadership is found in Patrick Overeem and Femke E. Bakker's "Statesmanship Beyond the Modern State," *Perspectives on Political Science* (2016), 1–10.

19. The most notable exceptions are conservative authors who typically gesture toward a classical or Lincolnian retrieval of the idea. See, e.g., the *Claremont Review of Books*, which prides itself as "A Journal of Political Thought and Statesmanship." This is mentioned not by way of deprecation—some discussion of the subject is better than none at all—but to point out the intramural nature of contemporary analysis of the topic. Incidentally, I say a good number of conservative academics would welcome more scholarly exchanges on the subject across the political aisle.

20. Richard S. Ruderman, "Democracy and the Problem of Statesmanship," *Review of Politics* 59, no. 4 (1997), 759–87.

21. John Rawls, *Political Liberalism*, expanded ed. (New York: Columbia University Press, 2005), 80–81. At least when applied to the international order, Rawls' confidence in institutions is not as resolute. In wars between liberal and non-liberal regimes, he stipulates the need for statesmen "to hold fast to the aim of gaining a just peace," while sedulously avoiding "the things that make achieving such a peace more difficult." Moreover, the political leader is tasked with setting the vanquished nation on the path toward a just and equitable political regime, if only by the example of his principled conduct. See his *The Law of Peoples* (Cambridge, MA: Harvard University Press, 2003), 98.

22. Robert A. Dahl, *Democracy and Its Critics* (New Haven, CT: Yale University Press, 1989), 52–79.

23. Richard Rorty, *Contingency, Irony, and Solidarity* (New York: Cambridge University Press, 1989). Consider also the French theorist Jean-François Lyotard's critique of "grand narrative" in his *Postmodern Condition* (Minneapolis, MN: University of Minnesota Press, 1984).

24. Benjamin R. Barber, *An Aristocracy of Everyone: The Politics of Education and the Future of America* (New York: Ballantine Books, 1992), 185. See also his *A Passion for Democracy: American Essays* (Princeton, NJ: Princeton University Press, 1998), 97.

25. Some scholars have suggested that statesmanship, whether desirable or undesirable as a normative matter, is no longer viable in the United States. See the reasons developed by James McGregor Burns (1978); John A. Gueguen, "Reflections on the Presidency," *Presidential Studies Quarterly* 12, no. 4 (1982), 470–484; and Herbert J. Storing, "American Statesmanship: Old and New," in *Toward a More Perfect Union: Writings of Herbert J. Storing*, ed. Joseph M. Bessette (Washington, DC: American Enterprise Institute Press, 1995), 403–30.

26. See Alexis de Tocqueville, *Democracy in America*, trans. George Lawrence (New York: Perennial Classics, 2000), II, 506–8, 691–5.

27. On this point see George Thomas, *The Founders and the Idea of a National University: Constituting the American Mind* (New York: Cambridge University Press, 2015).

28. Joseph Schlesinger, *Ambition and Politics: Political Careers in the United States* (Chicago, IL: Rand McNally and Co., 1966), 2.

29. Several scholars have stipulated that good leadership exerts an important pedagogical influence on citizens. For recent articulations of this view, see Marc Landy and Sidney M. Milkis, *Presidential Greatness* (Lawrence: University Press of Kansas, 2000), 4; James W. Ceaser, "Demagoguery, Statesmanship, and the American Presidency," *Critical Review* 19, no. 2 (2007), 257–98: 267; and Christopher E. Baldwin, "Franklin's Classical American Statesmanship," *Perspectives on Political Science* 41, no. 2 (2012), 67–74.

30. For defenses of this claim, see Janet Coleman, ed., *The Individual in Political Theory and Practice* (New York: Oxford University Press, 1996) and James T. Fetter, "The Great Man in Politics: Magnanimity in the History of Western Political Thought," (PhD diss., University of Notre Dame, 2012). For works that assess the influence of personality factors on political outcomes, see Fred I. Greenstein, "The Impact of Personality on Politics: An Attempt to Clear Away the Underbrush," *American Political Science Review* 61, no. 3 (1967), 629–41 in addition to his *Personality and Politics: Problems of Evidence, Inference, and Conceptualization* (Chicago: Markham, 1969); Margaret Hermann, "When Leader Personality Will Affect Foreign Policy: Some Propositions," in *In Search of Global Patterns*, ed. James Rosenau (New York: Free Press, 1976), 326–333; and Margaret Hermann, "Leaders and Foreign Policy Decision-Making," in *Diplomacy, Force, and Leadership: Essays in Honor of Alexander L. George*, eds. Dan Caldwell and Timothy J. McKeown (Boulder, CO: Westview, 1993), 77–94.

31. See Gordon A. Craig, *Germany: 1866–1945* (New York: Oxford University Press, 1978), 543.

32. Even so, Richard Ruderman (1997) points out (rather darkly) that not every statesman will be a predatory authoritarian, intent on imposing his or her agenda upon an unsuspecting people (784).

33. For defenses and applications of this argument, see Ian Shapiro and Judith Wagner Decew (eds.), *Theory and Practice: NOMOS XXXVII* (New York: New York University Press, 1995); Raymond Geuss, *Philosophy and Real Politics* (Princeton, NJ: Princeton University Press, 2008); Andrew Rehfeld, "Offensive Political Theory," *Perspectives on Politics* 8, no. 2 (2010), 465–86; Jeremy Waldron, *Political Political Theory: Essays on Institutions* (Cambridge, MA: Harvard University Press, 2016); and Matt Sleat (ed.), *Politics Recovered: Realist Thought in Theory and Practice* (New York: Columbia University Press, 2018).

Chapter One

Ambition and Flexibility in Plutarch's "Life of Alcibiades"

Among educated Romans of the imperial era, few works attracted as much attention as the Greek writer Plutarch's *Parallel Lives of the Noble Greeks and Romans*, which provided his readers with the kind of popular human-interest stories that in our time grab the attention of the casual shopper waiting in line at the supermarket. His literary formula was simple: pair a famous Greek political leader with a Roman counterpart to determine what educational value the similarities and differences between their respective lives and careers have for his contemporaries. Since his authorship of some twenty-two such couplets, Plutarch's appeal has extended beyond his intended general readership, as the *Lives* were read by and inspired several famous figures in their own right, including Shakespeare,[1] Napoleon Bonaparte,[2] Jean-Jacques Rousseau,[3] Ralph Waldo Emerson,[4] Friedrich Nietzsche,[5] many of America's founding fathers, and even American presidents such as John Adams and Harry Truman.[6] Yet the *Lives*, a book that once enjoyed immense celebrity in its own right, is seldom read by our generation, let alone by our politicians. Casting aside Plutarch's work would be unfortunate, however, because although the *Lives* are morality stories based on examples rather than systematic philosophical treatises, general reflections on politics and leadership are apparent in Plutarch's writings. Moreover, his subjects are not dead relics of the past but rendered by him into fifty individuals distinguished by their own relatable virtues and flaws.[7] He was not a political historian on the grand scale of Thucydides or Herodotus, nor did he aspire to such heights, believing that true character is revealed more by personal behavior than by great deeds and magnificent actions. Plutarch thought that the most effective way to encourage emulation was for his readers to use the human element of his statesmen as a means for examining one's own character, regardless of time and place.[8] He emphasized the telling cue, the revealing detail, or the fateful idiosyncrasy that hit upon the root of his subject's successes or failures. "It must be borne in mind that my design is not to write histories, but lives," he says of his undertaking, and more often than not a simple gesture or jest reveals a leader's virtues and vices more effectively than "the most glorious exploits."[9] Even so, Plutarch never loses the forest for the trees. The particularities he mentions never detract from Plutarch's overarching interest in statesmanship, as exemplified by the great leaders that Greece and Rome jointly produced.

It should thus come as little surprise that one expecting to find in the *Lives* a treasury of gilded hagiographies is soon disappointed. Indeed, Plutarch refused to plaster over the warts of even his most beloved stars.[10] To allow "the lessons of the past be a guide," in the words of Winston Churchill, Plutarch had to present the good with the bad.[11] The statesmen he surveys possess diverse combinations of good deeds and bad behavior, virtue and vice, making them capable of greatness as well as susceptible to bad habits. He understood that would-be statesmen of the classical era were often their own worst enemies, even as he harbored a classical distrust of democratic government and the wisdom of the *vox populi*.[12] As Simon Verdegem puts it, "Plutarch's protagonists are neither paragons of perfect virtue nor paradigms of pure vice," thus discouraging simple categorizations of "positive" and "negative" examples.[13] Moreover, as the *Lives* attests, he refused to limit his cast of great characters to any particular nation, race, or civilization.[14] Plutarch realized that political leaders were not some higher life form, but like the rest of mankind were jostled by passions, external obstacles, and events beyond their knowledge or control, and it is this realism that makes his portrayals more accessible to the everyday reader. If we are to renew the idea of statesmanship during these perilous political times, it behooves us to be like Plutarch: honest about the heroes we admire, acknowledging the virtues without denying the faults of those whom we entrust with the reins of power.

PLUTARCH'S ALCIBIADES

Perhaps Plutarch saw something of himself in the itinerant statesman Alcibiades, perhaps his most notorious subject in the *Lives*. Both men straddled cultural lines.[15] Plutarch was born into an affluent family at Chaeronea, a Greek hamlet that lies between Delphi and Athens.[16] While the exact year of his birth is uncertain, it occurred sometime during the reign of the Roman emperor Claudius (roughly A.D. 41–54). His parents' wealth obtained the best education money could buy, which included the study of philosophy as well as travels to Asia Minor, Egypt, and most significantly, Italy. In Rome, when not giving lectures on philosophy and ethics he immersed himself in the city's laws, history, and customs, even assuming the name Lucius Mestrius Plutarchus.[17] It was during this stay that Plutarch received the encouragement from his friends and students to begin writing the work that would become the *Lives*.[18] Upon returning to Greece some years later, he served in various political and religious positions while he continued his writing.[19] Though he became a great admirer of the awesome might of the Roman Empire, he maintained a lifelong love for Greece, once describing his native village as "a poor little place where I remained willingly so that it should not become even less."[20] There he died after an easy but active life sometime in his seventies, leaving behind a work that testified to his lifelong admiration for the figures that had a hand in making Greece and Rome great.[21] Thus he dedicated his *Lives* to his Roman patron, Quintus Socius Senecio—a symbolic bow to Roman ascendance by the child of Greece.[22]

A similar cosmopolitanism distinguishes Plutarch's vivid depiction of the Athenian general Alcibiades (431–404 B.C.). "Vivid" is indeed an apt description of Alcibiades, for by all accounts he was quite a sight to behold— beautiful, formidably so.[23] He looked the part of the leader, which was no small advantage for Plutarch, who notes that Alcibiades' "brilliant and extraordinary beauty" attracted many well-born persons who sought his company on a regular basis.[24] Endowed with a "happy constitution and natural vigour of body" that matched his "many strong passions," the uppermost being "his ambition and desire of superiority," he was raised by the hearthside of his cousin, the great Athenian general-statesman Pericles, and could trace the branches of his family tree to the most celebrated Athenian tribes (2, 1). Yet his master provided him with little guidance, for it was soon clear to all who knew Alcibiades that no authority could hope to tame his impetuous nature, not even the great Socrates, who for a short while took charge of his education only to eventually give up any hope of instilling moderation in his pupil (7).[25] Alcibiades reveled in freedom, adventure, action, instinct, and it was clear to all his tutors that nature, not convention, seemed to have already done the heavy lifting in shaping his character.[26] He enjoyed good food, good wine, and good company. In competitions, he was a fierce and courageous competitor, but not above using underhanded tactics to win, having once avoided a fall during a wresting match by biting his opponent "like a lion" (3). Above all, he was spirited—"*eros* personified" as one commentator has put it (or "high energy," to borrow a phrase from Donald Trump).[27] While others might have exploited such capabilities to indulge small pleasures or private gain, Alcibiades gratified his baser impulses while simultaneously pursuing a life that would fulfill his higher martial and political ambitions.[28] He wanted to win—often, and a lot. Inevitably, his gusto earned him friends and enemies alike, and his reputation as an arrogant, vain, and cavalier leader has been said to ensure his place in the pantheon of great Greek arch-villains.[29] While not immune to acts of flattery and self-abasement, there is no question that from the beginning of his life Alcibiades saw himself as different from his fellow Athenians, and he seemed to go out of his way to remind them of his purported superiority.[30] In all, his auspicious persona and advantages— "his noble birth, his riches, the personal courage he had shown in divers battles, and the multitude of his friends and dependents"—paved a road to fame, one made even smoother by his well-nigh instinctive ambition (10).

AMBITION

Ambition is often invoked as an integral element in any account of statesmanship. For the ancient Greeks, human grandeur and the pursuit of honor, albeit in guarded moderation, was often contrasted with the more servile pursuit of material gain. The virtue of magnanimity as extolled by Aristotle, or "greatness of soul" as elaborated by Roman statesmen such as Cicero, extolled the active use of one's talents to carry out political plans and reforms that supported the common good.[31] In the modern era, the role of individual ambition continued to be paid obeisance, even if only negatively, as Enlightenment thinkers ranging from Thomas Hobbes to Jean-Jacques Rousseau now cautioned against the dangers to civil peace posed by individual excess and pride.[32] Yet in the United States, the idea of political ambition continues to cast a seductive glow over our politics, an allure that many of the Constitution's framers sought to safely redirect through institutional channels rather than stamp out.[33] As Robert Faulkner has argued, political ambition—whether in the form of the candidate running for President of the United States or the local councilwoman intent on reforming zoning ordinances—is all around us.[34] The pursuit of superior power, reputation, and a name in history: these are the objects out of which a public career is made. On the whole, then, our contemporary attitude toward ambition is complicated, insofar as many recognize that ambition can be seen as advantageous and perhaps indispensible to sustaining the political order yet a potential danger to liberty if not properly curbed through legal checks and balances.[35] Like statesmanship itself, democratic theorists continue to grapple with the role of ambition in politics, a debate that is unlikely to wane so long as individuals continue to pursue and contend for political office.[36]

When the Peloponnesian War between Sparta and Athens erupted in 431 B.C., Alcibiades could hardly have hoped for a better outlet for his drive for distinction. Indeed, to be a genuine statesman he may have needed this crisis point on an international stage to quench what one scholar has called his "thirst for acclaim."[37] Certainly, he had spent a good deal of his life up until then preparing for the moment. As a young man of only eighteen, Plutarch relates that his martial bravery at the Battle of Potidaea in 432 drew praise from a good many Athenian generals (8).[38] He was a rising star in Athens, and would not be the last war hero to be pitched into the political arena—before, Plutarch intimates, he possessed any degree of personal maturity.[39] Combining early military success with "his own gift of eloquence," as a speaker in the assembly he was ready to push his fellow Athenians beyond their often self-imposed limitations, toward deeds that might chisel away the geographic and ethical limitations he saw as standing in the way of Athenian might in the Peloponnese (10). To that end, he succeeded in fomenting Athenian outrage against a group of Spartan diplomats and forming a confederacy of Greek city-states against the Lacedaemonians, "a great political feat" made all the more remarkable by the fact that it was authorized and coordinated in a single day (16).[40] Indeed, much seemed to be happening in a flash for Alcibiades and Athens.[41] The city and its allies were now hitching its fortunes to his ambition, and working in tandem they successfully put the Spartans and their allies on the defensive for a time. By way of his rhetoric, he successfully inflamed to new heights the simmering desire among the Athenians to acquire power and territory, urging them to strike quickly and boldly with an overwhelming armada against the small city-state of Sicily.[42] He wanted Athens to attain new heights in a forceful manner, Plutarch comments, but while the conquest of Sicily may have been "the utmost bound of [Athenian] ambition," it was only the beginning of his expectations for his countrymen and, even more, his personal legacy (19).[43] There was speculation that Alcibiades had his sights set on Carthage and Libya if all went as expected in Sicily. Fate, of course, had a different plan in store for him.

Give them credit: the Athenians sensed, however dimly, the danger to democratic rule that lurked in Alcibiades' outsized ambition. Prior to sailing for Sicily, he was appointed co-general of the Athenian army along with the veteran generals Lamachus and Nicias, the people hoping that the latter's famed caution would cool Alcibiades' notorious "heat" and impulsiveness (20).[44] "Co-general": the position was nothing short of an insult to one who would brook no equal, especially the comparatively milquetoast Nicias. But perhaps the division of authority served his goals after all. Alcibiades had long been annoyed by Nicias' reputation as a great general and envied the plaudits extended to him by the Athenian people for brokering the former peace between Athens and Sparta (14). Now, however, he had the chance to surpass his rival by rendering him a foil for his own deeds. When Nicias predictably urged conciliation on the eve of the Sicilian expedition, Alcibiades prevailed in swaying the Athenians to bestow manpower and resources without stint (20). It was one more notch in the belt of his ambition, but it came with a cost. In his absence, the malcontents he left behind in Athens spread salacious rumors about a wild party the night before Alcibiades' departure during which he was alleged to have done many debauched things, most seriously defiling stone markers of the city's gods (23).[45] The enraged

Athenians issued an immediate recall of Alcibiades to answer the charges, albeit one softened to prevent any mutiny among his men.[46] In deep trouble, Alcibiades refused to return to face the charges; indeed, he refused to return to Athens at all. "Seeing himself utterly hopeless of return to his native country," he sailed about the Peloponnesus, eventually seeking and receiving refuge in 415 from the very Spartans he had lately vilified (27). It was the beginning of his flight.

"I will make them feel I am alive," Alcibiades vowed when he heard of the sentence of death lain on him by the Athenians (26). And in short order the promise was made good. Thanks in no small part to the intelligence he provided to the Spartans, Athens fell to Spartan forces, and his native city groaned under the oppressive weight of the oligarchical government known as the Council of the Four Hundred. "Terrified into submission," the Athenians stood in need of rescue by a statesman that might lead it out of such dire straits (33). It was a circumstance too enticing to resist, and Alcibiades, now exiled from Sparta, soon aspired to return to Athens. There was a path open to him: throw out the occupying Spartans, replace them with hand-picked elites supportive of his own pretensions, and receive a hero's welcome as Athens greeted him with open arms. As it turned out, a coup succeeded without his direct involvement, but the new government was riven with its own internal discord and haphazard prosecution of the war with Sparta. The Athenian people, long frustrated with its military fortunes, softened their former anger toward Alcibiades. It was generally hoped that he would be the general—the statesman—who would restore Athenian democracy once and for all. Here was his opportunity to play the role of savior.

Yet Alcibiades demurred. If he returned to Athens it would be on terms of his choosing, not those dictated by the "mere grace and commiseration" of the people (34). As Plutarch puts it, Alcibiades saw himself under no obligation "to gratify and submit to all the wishes of those who, from a fugitive and an exile, had created him general of so great an army, and given him the command of such a fleet" (33). Alcibiades liked to lead military campaigns, not respond to schemes devised by others. He liked to initiate and control undertakings, not respond to the beckoning of malcontents. As it turned out, by declining to strike the match that would light a general conflagration of civil war in Athens, Plutarch suggests, Alcibiades saved the city-state from spinning into fragmentation and destruction.[47] What deserves notice, however, is the affront to Alcibiades' ambition and pride: if he would return to his homeland he would do so triumphantly, never hat in hand. If we are looking for a political leader whose ambition transcends petty material accolades, indeed, stands independent of the whims of a particular regime itself, Alcibiades' refusal is a case in point.[48]

Still in exile, Alcibiades continued to do what he did best as a youth, engaging in a variety of naval campaigns against Spartan forces, eventually reclaiming the Hellenesport for the Athenians (35). Following a few such victories, in the year 408 he at last felt ready to set eyes on his native country again that he might "show his fellow-citizens a person who had gained so many victories for them" (41). Having spent seven long years in exile, his return was a joyous occasion for the Athenian people, but Alcibiades still harbored resentment over their earlier betrayal.[49] Speaking in the Assembly shortly after his arrival, he complained of his ill-usage by his countrymen and with "courage and good hope" exhorted the Athenians to behave better in the future in both their treatment of him as their army's commander-in-chief (43). His ambition, he exhorted them, was something to celebrate rather than deride. Yet even as Alcibiades remained "exalted in his own thought," Plutarch notes, he could never shake the feeling that Athens' love for him was only a passing fancy (44). Public opinion, he now knew, was a slender reed on which to lay one's livelihood.

Alcibiades was right to be suspicious, for he was not the toast of the town for very long. His reputation in Athens now at an all-time high—"the lower and meaner sort of people" were reported to have pleaded with him to assume tyrannical powers—he decided once again to prove himself on the field of battle (45). Having climbed back to the heights of his former popularity, his ambition wanted to rise higher still. Yet his great reputation worked against him at the Battle of Notium in 406, the culminating naval battle against the great Spartan admiral Lysander. Alcibiades' fleet, undermanned and tired, kept coming up short against Spartan forces supported by the Persian prince, Cyrus the Younger (46). With hostilities apparently at a standstill, Alcibiades ventured to the adjacent islands supposedly to seek money and provisions for his starving soldiers.[50] It was a disastrous choice. Upon his departure, his men were lured into battle by the combined Spartan and Persian forces. The man whom Alcibiades had left in temporary command, his pilot and sometime drinking-buddy Antiochus, had been given a strict command not to engage the Spartans in battle. Placed in a do-or-die situation, however, Antiochus and his men had no choice but to return fire and an all-out naval engagement with the Spartans quickly ensued. The move played into Spartan hands: bereft of Alcibiades and no match for the superior intelligence and manpower of the Spartan fleets, fifteen Athenian ships were destroyed and Antiochus himself was slain. Though Alcibiades quickly returned to make amends for his departure, he was too late to reverse the fateful Spartan victory. Athens was soon besieged and razed by Lysander and the Spartan army, and, in a now familiar refrain, a new oligarchy—the Thirty Tyrants—was imposed on the people (49).[51]

Amid the chaos in Athens, the Notium fiasco offered Alcibiades' critics a new cause célèbre. In the aftermath of the fiasco, Alcibiades' recent exhortations to the people were forgotten as his behavior was represented by critics in the worst possible light as the result of his "self-conceited neglect of his duties" (46). Yet Plutarch reports that most Athenians had much to lament in "this sad state of affairs": the loss of their empire, their liberty, and their "most valiant and accomplished general," Alcibiades (49).[52] Presently choosing to roam the Thracian Chersonese in exile, Alcibiades was ruined, according to Plutarch, by his own glory and celebrity, torched by his own incandescence. "[H]is continual success had produced such an idea of his courage and conduct," he argues, "that if he failed in anything he undertook, it was imputed to his neglect" rather than his want of power or resources (45). No deed could be too difficult for him to accomplish, it was believed, provided "he went about it in good earnest." The Spartans, for their part, seemed to agree, believing that his ambition would not allow him "to live idly and at ease" and resist one last effort to save Athens from tyranny (49). Believing that the absolute extermination of Athenian democracy could only be guaranteed by the destruction of its foremost leader, they plotted Alcibiades' death (50).[53] In 404, he was tracked to the remote hamlet of Phrygia in what is now western Turkey, where he was residing in a hovel with a mistress. Late one night a fire was set by the house, and as Alcibiades fled from the blaze he was slain in a hail of arrows shot by a band of assassins (51).[54] He was not yet fifty years old.

Alcibiades' ambition was instrumental to his success as a statesman as well as a contributing factor to his downfall. Like many of the qualities we will examine, Alcibiades displays the Janus-faced role of ambition in human nature and public affairs: potent if directed toward the public good, but able to inflict great evil and destruction of self and state if not properly governed or restrained.[55] Yet despite all his efforts to appear independent from the people he lived among, his ambition was in fact highly conditioned by and dependent on their attitude toward him. Try as he might to separate them, his honor could not be divorced from the success of the people he led.[56] His ambition—indeed his very livelihood—was utterly state-centric and existed in the eyes of others, and it is not very surprising that his final status as a statesman without a state lasted only for a short duration. Left in isolation in Phrygia, fate had at last instilled in him a lesson no other teacher ever could: humility.

ADAPTABILITY

Along with ambition, a number of thinkers have identified adaptability as a core component of good leadership. In contrast to classical thinkers such as Plutarch who looked askance at character change in their political leaders, many writers of the modern era have praised the ability to alter one's temperament in response to new challenges and circumstances. Perhaps the most well-known spokesperson of this view was the notorious political counselor

Niccolò Machiavelli, who infamously advised his aspiring prince to know how to imitate the behavior of the lion and the fox—that is, to act either boldly or with subterfuge—to counteract the obstacles that fortune rises before the political leader.[57] In the United States, Progressive Era thinkers such as Herbert Croly made a similar point, holding up Abraham Lincoln as the statesman whose political flexibility might serve as an exemplar for addressing twentieth-century economic and political upheaval.[58] More recently, a host of scholars have pointed to a leader's willingness to vary his or her behavior as the defining feature of "adaptive" or "situational" leadership in such diverse arenas as politics, education, and human resource management.[59] Overall, perceptions of the necessity and even merits of a leader's embrace of flexibility have dissipated earlier suspicions, and we now live in an age in which adaptability is a quality for praise rather than derision in a political leader.

For his part, Alcibiades possessed adaptability in spades. If his ease in "plac[ing] himself upon good terms with all that he met" was some sort of vice, he certainly never recognized it as such (105–6). Indeed, much of his success owed to his ability to respond quickly and adapt to changing circumstances, dangers, and environments. The milieux that honed his fly-by-night behavior are impressive both in their number and variety: his adaptability served him well as an Athenian, Spartan, Persian, and Athenian once again.[60] He was nicknamed, Plutarch reports admiringly, "the chameleon," based on his "peculiar talent and artifice for gaining men's affections" and entering seamlessly into the "habits and ways of life" of a people (28). As an Athenian, he possessed and reflected back to the people the public spiritedness that made Athens great. As a Spartan, he was abstemious to the envy of even the most austere hoplite. In Persia, he once again swung back to his former extreme, conducting himself with the utmost pomp and magnificence. Nor was his resourcefulness always a product of necessity, though his malleability led him through more than one narrow escape. Change suited his restlessness and appeared to have an inherent appeal for one who thrived on presenting himself with new challenges and carrying out the seemingly impossible.[61] Despite Alcibiades' hunger for public recognition, the many drastic about-faces recounted by Plutarch suggest a survival instinct that made loyalty to any particular regime a tenuous proposition indeed.[62]

Perhaps the most striking illustration of Alcibiades' adaptability occurred during his time with the Spartans, whose sanctuary he accepted following his initial exile from Athens. What a lifestyle change for the supposed descendent of Ajax (1)! Having until then reveled in the finer things of life, he took to his new regime like a fish to water. In terms of military strategy, he disclosed Athenian battle plans and recommended without reservation measures that would thwart the very maneuvers he had so recently counseled on his former city-state's behalf.[63] But even more dramatic was Alcibiades' personal transformation and the total makeover of his outward appearance. Gone were the Milesian robes, the dainty victuals, and the streak of nonconformity. As a dour Spartan, Plutarch takes pleasure in dwelling on Alcibiades' clipped hair, baths in ice-cold water, nights spent on rough pallets, and meals of "black broth," a soup consisting of boiled pigs' legs, blood, salt, and vinegar (27).[64] He carried the new identity off well, however, captivating and winning over many skeptical Spartans by his quick adoption of their lifestyle. Yet such extravagant attempts to curry favor eventually sowed distrust. Alcibiades had to outdo everyone, going to extremes even in asceticism. Moreover, in spite of his professed allegiance to the Spartans, jealousy and suspicions among Spartan elites revolving around his ultimate loyalties grew as his victories on behalf of the Lacedaemonians piled up. When rumors began making the rounds that Alcibiades was carrying on an affair with the wife of the Spartan king, Agis II—confirmed, so it seems, by a love-child he shared with the woman—it was not difficult for the city's magistrates to persuade Spartan elites to set upon and execute the Athenian-turned-Spartan (28). The plot was unsuccessful—this time.

Having gotten wind of the Spartans' plan, Alcibiades was again on the lam (29). This time he made off further east to Persia, where he once more tried to endear himself to his countrymen by making a new pledge of allegiance to the Persian prince, Tissaphernes (445–395 B.C.), "a cruel character" and avowed "hater of the Greeks" (30). Alcibiades was again compelled to dramatically alter his self-presentation, though perhaps he welcomed the change to the more luxurious Persian lifestyle. Even more significant than his outward changes, however, were those he made in his approach to foreign affairs. Quickly he became one of the most influential figures about the prince as he now participated in matters of diplomacy rather than military strategy, urging a policy of conservative neutrality toward the outside world. It was a move more characteristic of Nicias than Alcibiades, but neither the latter nor Plutarch let on any indication of inner conflict. Alcibiades' recommendation to his new patron "was to furnish [Spartans and Athenians] but sparingly with money, and so wear them out, and consume them insensibly" by depleting their resources to the extent that they would be ready to submit to the Persian prince. Plutarch notes that Tissaphernes, a "lover of guile and wickedness" in his own right, could not but help but admire the ingenuity of the plan, and it was not long before Alcibiades' efforts endeared himself to even those Persians that had most feared and envied him (29).[65] In due course, he would abandon the Persians just as he had the Spartans and Athenians before. From a political standpoint, Alcibiades' malleability never stopped raising him to new levels of success and positions of leadership. "Whether with good men or with bad," Plutarch remarks with no little admiration, Alcibiades was able to quickly "adapt himself to his company, and equally wear the appearance of virtue or vice" (28).

Alcibiades' flexibility was not simply a survival mechanism during a time of interstate conflict, but guided his conduct in matters large and small. He was a chameleon, certainly—but also slippery as a snake. No matter where he happened to be, Plutarch suggests that Alcibiades' day-to-day relations were marked by an easygoing cunning, especially in the political and financial realm, where he often engaged in bribery and flattery in order to have his way.[66] Alcibiades, in comparison to the "simple and straightforward" Roman statesman Coriolanus, is described by Plutarch as unscrupulous, cunning, and false.[67] To Plutarch, he was a sharper, admittedly, but good at what he did. Alcibiades could never manage to make himself hated by the Athenian people, notwithstanding the harm his schemes sometimes inflicted. In comparison to the ethereal Socrates, Alcibiades was not an unpleasant gadfly but instead "always tried to place himself upon good terms with all that he met."[68] He was a sociable man, and was forthright about his desire for winning recognition from others according to their, not his, standards for praise. As Plutarch puts it, he never denied his "love of distinction" or that it was pleasant for him "to be honoured, and distasteful to him to be overlooked."[69] The dependence of his self-image on public opinion was a great strength as well as weakness for this political leader, for all political leaders.

The engine that powered Alcibiades' ambition was his capacity for reinvention. His conduct "displayed many great inconsistences and variations," Plutarch remarks, all serving the "ambition and desire for superiority" which defined "his real character" (2). Wherever in the world he was driven, he seemed to fit in—until he didn't, and then he went elsewhere and started over. He did nothing in half-measures: "at Sparta, he was devoted to athletic exercises, was frugal and reserved; in Ionia, luxurious, gay, and indolent; in Thrace, always drinking; in Thessaly, ever on horseback; and when he lived among the Persians, he exceeded them in displays of magnificence and pomp" (28). Such elasticity often put would-be foes at ease, no small feat for a political leader, but his permutations also testified to his refusal to accept, as Plutarch puts it, "the many and wonderful vicissitudes of his fortunes" (2). Plutarch indicates that good statesmanship must show resourcefulness, if not of the extreme Alcibiadean variety than at least some approximation thereof, displaying a readiness to influence opponents and events rather than resignation to being controlled by them. Thus it is not simply Alcibiades' great ambition that deserves our consideration in the *Lives*, but how that ambition dovetailed with his adjustments to the wildly different regimes in whose circles of power he so easily moved. Unpredictable as the gods, one never really knew what he would do or where he would be next.

CONCLUSIONS

Plutarch's Alcibiades typifies two qualities—ambition and flexibility—that it is appropriate to include within any general definition of statesmanship.[70] Many Americans still clamor for leaders who have the gumption to seek out opportunities for public service along with the facility to meet their fellow and sister citizens at their own level. While the perils of the professionalization of American politics have been well documented, citizens nonetheless are attracted to representatives who genuinely want to be active participants and contributors in the political arena. Alcibiades was just such a figure, a wild, fantastic soul, unsurprising only in his readiness to take risks that might further his goals and willing to take up and abandon projects that might enhance his own glory first, and the good of the community second.[71] Such a temperament was buttressed by a gift for what the sociologist Max Weber famously referred to as charismatic authority, a rarefied, almost supernatural ability to move people by the sheer force of one's "specific gifts of body and spirit."[72] This common touch made it easier for his drive for glory—his vainglory, it would not be inappropriate to call it—to frequently coincide with the desires of those he led, the times he lived in being as frenetic and unpredictable as his own personality. As Plutarch saw him, for all his seeming independence Alcibiades was not just *eros* embodied, but an incarnation of Athens itself, his insatiable quest for valor only a silhouette of the self-aggrandizement of its citizens.[73] The Athenian people he led were given a statesman that reflected back their most praiseworthy and problematic ambitions, martial or otherwise. The city required Alcibiades' superior martial and political abilities, yet simultaneously could hardly tolerate him for very long.[74] In the end, it was precisely this frequent congruence between Alcibiades' ambition and Athenian politics that threatened its democratic government.[75] Both Athens and Alcibiades became caught up in confounding his personal policy with public policy, mistaking his private good for the common good, and in turn his statesmanship subtly assumed the form of a benevolent parent protecting and reprimanding his charges rather than educating and preparing citizens to deal with political crises on their own.[76]

The weaknesses of Alcibiades' leadership should not obscure the positive aspects of his political career as described by Plutarch. Indeed, Alcibiades' adaptability suggests that one need not be morally faultless in order to accomplish a great deal on behalf of the good of the community.[77] From an early age, he did not try to exorcise or mortify his natural spiritedness, but lived with it alongside his more elevated political objectives and thirst for glory. In Alcibiades' successes on behalf of the Athenian and Spartan regimes, Plutarch illustrates that great deeds on behalf of a political cause might be performed in spite of (and even partly thanks to) the all-too-human passions that draw us away from their accomplishment. Alcibiades reached for a life that was unburdened by social restrictions, received traditions, and expectations, one that would give the most generous field of play to his ends and whatever means used to achieve them. For a considerable period of his brief time on earth, he satisfied both of these seemingly contradictory sides of his personality. Like his Roman counterpart Coriolanus, when Alcibiades was in his country, Plutarch writes, he "eminently sustained it"; when in exile, he "eminently damaged" it.[78] These are the type of people that make for statesmen in Plutarch's time and in our own.

Yet in the end, Plutarch's Alcibiades points to some qualities that are necessary but ultimately insufficient for a theory of statesmanship. While we may pine for elected officials that are more responsive to public opinion, his is a cautionary tale of the dangers invited by the statesman that rests his finger too heavily on the pulse of the people.[79] Plutarch teaches that Alcibiades never learned or even seriously attempted to stand up for a higher principle and master his temptations; he is fundamentally an irrational character, totally dependent on and responsive to forces, events, and whims outside his ken.[80] Despite all his magnificent deeds and words, all his acknowledged persuasiveness, great wantonness and luxury were mingled with these qualities, in his drinking, eating, and living (17). So much of his personality was for show; so little of it was for substance. "The truth is," Plutarch confesses, that Alcibiades' "liberalities, his public shows, and other munificence to the people, which were such as nothing could exceed," often served to indulge the people rather than invite critique (18). By spurning private virtue, Alcibiades had done more than repudiate the Socratic way of life based on moderation and philosophy. He had rejected any personal code or standard to live by that transcended his own visceral quest for glory, and the vices that attended such single-mindedness resulted in his downfall on more than one occasion.[81] Try as he might, his skill in changing his colors in response to events without could not guard him from the consequences of the flaws within. Alcibiades' statesmanship was at once a standing reproach to and ultimately a verification of the rule of life inscribed above Plutarch's beloved Delphic temple: "Nothing in Excess."[82]

For Plutarch himself, the bad in Alcibiades outweighed the praiseworthy. With nothing of "temperance, continence, and probity" in his makeup, Plutarch concludes, he was "the least scrupulous and most entirely careless of human beings in all these points."[83] Alcibiades was a good, even great statesman, exhibiting a quickness of mind that any effective political leader must have at his or her disposal. Yet what he possessed in terms of resourcefulness he lacked in principle, or even genuine independence. There lies in him little of the loyalty, sturdy republican virtue, and aversion to civic corruption ingrained granite-like in the Roman statesman Cato the younger. As we turn to Plutarch's assessment of his republicanism, think of him hazarding his dignity in an alcohol-fueled night of debauchery.

NOTES

1. Christopher Pelling, *Plutarch and History: Eighteen Studies* (London: Gerald Duckworth & Co., 2002), 387–411.

2. Robert Lloyd George, *A Modern Plutarch: Comparisons of the Most Influential Modern Statesmen* (New York: Overlook Duckworth, 2016), 3.

3. The philosopher once referred to Plutarch as his "master and consoler." Quoted in Bertrand de Jouvenel, "An Essay on Rousseau's Politics," in *Jean-Jacques Rousseau: Critical Assessments of Leading Political Philosophers*, ed. John T. Scott, 4 vols. (New York: Routledge, 2006) I, 79–140: 90.

4. Emerson praised Plutarch as "among prose writers, what Chaucer is among English poets, a repertory for those who want the story without searching for it at first hand. . . . His delight in magnanimity and self-sacrifice has made his books, like Homer's Iliad, a bible for heroes." Quoted in his introduction to *Plutarch's Morals*, ed. William W. Goodwin (Boston, MA: Little, Brown, and Co., 1878) I, ix–xxiv: xi.

5. Nietzsche viewed the *Lives* as a kind of rude self-help book, an example of those biographies "upon whose title-page there would stand 'a fighter against his age.'" Feed your soul with Plutarch, he proclaimed in 1873, "and when you believe in his heroes dare at the same time to believe in yourself." See his "On the Uses and Disadvantages of History for Life," in *Untimely Meditations*, trans. R. J. Hollingdale (New York: Cambridge University Press, 1997), 57–123: 95.

6. After his presidency, Truman recalled that his "father used to read me out loud from [Plutarch]. And I've read Plutarch through many times since. I have never figured out how he knew so much, I tell you. They just don't come any better than old Plutarch. He knew more about politics than all the other writers I've read put together. When I was in politics, there would be times when I tried to figure somebody out, and I could always turn to Plutarch, and nine times out of ten I'd be able to find a parallel in there." Quoted in Meyer Reinhold, *Classica Americana: The Greek and Roman Heritage in the United States* (Detroit, MI: Wayne State University Press, 1984), 264.

7. The classicist D. A. Russell points out that the *Lives* "has little room for the larger elements of historical composition—speeches, battles, geographical excursuses. [Plutarch] is not bound to relate everything; he can epitomize at one point and expand at another. He is not bound to chronology, but can arrange his material in other ways if he likes. He does not have to assume the Olympian, half-poetical grandeur of history, but can descend on occasion to trivialities or to the informality of personal comment or philosophical argument." See his "On Reading Plutarch's *Lives*," *Greece & Rome* 13, no. 2 (1966), 139–54: 148. Elsewhere, Russell has attributed the influence and charm of the *Lives* to its dramatic literary quality rather than historical accuracy. See his "Plutarch and the Antique Hero," *The Yearbook of English Studies* 12 (1982), 24–34: 34.

8. On the pedagogical function of the *Lives*, see Hubert M. Martin, "Moral Failure Without Vice in Plutarch's Athenian *Lives*," *Ploutarchos* 12, no. 1 (1995), 13–18, and Philip Stadter, *Plutarch and His Roman Readers* (New York: Oxford University Press, 2014), 231–45. Stadter in particular has portrayed the *Lives* as furnishing a kind of "adult education" in which readers are expected to engage in a form of self-analysis comparing their own lives to those narrated by Plutarch. See his "The Rhetoric of Virtue in Plutarch's *Lives*," in *Rhetorical Theory and Practice in Plutarch*, ed. L. Van Der Stockt (Louvain: Peeters, 2000), 493–510: 504.

9. Plutarch, "Life of Alexander," in *Plutarch's Lives*, trans. John Dryden as revised by Arthur Hugh Clough, 5 vols. (Boston: Little, Brown, and Co., 1906), IV, 159–255: 159. On Plutarch's authorial aspirations, see Pelling (2002), 143–70. Reginald Barrow justifies Plutarch's discursive style as consistent with classical approaches to reading, noting that "[i]f the writer had time to stray from the high road, so had the reader; and the digressions of Plutarch were no more tedious to his readers than those of Herodotus to his hearers. . . . In those days reading must have been more leisurely than now; books were fewer and their pages could not be flicked over." See his *Plutarch and His Times* (Bloomington, IN and London: Indiana University Press, 1967), 64.

10. For this point, see Laurel Fulkerson, "Plutarch on the Statesman: Stability, Change, and Regret," *Illinois Classical Studies* 37 (2012), 51–74. Fulkerson notes that Plutarch often portrays a particular character trait in positive or negative lights depending on the context (52). For a particular example of this variability applied to the Greek concept of *philotimia* ("the love of honor"), consider Tim Duff, *Plutarch's Lives: Exploring Virtue and Vice* (Oxford: Clarendon Press, 1999), 83–89.

11. Winston S. Churchill, *The Second World War: The Gathering Storm* (Boston, MA: Houghton, Mifflin, and Co., 1948), 255.

12. On Plutarch's low view of democratic politics, consider Margaret Thornton, "Plutarch and Athenian Democracy," *Ancient Society* 1, no. 4 (1971), 3–22: 11; G. J. D. Aalders, *Plutarch's Political Thought*, trans. A. M. Manekofsky (Amsterdam, Oxford, and New York: North Holland Publishing Co., 1982), 28–32; Duff (1999), 90; Laurel Fulkerson, *No Regrets: Remorse in Classical Antiquity* (Oxford: Oxford University Press, 2013), 209; Suzanne Saïd, "Plutarch and the People in the *Parallel Lives*," in *The Statesman in Plutarch's Works*, eds. Lukas de Blois, Jeroen Bons, Ton Kessels, and Dirk M. Schenkeveld (Leiden and Boston, MA: BRILL, 2005), 7–25; and Stadter (2014), 23–24, 28–32.

13. Simon Verdegem, *Plutarch's Life of Alcibiades: Story, Text and Moralism* (Leuven: Leuven University Press, 2010), 25. A similar point is raised by Duff (1999), who sees degrees of good and bad in Plutarch's moralism and a dearth of "comfortable black or white characters" (64).

14. Robert Lamberton contrasts Plutarch's interest in statesmanship with the lack of opportunities for its demonstration during his lifetime, nothing that his paeans to the "active, engaged life" and the great leaders and statesmen of the past were at odds with his own existence in "a place and an age without politics, where there was no foreign policy, no scope for military excellence—except at the limits of the [Roman] empire, a part of the world that on the whole does not seem to have interested him much." See his *Plutarch* (New Haven, CT: Yale University Press, 2001), 2.

15. Christopher Pelling points out that it was unusual prior to Plutarch's *Lives* for a biographer to chronicle an individual from cradle to grave. See his "Greek Lives," *Ploutarchos* 2 (2004/2005), 71–88: 77.

16. Much of the following reconstruction relies on D. A. Russell's excellent *Plutarch* (London: Longwood, 1973).

17. Barrow (1967), 39.

18. Barrow (ibid.) notes that Plutarch probably did not set out to write the entire *Lives* at once, but after publishing a couple of biographies was probably encouraged by his Roman friends to continue the work (52).

19. For Plutarch's activities as a priest of Delphi see Christopher P. Jones, *Plutarch and Rome* (Oxford: Clarendon Press, 1971), 10, 26, 28–34 and Simon Swain, "Plutarch, Hadrian, and Delphi," *Historia* 40 (1991), 318–30.

20. As quoted in C. J. Gianakaris, "The Legacy of Plutarch," *Western Humanities Review* 22, no. 3 (1968), 207–13: 208.

21. According to Hugh Liebert, "Plutarch was simultaneously a citizen of a city and of an empire; he was Chaeronean and Roman. His ambitions, both political and literary, found outlets on both levels, without one evidently outranking the other in his affections. And yet he seems to have felt that in his time Rome was more of a threat to what he cherished in Chaeronea than Chaeronea was a threat to what he admired in Rome." See his *Plutarch's Politics: Between City and Empire* (New York: Cambridge University Press, 2016), 42.

22. George (2016), 2. But cf. Simon Swain's *Hellenism and Empire: Language, Classicism, and Power in the Greek World, AD 50–250* (Oxford: Clarendon Press, 1996), who argues that Plutarch always saw the heroes of Greek culture as the only models fit for emulation (143).

23. Martha Nussbaum describes Alcibiades as "endowed with a physical grace and splendor that captivated the entire city. They did not decline as he grew, but flourished at each stage with new authority and power," enlarging his vanity over time. See her *The Fragility of Goodness: Luck and Ethics in Greek Tragedy and Philosophy*, revised edition (New York: Cambridge University Press, 2001), 165. For a critical portrayal of Alcibiades as an aristocratic fop, see Charles Baudelaire, *The Painter of Modern Life and Other Essays*, trans. Jonathan Mayne

(London: Phaidon, 1995), 26–27. Alcibiades' only notable physical defect was a lisp that made it a challenge for him to pronounce the letter "r," a handicap ridiculed by the comic playwright Aristophanes in his *Wasps*.

24. Plutarch, "Life of Alcibiades," in *Plutarch's Lives* (1906), II, 1–51: 4. Unless otherwise specified, parenthetical references in this chapter apply to this source. For a thorough discussion of the link between outward appearance and inner excellence in the *Lives*, see W. Jeffrey Tatum, "The Regal Image in Plutarch's *Lives*," *The Journal of Hellenic Studies* 116 (1996), 135–51.

25. On Alcibiades' rejection of Socratic virtue, see Michele A. Lucchesi, "Love Theory and Political Practice in Plutarch: The *Amatorius* and the *Lives of Coriolanus and Alcibiades*," in *Erôs in Ancient Greece*, eds. Ed Sanders, Chiara Thumiger, Chris Carey, and Nick J. Lowe (Oxford: Oxford University Press, 2013), 209–28: 223. The brief pairing of Socrates and Alcibiades—the squat philosopher juxtaposed with the strapping young Athenian—was "a matter of general wonder" among the Athenian people, especially when the two were seen dining, encamping, and eventually fighting alongside each other as soldiers in the Battle of Potidaea (5). Although Socrates eventually surrendered his attempts to make Alcibiades "humble and modest, by showing him in how many things he was deficient," Plutarch notes that only Socrates' speeches were able "to draw tears from [Alcibiades'] eyes, and to disturb his very soul" (7). The complex relationship between the two famous Athenians has received extended treatment in Ariel Helfer's *Socrates and Alcibiades: Plato's Drama of Political Ambition and Philosophy* (Philadelphia: University of Pennsylvania Press, 2017).

26. In light of this description, consider Timothy Duff's suggestion that Plutarch views character as being largely fixed in childhood, "and adult character may be more or less stable or unstable depending on the extent to which nature has been 'mixed' or tempered by education and reason." See his "Models of Education in Plutarch," *Journal of Hellenic Studies* 128 (2008), 1–26: 2. On the theme of unstable personality in Plutarch's thought, see also Christopher Gill, *The Structured Self in Hellenistic and Roman Thought* (New York: Oxford University Press, 2006), 412–21.

27. Barry Strauss, *Fathers and Sons in Athens: Ideology and Society in the Era of the Peloponnesian War* (Princeton, NJ: Princeton University Press, 1993), 152.

28. Eric Hoyer, "Alcibiades' Challenge to Democratic Politics" (PhD diss., University of Pennsylvania, 2011), 30–31, 84.

29. On Alcibiades' tendency to get under the skin of his fellow Athenians, see Grace Harriet Macurdy, "Alcibiades: A Study of a Greek Statesman from the Pages of His Contemporaries," *The Classical Weekly* 2, no. 18 (1909), 138–40 and Matthew A. Sears, *Athens, Thrace, and the Shaping of Athenian Leadership* (New York: Cambridge University Press, 2013), 90.

30. Alcibiades adorned himself, Plutarch relates, with "long purple robes like a woman, which dragged after him as he went through the market-place," carried around the city a garish, "richly gilded" shield emblazoned with an image of Cupid, and enjoyed good food, drink, and women (17).

31. See Kenneth L. Deutsch, "Thomas Aquinas on Magnanimous and Prudent Statesmanship," in *Magnanimity and Statesmanship*, ed. Carson Holloway (Lanham, MD: Rowman & Littlefeld, 2008), 49–65: 49–50.

32. In his *Leviathan* (ed. Edwin Curley; Indianapolis, IN: Hackett, 1994), Thomas Hobbes maintains that mankind's "perpetual and restless desire of power after power," often manifesting in the form of pride or vainglory, can only be safely subdued by an almost omnipotent sovereign (58, 89–100). Jean-Jacques Rousseau, while recognizing the need for a lawgiver of extraordinary virtue and independence in his *Social Contract*, nonetheless viewed such a person as ultimately instrumental and epiphenomenal. See his "On the Social Contract," in *The Collected Writings of Rousseau*, trans. Judith R. Bush, Roger D. Masters, and Christopher Kelly (Hanover, NH: University Press of New England, 1994) IV, 127–224: 154–7.

33. See, e.g., James Madison's famous *Federalist #51*. In the course of arguing that "ambition must be made to counteract ambition," Madison lauded the Constitution's potential to connect the interest of the elected representative to the constitutional rights and prestige of office, thus preventing the concentration of political authority in any single department. See Hamilton et al. (2001), 267–72: 268.

34. Robert K. Faulkner, *The Case for Greatness: Honorable Ambition and Its Critics* (New Haven, CT: Yale University Press, 2007), 2.

35. In his famous study of the American founders, the historian Douglass Adair pointed up "the love of fame" as "a noble passion because it can transform ambition and self-interest into dedicated effort for the community." Interestingly, Adair claimed that "the concrete type of fame" found in Plutarch's *Lives* and other ancient sources formed the template the framers adopted as lawgivers and founders of a modern commonwealth. See his "Fame and the Founding Fathers," in *Fame and the Founding Fathers: Essays by Douglass Adair*, ed. Trevor Colburn (New York: W.W. Norton and Co., 1974), 3–26: 12, 13.

36. For recent works that grapple with the relationship between ambition and democratic politics, see Joseph Romance and Neil Riemer (eds.), *Democracy and Excellence: Concord or Conflict?* (Westport, CT: Praeger, 2005); Faulkner (2007); and Jeffrey A. Becker, *Ambition in America: Political Power and the Collapse of Citizenship* (Lexington, KY: University Press of Kentucky, 2014).

37. Steven Forde, *The Ambition to Rule: Alcibiades and the Politics of Imperialism in Thucydides* (Ithaca, NY: Cornell University Press, 1989), 183.

38. In Plato's *Symposium*, Alcibiades indicates that Socrates was responsible for saving his life during this campaign. See Plato, *The Symposium*, trans. M. C. Howatson (New York: Cambridge University Press, 2008), 60.

39. Gill (2006), 418–9. In Thucydides' *Peloponnesian War* (Chicago: University of Chicago Press, 1989), Alcibiades' youth is a chief line of attack for his cautious rival, Nicias, who decried military campaigns "such as it is not fit for a young man to consult of, much less hastily to take in hand" (383).

40. Alcibiades had secretly convinced the ambassadors to present themselves to the Athenian people as treating informally on behalf of Sparta (15). When the ambassadors did as he suggested, Alcibiades welshed on his oath of goodwill and publicly accused the men of duplicity, sending the people into a rage and Nicias, who had orchestrated the negotiations, into bewilderment (16).

41. Martin Ostwald characterizes Alcibiades' political triumph over Nicias as a clash between "youth, dash, and color" and "dull and staid" experience, noting that while "Alcibiades was entering the political stage in a flash . . . Nicias had earned his spurs the hard way, serving with Pericles before getting a command of his own." See his *From Popular Sovereignty to the Sovereignty of Law: Law, Society, and Politics in Fifth-Century Athens* (Berkeley, CA: University of California Press, 1986), 301.

42. A more notorious example of Alcibiades' rhetorical power, to say nothing of his ruthless foreign policy, was his successful effort to persuade the Athenians to slaughter the inhabitants of the small Spartan colony of Melos. According to Thucydides (1989), after the town of Melos surrendered to the Athenians in 416, the Athenians "slew all the men of military age, made slaves of the women and children, and inhabited the place with a colony sent thither afterwards of five hundred men of their own" (372).

43. On the complex relationship between Alcibiades and the Athenian people in the *Lives*, see Leo Strauss, *The City and Man* (Chicago: University of Chicago Press, 1964), 199, 204–5; Michael Palmer, *Love of Glory and the Common Good: Aspects of the Political Thought of Thucydides* (Lanham, MD: Rowman & Littlefield, 1992), 79–110; and David Gribble, *Alcibiades and Athens: A Study in Literary Presentation* (Oxford: Clarendon Press, 1999), 270.

44. Alcibiades despised the so-called "peace of Nicias" between Athens and Sparta and sought to undermine Athenian confidence in both the treaty and its namesake. Plutarch notes that the more Alcibiades' fellow citizens celebrated the treaty, the more he bristled with envy toward its architect (13–14).

45. Alcibiades was charged with sacrilegious behavior offending the goddesses Ceres and Prosperine, to wit, "representing in derision the holy mysteries, and showing them to his companions in his own house . . . [and] nam[ing] himself the chief priest . . . contrary to the laws and institutions of the Eumopidae" (26). It was considered a form of blasphemy to imitate such rites outside the walls of the temple-precinct without the authorization and supervision of a priest. On Plutarch's telling, however, "[Alcibiades'] accusers alleged nothing that was certain or solid against him" (24). Stephen Usher notes that the culprits of the desecration were

never ascertained, and speculates that the deed may have been perpetrated by Alcibiades' enemies in an effort to frame him. See his "Alcibiades and the Lost Empire," *History Today* 21, no. 2 (1971), 116–22: 119 and cf. the account detailed by Thucydides (1989), 392–3.

46. Despite the efforts of the Athenians to deal with the accusations against Alcibiades in a manner that would not damage the war efforts, Plutarch notes that the Athenian soldiers were dispirited to learn that Alcibiades, their great "spur to action," had been ordered away from the field of battle (26).

47. Plutarch declares that "It was Alcibiades, alone, or, at least, principally, who prevented [insurrection] . . . for he not only used persuasion to the whole army, and showed them the danger, but applied himself to them, one by one, entreating some, and constraining others" (33–34).

48. Thus as Helfer (2017) notes in his discussion of Alcibiades, "political ambition, even at its most virtuous, is never simply selfless. . . . The democracies of ancient Greece consistently produced ambitious figures whose zeal for political honor was so great it threatened to outstrip or distort the intention to win that honor through honorable service" (2).

49. Alcibiades was said to be "full of fear" about returning to Athens, the lone mention of the emotion in Plutarch's narrative of his life (42). But initially the Athenians' celebrated his return, and the only thing to dampen their spirits was "the remembrance of the miseries [the Athenians] had endured" since his departure. Plutarch records a widespread belief that Athens' misfortune may have been avoided "if they had left the management of their affairs formerly, and the command of their forces, to Alcibiades."

50. At least, this is the explanation offered by Plutarch, but disagreement abounds concerning Alcibiades' exact whereabouts. Regardless of his location, he was absent from his fleet at a pivotal moment.

51. Quoted in John Finlay, "The Night of Alcibiades," *The Hudson Review* 47, no. 1 (1994), 57–79: 65.

52. Indeed, Plutarch relates that the Athenians in their misery still held out "faint hopes" that so long as Alcibiades drew breath he might one day return to Athens and re-establish democratic government (49).

53. During this period, Alcibiades apparently became a pirate. After leaving the Athenians a second time, Alcibiades and a band of mercenary soldiers took to making war upon "those Thracians who called themselves free, and acknowledged no king. By this means he amassed to himself a considerable treasure, and, at the same time, secured the bordering Greeks from the incursions of the barbarians" (47).

54. Plutarch mentions other reports that Alcibiades' death ensued from his debauchment of a young lady of patrician birth, and that it was her angry brothers, not hired assassins, who were his executioners (51). Whichever story we choose to believe, in both cases Alcibiades' passionate nature, so instrumental to his early political success, is accessory to a rather inglorious demise.

55. Jeffrey Beneker has described the concept of *erōs* in the *Lives* as a barometer for "the presence of self-control in general, and by extension, for revealing a statesman's ability to take aim at a political or military goal, and then to pursue that goal to its fruition without distraction." See his *The Passionate Statesman: Erōs and Politics in Plutarch's Lives* (New York: Oxford University Press, 2012), 223.

56. This feeling was mutual, at least if we are to take the word of Aristophanes, who once summed up the fraught relationship between Alcibiades and the Athenians in the following terms: "They love, and hate, and cannot do without him" (18).

57. Niccolò Machiavelli, *The Prince*, trans. Harvey C. Mansfield, 2nd ed. (Chicago: University of Chicago Press, 1998), 61–62.

58. Herbert Croly, *The Promise of American Life* (Princeton, NJ: Princeton University Press, 2014), 89–122. In a similar vein, consider President Franklin Delano Roosevelt's description of the Constitution as a document characterized by "generality, implication and statement of mere objectives" permitting "flexible statesmanship of the future . . . [that is] adapt[ed] to time and circumstance." See his famous "Address on Constitution Day, September 17, 1937" in *The Public Papers and Addresses of Franklin D. Roosevelt*, ed. Samuel I. Rosenman (New York: Macmillan, 1941) VI, 359–66: 363.

59. See, e.g., Fred Fiedler, *A Theory of Leadership Effectiveness* (New York: McGraw-Hill, 1967); John Colville, "The Qualities of a Statesman," *Schweizer Monatshefte: Zeitschrift fur Politik, Wirtschaft, Kultur* 59, no. 2 (1979), 1–11: 6–8; Paul Hersey, *The Situational Leader* (New York: Warner, 1985); Gene E. Hall and Shirley M. Hord, *Change in Schools: Facilitating the Process* (Albany, NY: State University of New York Press, 1987), 16–18; Ronald A. Heifetz and Donald L. Laurie, "The Work of Leadership," *Harvard Business Review* 75, no. 1 (1997), 124–34; Gary Yukl, "How Leaders Influence Organizational Effectiveness," *The Leadership Quarterly* 19, no. 6 (2008), 708–22; Ronald Heifetz, Alexander Grashow, and Marty Linsky, *The Practice of Adaptive Leadership* (Boston: Harvard Business Press, 2009); and Gary Yukl and Ribina Mahsud, "Why Flexible and Adaptive Leadership is Essential," *Consulting Psychology Journal: Practice and Research* 62, no. 2 (2010), 81–93.

60. The cosmopolitan philosopher Michel de Montaigne once applauded Alcibiades' ability to "conform to [the] custom" of any habitation, thus avoiding drawing unwanted attention to himself amid the "strangeness and oddness" of his surroundings. See Michel de Montaigne, *The Complete Essays*, trans. E. A. Screech (New York: Penguin, 1993), 187.

61. Hoyer (2011) notes that Alcibiades' adaptability to different regimes betrayed a "love of politics for its own sake" that went beyond the welfare of the people he purportedly served (32).

62. Forde (1989), 122.

63. Alcibiades' recommendations included sending forces to help the besieged Syracusans and fortifying a Spartan raiding-post in the village of Decelea near Athens, where an important trading route connecting Athens to the island of Euboea was located (27).

64. Robert Flacelière, *Daily Life in Greece at the Time of Pericles*, trans. Peter Green (London: Phoenix Press, 2002), 171.

65. Plutarch notes that Tissaphernes was so won over by Alcibiades' charm that he named his most "royally and exquisitely adorned" park after him (30).

66. Plutarch notes that on matters of finance, Alcibiades "was often guilty of procuring [funds] by accepting bribes, and spent it ill in luxury and dissipation." See his "Comparison of Alcibiades with Coriolanus," in Plutarch's *Lives* (1906; II), 101–106: 103. Plutarch pays a sort of backhand compliment in declaring that Alcibiades never ruled by means of violence, terror, or oppression.

67. Ibid., 102.

68. Ibid., 105–6.

69. Ibid., 106, 105.

70. See Forde (1989), who argues that in orienting his self-interest exclusively toward honor and politics, Alcibiades' ambitions reflect the fondest aspirations of all statesmen (183, 204).

71. On the idea that Alcibiades is a figure who scorns chance and in so doing exemplifies an older Athenian notion of risk-taking, see Lowell Edmunds, *Chance and Intelligence in Thucydides (*Cambridge, MA: Harvard University Press, 1975), 110.

72. Max Weber, "The Sociology of Charismatic Authority," in *From Max Weber: Essays in Sociology*, trans. Hans Heinrich Gerth and C. Wright Mills (New York: Oxford University Press, 1977), 245–54: 245. For a more recent application of Weber's idea, see Carnes Lord's *The Modern Prince: What Leaders Need to Know Now* (New Haven, CT: Yale University Press, 2003), 19, 23.

73. These parallels are brought into greater relief by Pelling (2002), 125–8; Jeffrey Alan Becker, "Statesmanship and Power: A Biography of Ambition in America" (PhD diss., Rutgers University, 2004), 63; and Fulkerson (2013), 70.

74. Faulkner (2007), 58.

75. As Hoyer (2011) puts it, "Ambition is a key component of much of the literature on statesmanship and it always poses a threat to democratic bodies. How are we to let one individual sit above the rest, even if we need this person's expertise? Alcibiades' character flaws and his excellence put this question in a most useful, if troubling, way" (228).

76. Ibid., 84. Alcibiades' own sensitivity to the danger he posed to Athenian democracy is epitomized in an anecdote Plutarch tells about Alcibiades' large, beautiful, and expensive dog. He cut off the animal's tail, and when his friends told him the people were speaking badly

about him for having done so, he laughed and replied, "Just what I wanted has happened, then. I wished the Athenians to talk about this, that they might not say something worse of me" (10).

77. Finlay (1994) suggests that Alcibiades may have been the real-life model for Socrates' infamous description of the democratic soul in book eight of Plato's *Republic*, wherein the democratic individual is depicted as a chaos of passions and hedonistic pleasures (58).

78. Plutarch (1906; II), "Comparison of Alcibiades with Coriolanus," 101.

79. See Aalders (1982), 30 and Fulkerson (2012), 70.

80. On the importance Plutarch attributes to "static" character traits in the *Lives*, see Simon Swain, "Character Change in Plutarch," *Phoenix* 43, no. 1 (1989), 62–68, Duff (2008), 22–23. As Fulkerson (2012) puts it, "In general, Plutarch favors consistency—sticking to the same plan or behaving in the same way—over flexibility of behavior or mindset. While he is certainly capable of seeing the drawbacks to consistency and the benefits of its opposite, he, like nearly all other ancient authors, seems to believe that a change of behavior, even for a good reason (e.g., flexibility in meeting changed circumstances or in order to appease the popular temper) often bespoke some larger, often troubling, inconsistency within the self" (51).

81. Simon Verdegem, "Parallels and Contrasts: Plutarch's *Comparison of Coriolanus and Alcibiades*," in *Plutarch's Lives: Parallelism and Purpose*, ed. Noreen Humble (Swansea: Classical Press of Wales, 2010), 23–44: 28.

82. Usher (1971) argues that Alcibiades "had conceived no limits to his ambitions, and brooked no impediment to them, neither law, nor religion, nor convention," concluding that "[i]f it had been possible to harness the talents of Alcibiades, Athens might have kept her empire as well as her cultural pre-eminence" (122). Similarly, Nussbaum (2001) sums up the life of Alcibiades as "a story of waste and loss, of the failure of practical reason to shape a life" (166).

83. Plutarch (1906; II), "Comparison of Alcibiades with Coriolanus," 106.

Chapter Two

Principle and Resistance in Plutarch's "Life of Cato the Younger"

Into the cruel world of reality he was born too late. Marcus Porcius Cato Uticensis, commonly called Cato the younger, was a man out of his time, or as Plutarch describes him, a fruit ripe before its season.[1] If Alcibiades' chief attribute was his ability to camouflage himself to the times, Cato refused to disguise his own solid and substantial character in response to fortune's whims. Guided by firm convictions concerning both individual and political conduct, Cato's statesmanship testifies to how an inner code may both guide political decisions and serve as an engine of resistance in times of change. Alcibiades, like many politicians today, could never tolerate being unpopular for long. Cato would accept ignominy with pride if it meant preserving the Roman republic—that is, if pride could ever break through his virtue. Centered on ideas of restraint and resistance to political corruption, Plutarch's portrayal of Cato's statesmanship provides a counterbalance to Alcibiadean leadership. Nevertheless, his life brings to the surface difficulties attending any quest for a more ethical form of political leadership today.

In light of Cato's abiding place as a torchbearer in American political history, it is somewhat surprising that political theorists have not had more to say about either the younger Cato's statesmanship or Plutarch's analysis of its significance. Indeed, Roman political thought has been viewed as an afterthought by many scholars of the ancient world. As Benjamin Straumann has argued, political theorists are often prone to lumping Greece and Rome together, leading to a dull perception of distinctly Roman political ideas or an overconcentration on matters of Roman institutional or constitutional design.[2] Moreover, when Cato is studied by scholars today, it is rarely via Plutarch's *Lives* but through the lens of the Roman historians Sallust or Tacitus, whose works typically invoked Cato's severity as a point of contrast with his more opportunistic peers.[3] Plutarch's "Life of Cato the Younger" is more detailed than these broader accounts of Roman politics and conveys, above all, a lesson in statesmanship that brings into clearer view the idiosyncratic positive and negative attributes of Rome's republican hero.[4] For its bearing on understanding political leadership today as well as its value for sharpening our perception of Roman political theory, Plutarch's Cato merits closer attention than it has hitherto received.

Plutarch, like many others since his time, was quite seduced by Cato's charms. Even a cursory reading of the "Life of Cato" shows that Plutarch admired his subject immensely, at times heaping such fulsome praise on his character that many scholars have questioned the reliability of his narrative.[5] Yet even allowing for literary embellishments, Cato is a figure one would expect to find in any catalogue of history's great statesmen as a symbol of the responsibilities of republican liberty and, relatedly, the duty of resistance to political corruption and tyranny.[6] Certainly his example gave solace to many eighteenth-century Americans, who drew parallels between his critical stance toward corruption and their own.[7] Thanks to the popularity of the playwright Joseph Addison's *Cato*, many of the founding generation, notably George Washington, came to appreciate the nobility as well as tragedy involved in risking life and limb on behalf of a civic ideal.[8] Following the American Revolution, anti-federalist opponents of the federal Constitution claimed to be inheritors of his legacy in their defiance of expanded national power. Guard your liberties jealously, the anti-federalist writer "Cato" admonished his readers, lest "great power connected with ambition, luxury and flattery" create an American Caesar "as the same causes did in the Roman empire."[9] Similar references have extended into the twenty-first century, as Cato and his identification with the public good continue to be invoked by citizens concerned about government corruption and overreach. Without question, Cato has had a good deal to teach American citizens and political leaders of the past and present. What might be his message for those of the future?

PLUTARCH'S CATO

Fate decreed that Cato would live in the shadow of his great-grandfather of the same name (234–194 B.C.), the famed conservative orator and senator most often recalled for defending native Roman values against the spread of Greek culture.[10] Born a century and a half later, the younger Cato (95–46 B.C.) seemed to have some of this same conservatism sewn into his character. From his very infancy, according to Plutarch, in Cato's "speech, his countenance, and all his childish pastimes, he discovered an inflexible temper, unmoved by any passion, and firm in everything."[11] Although an orphan, the great statesmen and orators of the republic's heyday seemed to stand in as ghostly father figures for him, teaching virtue through their example and checking whatever vices arose during his youth (370).[12] Indeed, emulating their traits and talents seemed to inoculate Cato against manipulation of all sorts. Rough toward flatterers and even more belligerent toward those that dared to bully him, he would never suffer fools gladly. Independent of patrician and plebeian alike, he was free to chart his own political path through the city's bruising hierarchies with only his unwavering principles for company.

Throughout his life, Cato would have a complicated relationship with his Roman contemporaries. To begin with, he was not very well liked. His "strict and austere" habits could be mistaken for putting on airs, and while his distant attitude elicited "awe and respect" among members of the public it also led to ridicule and suspicion (374, 386). His colleague Cicero, himself a loyal republican, once remarked that notwithstanding Cato's integrity and patriotism, he often spoke in the Senate as though he were living in Plato's republic rather than "among the dregs of Romulus's posterity."[13] In truth, Cato was always a little out of sync with the times: he adopted an unusual course of self-mortification and inner composure that jarred with the civic upheaval of his day. In a way, this was how he sought to lead others, having "esteemed the customs and manners of men at that time so corrupt, and a reformation in them so necessary," that he was willing "to go contrary to the ordinary way of the world" in his habits (376). Yet he never became indifferent toward the *res publica*, the "public thing," in Rome. He did not care if he offended the sensibilities of grandees, since he believed that the republic was more important than any one man, and that in the grand scheme of things personality and popularity mattered little in comparison to defending the common good.[14] Yet neither was he anti-social: Cato was a child of the republic insofar as he understood that the individual pursuit of justice, moral rectitude, and the good life were facilitated and perfected through society and participation in its political life. Passing between the boundaries separating public and private life effortlessly, in all his diverse public offices—prætor, quæstor, senator, and tribune—Cato adhered to an admirable if Quixotic mission to purge Roman politics of financial and civic malfeasance, envisioning a body politic as free from vice and corruption as his own.[15]

Long before ever stepping foot in Roman politics, Cato volunteered to defend republican values on the field of battle. As a soldier in the Roman army, he helped organize the men who put down the slave uprising instigated and led by the Thracian gladiator Spartacus, and his heroism coupled with his noble lineage gained him a speedy entry into the world of statecraft (377).[16] Unlike Alcibiades, however, Cato used his military reputation to become one of the most rare of birds: the honest politician.[17] He did not conceive politics as a moneymaking enterprise, but as the highest duty of a citizen, a duty made all the more critical in light of the republic's woes. Thus Plutarch pronounces that Cato's political undertakings, like his military campaigns, were performed not to attain "honour or riches," nor persecuted "out of mere impulse, or by chance," but because Cato believed "the service of the state [to be] the proper business of an honest man, and therefore he thought himself obliged to be as constant to his public duty as the bee to the honeycomb" (389). Dedication to the republic would be Cato's sword to carry and fall on—figuratively and literally.

SELF-GOVERNMENT

At least in the classical era, the ability to govern oneself was inseparable from that of governing others. The city is merely the soul writ large, as Socrates famously suggested to his interlocutor Adeimantus in Plato's *Republic*, and detecting the presence or absence of justice on a grand scale is not unlike identifying its existence in the individual.[18] Nor was the relationship between private and public character a byproduct of the Greek world alone. Many Roman thinkers and politicians continued to pay heed to the virtue of moderation, emphasizing the importance of restraint, equanimity in the face of adversity, and the subordination of the passions to reason. As Cicero once remarked with uncharacteristic pith, "the more we excel, the more humbly should we behave."[19] On such accounts, good leadership was wedded to notions of moderation, sobriety, and a sense of proportion necessary to keep one from veering toward political extremes.[20] Today, modern citizens are more inclined to show lenience regarding private failings and moral imperfections, emphasizing credentials and results frequently at the expense of character and integrity. Nonetheless, the idea that private and public personae are intertwined and have some bearing on one's leadership capabilities continues to have currency.[21] We often express indignation toward the personal failings of politicians, even if election results tell a different story.

Few if any men of his time took his private character as seriously as Cato.[22] His moral code, hammered on the forge of self-denial, was rooted in Stoicism.[23] He was in fact a natural fit for its rigorous and "severe way of living," whose tenets he learned at the knee of an obscure teacher of the doctrine, Antipater of Tyre (425, 374). Even as a young child, Plutarch reports, Cato was mature beyond his years—"it was difficult to excite him to laughter, [and] his countenance seldom relaxed even into a smile"—but he did his best to turn his "natural stubbornness and slowness to be persuaded" from an impediment to an asset in his formal education (370). He assumed a monk-like lifestyle of self-denial that inured "his body to labor and violent exercise," retiring from human contact for long stretches of time and surrendering his possessions and inheritance (375).[24] When he did go out in public, he was often seen roaming bareheaded and shoeless no matter the season in order to strengthen his physique. Eccentric? Certainly. Yet this was an education of mind as well as body. As Plutarch describes, Cato's efforts to root out vice were reinforced by the study of philosophy, particularly ethics, which instilled in him an affinity for every virtue, the foremost being "that steady and inflexible justice which is not to be wrought upon by favour or compassion" (374). Altogether, Cato's regimen resulted in his possession of almost superhuman levels of self-abnegation and restraint, arguably unparalleled among political leaders before or since his time.

One might expect such an upbringing to lead to a quiet, hermetic life somewhere far removed from the welter of public affairs. Yet Cato's principled moderation was channeled into both his military and political career, thereby testing and solidifying his education by means of experience. As commander of the Roman army, Cato made every effort to make his men like himself by blending reason with authority (379).[25] He was no impetuous leader but a disciplined commander that meted out rewards and punishments in accordance with desert, and by his example "it was hard to say whether [his soldiers] were more peaceable or more warlike, more valiant or more just." Indeed, Cato did not shy from the hardships of war. While his "character, high purpose, and wisdom" were unmatched, Plutarch relates, he adopted the diet, apparel, and mode of transportation of his subordinates, earning the love as well as respect of the soldiers. Yet even though his even temper proved valuable in the heat of battle, it often befuddled his contemporaries in the arena of civil society. When he declined accolades for his service during the slave uprisings, Plutarch relates that Cato was regarded by many Romans as "a man of a strange and eccentric temper" for rejecting public recognition (377).[26] In fact, such disavowals were of a piece with his republicanism: Cato recognized that the republic's successes, whether in war or politics, should not be ascribed to any single person, himself included.

Cato's core principles of self-government and moderation were taxed by the often-duplicitous and opportunistic behavior of his peers. Yet just as his education prepared him for battle against unruly slaves, it also equipped him for dealing with political adversaries. It helped that the distinctly Roman Stoicism he imbibed was not focused exclusively on abstract philosophy, metaphysics, and contemplation, but involved precepts governing immediate, day-to-day conduct.[27] Cato had another advantage going into politics: a thorough education in and facility with the art of rhetoric and debate, a skill he wielded not as a tool for self-promotion but as a means for defending the republican regime.[28] He believed that "the art of speaking and debating in public" was necessary to preserving the martial or warlike spirit of the state, an indispensible element in any great commonwealth (374). While there was no grandstanding in Cato's speeches, Plutarch writes that if something needed to be spoken, he could be counted on to say it—with a "full and sounding voice" in language that was "straightforward, full of matter, and rough" (375).[29] Certainly, at times Cato's integrity and subdued demeanor made him appear to be ill-suited for the kind of political combat carried out among Roman elites. Nonetheless, Cato's speech was capable of moving the emotions of his audience, as was evident before a battle at Dyrrhachium in the twilight of the republic when, Plutarch notes, he outdid the general Pompey in rallying the spirits of the Roman army with repeated invocations of "liberty, manly virtue, death, and a good name" (426).[30] His oratory was intended to recall his fellow Romans to the basic principles of civic duty that held together both his moral constitution and, he hoped, that of the Roman republic. Cato embraced philosophy in a way that Alcibiades neither would nor could, Plutarch suggests, as he served the republic as a kind of philosopher-rhetor concerned foremost with improving the body politic by correcting its ignorance rather than exploiting office to his advantage through flattery or manipulation (385).[31] Whether in armed or political conflict, he was prepared to speak and fight on behalf of his principles, win or lose.

In the political realm, Cato's discipline found expression in his professional conduct. He was concerned not with the "title and honor" of public office, Plutarch states, but "the knowledge and understanding" of its responsibilities, and so was unwilling to rush into any position without having first acquired an understanding of its authority and obligations (385). Out of concern for the republic, he found his niche as a defender of tradition, fiscal responsibility, and thrift, logging long hours—"he always came first of any of his colleagues to the treasury, and went away the last," Plutarch reports—that underscored his dedication to the commonwealth (387). Unsurprisingly, Cato avoided the circles of the political elite and social climbers, preferring instead to absorb himself in the task of protecting the republic from even the smallest financial mismanagement or self-dealing. Combining in Plutarch's words "an admirable mildness of temper and greatness of spirit," Cato sought to stem the tide of growing political acrimony, power politics, and civil unrest—in short, profligacy of all kinds, as he could never stand any kind of waste (383). Occasionally this devotion won cheers, as was the case when he bravely prosecuted a group of assassins in the employ of the dictator Sulla for their "unlawful and impious actions" against the republic (387).[32] But despite being returned to public office on many occasions, he was not always an object of applause. In an effort to shut down bribery, he championed a law requiring public officials to answer questions under oath about their financial transactions during the preceding election (414). In response, candidates for office and their well-heeled supporters dreaded to exchange money even as they feared their competitors would figure out some way to skirt the law. Rival politicians were at one, however, in their dislike for Cato's hard medicine (416). Political elites and their votaries took to pelting Cato with stones as he made his way through the streets of the city (415). Undaunted, Cato took it upon himself to act as a kind of election monitor so that he might keep a watchful eye over the new regulations governing candidate expenditures, a move that provoked admiration as well as resentment.[33] Plutarch teaches that the statesman committed to moderating the immoderate regime must, at least for a time, be prepared to endure some unpopularity.

Indeed, Cato made few friends in politics. Recognizing that draining the Roman swamp would be no easy task, he remained undeterred by any opposition, no matter how many would-be dictators attempted to thwart his reforms. Moreover, a significant portion of his ire was directed toward the Roman people themselves, whom he did not flinch from rebuking for their complicity in the republic's corruption (391).[34] It was a daring move for one who could never fall back on a winning personality. With a stony disposition "not to be wrought upon by favor or compassion," he could hardly count on launching a charm offensive in support of his proposals (374).[35] Yet he kept at the work of endearing himself, however obliquely, to friend and foe alike by means of his example. At one point, Plutarch notes, Cato dedicated himself to reviving a rarely observed law requiring candidates for office to memorize the names of their fellow citizens, and soon learned "by his own knowledge" the names of all he spoke with, to the praise and derision of his colleagues (378).[36] Only with time did his peers warm to him, though it surely helped matters that he was willing to accept both praise and blame for the stringency of his political reforms. It was all Cato's fault, critics could cry to citizens who begged for favors: neither the rich nor the poor could gain a foothold on public affairs under his watchful eye (415).[37]

Moderation distinguished Cato's personal, military, and political conduct, a leitmotif that has been occasionally portrayed tragically or even negatively.[38] As the classical historian Edward Gibbon concluded somewhat unfairly, Cato illustrated "that a character of pure and inflexible virtue is the most apt to be misled by prejudice, to be heated by enthusiasm, and to confound private enmities with public justice."[39] It is true that Cato's intransigence never allowed him to bend principles to suit the exigencies of the day, resulting in a slowness to act that perhaps explains Plutarch's sometimes critical tone toward his life.[40] Perhaps this lack of versatility is the price one must pay for living in accordance with a single ethical code or rule. Yet if Cato's notorious stubbornness in some instances constrained the scope of his leadership, it did not defang him as a political opponent. Few public figures resisted the approaching imperial age as vigorously as he did.

RESISTANCE

In contrast to politicians who kowtow to or exploit popular sentiment, statesmanship is often seen as entailing a type of courageous resistance to the prevailing winds of majority opinion and political change. On such accounts, the courage of one's convictions, not the shifting sands of public opinion, should be the ground on which one stands. At least this idea of statesmanship was the hope of many of the Constitution's framers, who believed that its rules and procedures would not only inoculate ambition but also facilitate leadership capable of resisting factious influences and demagoguery.[41] Distrust of the people and the politicians that indulged their whims was not unique to North America, however. "In history a great volume is unrolled for our instruction," British Member of Parliament Edmund Burke wrote in his *Reflections on the Revolution in France* (1790), "drawing the materials of future wisdom from the past errors and infirmities of mankind."[42] For Burke and other critics of mass democracy, past experience teaches the grave consequences wrought "by pride, ambition, avarice, revenge, lust, sedition, hypocrisy, ungoverned zeal, and all the train of disorderly appetites"—vices that he believed the statesman must withstand rather than placate. For such thinkers, the epitome of the statesman consists in the willingness to resist the momentary whims and passions of the general public, inspired as they often are by the overall weakness of human reason. Yet resistance need not be confined in its expression to anti-populist screeds declaiming against the wisdom of crowds. Throughout American political history and into the present day, statesmanship as resistance to the powers-that-be has been preached from a range of pulpits, spanning right-wing Jerimiahs such as Pat Buchannan to centrist-liberals like Daniel Patrick Moynihan to recent far-left-leaning "anti-fascist" resistance movements.[43] Amid this diversity of voices is a common refrain of praise for the political leader who has the strength to swim against the stream of public opinion and stand up for what he or she believes is right, personal or political fortunes be damned.

For Plutarch, Cato was as impervious as the legionnaire's shield, standing almost alone against the erosion of Roman republicanism. Perhaps he was destined for such a role, being from his adolescence "resolute in his purposes, much beyond the strength of his age, to go through with whatever he undertook" (370). His political outlook was traditionalist, not that of a fly-by-night revolutionary, and he was intent on learning from the wisdom of the ages rather than litigating its inadequacies. The best of this past was gathered in what was called the *mos maiorum* (roughly, the "way of the ancestors"). The Roman republic did not have a written constitution, but rather a widely agreed upon set of principles, traditions, and social norms forming a way of life that guided law-making on the solid basis of immemorial custom.[44] Cato did his best to anchor the ship of state to this history during his "stormy and tempestuous" time, lending his "fixed and immovable bent to all virtuous and honest action" to the task of preserving the civic standards that had made the republic a success.[45] For Cato, there were practical as well as sentimental reasons for defending such traditions. The Roman constitution, like the common law in Great Britain today, was flexible—certainly more flexible than Cato himself—and this quality had on more than one occasion prevented the periodic clashes between aristocrats and plebeians from spilling over into outright anarchy or civil war.[46] Indeed, over the centuries-long growth of Rome from provincial city-state to cosmopolitan metropolis, its republican ethos had been a touchstone of consistency and familiarity amid great political, cultural, and geographic upheaval and expansion. Here was the tradition, identity, and political system that Cato resolved to defend, "inflexible to pleasure, fear, or [the] foolish entreaties" of opponents or purported friends (380).

Cato's personality as well as his commitment to stemming the tide of corruption met a dramatic antagonist in the form of one of history's most notorious political figures: Julius Caesar. The public lives of these two figures tracked closely, not merely in time but also in their possession of a clear-eyed vision of the future Rome. Yet a collision course between the two titans was inevitable. There were too many differences in their personalities, their ultimate loyalties. Cato did all things with the utmost care; Caesar acted quickly, both in war and politics. Indeed, Caesar did little to restrain his passions, especially his impulse toward political rule, power, and glory. Yet as a military commander he was no voluptuary, instead coveting all manner of danger, hardship, and labor during his several military campaigns.[47] He was in Plutarch's estimate "born to do great things," with his "passion after honor" always impelling him to surpass all past efforts with new claims to fame.[48] While rivaling Caesar in military prowess, Cato is portrayed by Plutarch as the lone voice in the wilderness remonstrating against his fellow Romans' dangerous ambition. There were not many listeners. Caesar appealed not to immemorial custom and principles, but to Romans as he found them in the republic's late hour: hungry for territory, politically anxious, and civically apathetic. Cato, like Marcus Brutus, spoke the language of pious virtue in hopes of reclaiming an ever-more distant past. For his part, Caesar's power, driven by his own pretensions to glory, was built on fear, an basis of support that overpowered whatever reverence the people had for Cato (433). Even if his opponent's designs had been frankly admitted, however, Cato's cause would have faced an uphill climb: it would take more than one man to fell Caesar.

An early showdown with Caesar pitted Cato's resistance against the wishes of the people and those of the future emperor. In an effort to win popular support to their side, Caesar and his allies set themselves against the aristocratic Roman Senate, proposing land reform laws that would redistribute arable land to the poor and needy. From the outset, Cato saw through the proposal as well as its instigator. While he stated he did not oppose "the advantage the people should get by this division of the lands," he was chagrined that political leaders should advance their causes "by thus courting and cozening the people" (402). Sensing their plan in growing peril the longer Cato spoke, Caesar's supporters quickly strong-armed the Senate into supporting and defending the land reforms.[49] Even with the writing on the wall, only Cato's close friend Cicero could persuade him to reluctantly accede to the proposal on behalf of the people—"though Cato have no need of Rome, yet Rome has need of Cato, and so likewise have all his friends," Cicero is reported to have pleaded—but he did not hold his tongue for long (403). When a confident Caesar introduced another law that would designate most of the Campania region in Southern Italy for a similar division, nobody dared to speak against the proposal except an enraged Cato. He minced no words, lambasting not only the so-called reforms but the people for having set a "a tyrant in their citadel," with such language that Caesar signaled his removal from the rostrum to prison, Cato continuing to rant against him the whole way (403, 404).[50] The episode tested the mettle of Cato's resistance just as it revealed Caesar's growing insecurities about his authority. Criticizing both Caesar and those senators and citizens who supported him, his principled republicanism worked hand-in-glove with his resistance to one-man rule and those that supported it.

Throughout Caesar's rise to power, Cato continued to be a stubborn thorn in the future autocrat's side. After Cato helped quash an attempt by the Roman Senator Lucius Catilina to overthrow the consulship of Cicero, Caesar realized seizing control of Roman government would be no easy task.[51] He was under suspicion and would need protection, which is why in 60 B.C. he formed a party comprising the "most corrupt and dissolute elements of the state" (395). As his power continued to expand, Plutarch depicts Cato as one of the few major figures that resisted figures such as the military commander Pompey and the wealthy aristocrat Marcus Crassus in their attempts to join with Caesar to "subvert the constitution and parcel out the empire" for their mutual benefit (410). Often taking his life into his own hands, it was Cato, Plutarch argues, who "void of all fear, and full of assurance" stood firm against their combined efforts to assume office and divide the spoils of power among themselves (397). It was Cato who urged the Senate to see through and oppose Caesar's "soft words and popular speeches" that would lead to the ruin of the republic (393). Later, it was Cato who, by standing for the prætorship, opposed the combined might of the First Triumvirate—consisting of Caesar, Pompey, and Crassus—reasoning "that he might not act as a private man, when he was to contend with public magistrates" (411).[52] And in a twist of fate, it was Cato who, in declining to accept a marriage alliance with the family of Pompey, perhaps led to the institution of the Triumvirate in the first place (400).[53] On this last point, in Plutarch's view, his principled resistance may have cost the republic dearly.[54] For his part, Cato believed that his opposition to Caesar, even if unsuccessful, was the right thing to do: the Roman constitution could survive only if good citizens were willing to speak up and in their personal and political conduct do what was right. Far better to lose gracefully with "justice and honesty," he reasoned to his fellow Romans, than suffer Caesar's fate, that is, to be "found guilty of those designs against his country, which he had so long practised and so constantly denied" (436). Cato's statesmanship is most distinctive in moments such as these. Civic virtue is essential to leading a nation to victory or new heights; it may also be a balm in defeat.

It was not long before Cato's prophecies concerning Caesar's designs were fulfilled.[55] As enemies to Caesar were eliminated, Cato was increasingly becoming public enemy number one. Yet to the end he continued to resist the inevitable as much as he could, continuing to repeat to his fellow senators the "severe truths" concerning Caesar, reiterating a now familiar refrain to his fellow listeners that "it was not the sons of the Britons or the Gauls they need fear, but Caesar himself, if they were wise" (422). Buoyed by a spate of military successes, in 49 B.C. Caesar, "in a sort of passion, casting aside calculation, and abandoning himself to what might come," traversed the Rubicon river and took possession of the Italian trading route in the city of Ariminum.[56] Beginning a forward march on Rome, violence appeared imminent, and all eyes looked with regret on the prophetic Cato, "who had alone foreseen and first clearly declared Caesar's intentions" (423). "If you had believed me, or regarded my advice," Plutarch reports him as scolding, "you would not now have been reduced to stand in fear of one man, or to put all your hopes in one alone." Nonetheless, he dug in his heels even deeper and took both diplomatic and military measures to forestall the republic's demise and counterbalance Caesar's authority, even going so far as to support his former foe Pompey as consul (418).[57] With battle looming, he urged his fellow Romans to take heart in their participation in either a happy victory or glorious defeat (432). The republic lying in its death throes, Cato's virtue had perhaps never appeared more impressive, striking every citizen not with admiration but remorse. His predictions had not been so farfetched after all.

Cato's death represents his last and most dramatic act of resistance. When the fall of the republic appeared inevitable, Cato was forced to determine what role he would play in the new imperial order. He initially chose exile from Rome, defending the small city of Utica in Africa with the same freedom "from any secret motives or any mixture of self-regard" he had shown throughout his public life (435). When Utica also fell to Caesar's army, however, Cato had seen enough. The path back to republicanism seemed lost. Following a lively supper party with close friends and colleagues, the party talked over various topics, including the Stoic philosophy that Cato had imbibed as a youth (438). So earnest was his defense of one of the doctrine's core tenets—"that the good man only is free, and that all wicked men are slaves"—that Plutarch remarks it became obvious to all those present that Cato intended to end his life (439). He spent the remainder of the night reading Plato's *Phaedo*, perhaps meditating on the similarities between his own principled way of life and that of the Athenian philosopher (441). Early the next morning, he committed suicide, tearing open his abdomen with his own sword, in and out, and then casting his intestines across the room when a physician attempted to save his life (442).[58] When Caesar learned of his antagonist's demise, Plutarch relates, he was dismayed. "Cato, I grudge you your death," he quipped, "as you have grudged me the preservation of your life."[59] In truth, Cato was more valuable to the reigning Caesar alive than dead: had Cato owed his life to Caesar he would have simply augmented the Emperor's glory and further diminished that of the republic.[60] What to make of his last gesture of resistance to imperial rule? For some, it was the coward's easy way out; for others, it was the final, dramatic act of one who now wished to join the stately company of his republican relations rather than live under the thumb of Caesar. Without unduly romanticizing the deed, we can admit that Cato's suicide made him a republican martyr, his refusal to serve Caesar establishing a timeless reproach to autocratic power.[61] His sacrifice guaranteed his status as republican statesman in his age—in all ages.

Plutarch's Cato shows how the statesman in the mold of reformer must have sufficient strength to endure the fickleness of public opinion, the hostility of civil authorities, and the buffets of fortune itself. In the eyes of many of his Roman contemporaries, Cato was deemed a projection of "Virtue herself, and in all his acts he revealed a character nearer to that of gods than of men."[62] Even so, there was a grain of truth to the many criticisms lodged against Cato. Can there be too much virtuous principle in the statesman's pursuit of the public good? One is reminded of Ralph Waldo Emerson's remark that "a foolish consistency is the hobgoblin of little minds, adored by little statesmen and philosophers and divines."[63] Particularly in the modern era, politics often involves "dirty hands," that is, to be effective in governing, one must inevitably lose one's moral innocence.[64] Consequently for many political thinkers, politics is not a battle of ideas so much as a competition of power, in which one's practicability, not principles, dictate success.[65] Cato would never live a life of such grit, and so his resistance, however noble in the abstract, is not without some trace of futility.

CONCLUSIONS

Cato's personality set him apart from his contemporaries as well as most political leaders today. He stood against not merely political corruption and demagoguery, but excess of all kinds. To be sure, he was on occasion given to spitfire, taking on the appearance of what Plutarch called "a kind of ecstasy of contention in the cause of what was good and just" when the situation called for it (396). But in spite of the occasional outburst, his self-government and steady resistance to the enemies of republican government are the qualities that stand out most in Plutarch's portrayal of his statesmanship. Cato exemplified what was best about the Rome of an earlier era: a straight-shooter grounded in a political and ethical philosophy allowing him to assess, overcome, or at least bear patiently political hardships, pitfalls, and set-backs.[66] For our purposes, his ultimate value as a leader lies in the fact that he was not a political weathervane but a pillar of civic virtue, unmoved by the sources of potential influence that swirled around him. In modern par-lance, Cato was no flip-flopper eager to broker "deals," with a mental hori-zon stretching only to the next political news cycle. Rather, he supported policies on the basis of their conformity with the republic's history, customs, laws, and institutions. These were the standards against which he measured political proposals, judging their merits in light of the guidance provided by the past. Cato's personal as well as political moderation, his resistance to the republic's imperial drift, and his unyielding defense of the most praiseworthy aspects of Roman republicanism merit the consideration of all would-be statesmen today. There is something refreshing in his willingness—his readi-ness—to be unpopular.

Yet having acknowledged Cato's great virtue, his life also offers a cau-tionary tale for those that would emulate his example. His commitment to principle at times boxed himself in as a political leader. Cato was a throw-back, with an "old-fashioned virtue out of the present mode" in which greed, ambition, and gamesmanship ran unchecked.[67] His "remarkable and wonder-ful" behavior was too out of sync with the world he lived in, as indicated by Plutarch's concession that Cato may have been "too great and too good to suit the present exigencies, being so out of all proportion" to the "stormy and tempestuous" time in which he lived.[68] His strict adherence to justice, which in Plutarch's estimate "acquires a man power and authority among the com-mon people," limited the range of options he might deploy against Caesar (416).[69] So pristine was his moral and civic virtue that any attempts to save the republic that would compromise Rome's longtime conventions were usu-ally political non-starters: the rules of the game were more important to him than victory.[70] As a figure concerned foremost with motives rather than consequences, there was no wiggle room in his statesmanship to countenance an occasional ends-justify-the-means detour. To the end, he was resolved to follow the bright letter of the law rather than its amorphous spirit.[71] He would not be party to the pragmatism, paradoxes, and virtuosity we find in the savvy Alcibiades, nor take the shorter leap to the prudential behavior that is perhaps the most important element of good statesmanship in all times.

Together, Alcibiades and Cato provide two inspiring but ultimately flawed portraits of statesmanship. Plutarch's Alcibiades possessed many of the qualities we associate with good political leadership: ambition, adaptabil-ity, popular appeal, and a grand vision for the political community. Yet his overweening pride and inability to curb his all-too-human passions proved to be his downfall, both politically and personally. In contrast, Plutarch's Cato exhibits a loathing of "fatal ambition," a principled dedication to the good of the republic, and a courageous if ill-fated resistance to Rome's financial, political, and civic corruption (326). However praiseworthy, his nature foreclosed the kind of flexibility, quick thinking, and risk-taking the republic in its hour of crisis required. Cato dies a victim rather than shaper of political events, with his convictions intact but his beloved commonwealth in tatters. Together, the lives of Alcibiades and Cato highlight the nobility of a life lived in accordance with a single ambition or ethical guideline. Yet their fates also reveal pitfalls of living on the edge of these extremes. As the religious writer Orestes Brownson once put it, "private virtues never saved, private vices never ruined a nation."[72]

Among the more measured critiques of Cato, the assessment of the great medieval theologian Saint Augustine of Hippo stands out for its praise of Cato's repudiation of worldly fame and criticism of his suicide as an act of cowardice.[73] Cato is fortunate to receive across the mists of time even a grudging nod from Augustine, for whom grand statesmanship on the Greek and Roman scale was a thing of the past. Unlike Plutarch, Augustine would not try to pry open and inject new life into those antique models for his readers. He was after something else, a project that self-consciously rejected the kind of world-defying feats that characterized Plutarch's heroes. In his *City of God*, a more humble form of statesmanship emerges, one that would be scarcely fathomable to a Greek or Roman of an earlier epoch. Indeed, even now it is almost unthinkable to expect any notion of statesmanship at all in the Catholic bishop's bleak and famously "realistic" portrayal of politics.[74] But miracles abound.

NOTES

1. See Plutarch's (1906; IV) description of Cato in his "Life of Phocion," 329–369: 332.
2. Straumann (2016), 2.
3. See Kapust (2011), 65; Dean Hammer, *Roman Political Thought: From Cicero to Augustine* (New York: Cambridge University Press, 2014), 161–4; and Jed W. Atkins, *Roman Political Thought* (New York: Cambridge University Press, 2018), 129.
4. As the classicist Robert Goar once claimed, Plutarch's narration "brings us as close to the historical Cato as it is possible for us to come." Quoted in Rob Goodman and Jimmy Soni, *Rome's Last Citizen: The Life and Legacy of Cato, Mortal Enemy of Caesar* (New York: St. Martin's Press, 2012), 320. Good modern treatments of Cato include Charles Oman, *Seven Roman Statesmen of the Late Republic* (London: Edward Arnold, 1910), 204–33; Lily Ross Taylor, *Party Politics in the Age of Caesar* (Berkeley, CA: University of California Press, 1949), 119–39, 162–82; and Lucy Hughes-Hallett, *Heroes: Saviors, Traitors, and Supermen: A History of Hero Worship* (New York: Knopf, 2004), 76–130.
5. It must be noted that Plutarch's primary sources were two figures highly sympathetic to Cato's twin commitments: the republican statesman Cicero and the Stoic senator Thrasea Paetus.

Plutarch's praise of Cato may be explained by evidence that he may have subscribed to the same principles of Stoicism that attracted Cato. On this head, see Jan Oposomer, "Is Plutarch Really Hostile to the Stoics?" in *From Stoicism to Platonism: The Development of Philosophy, 100 BCE–100 CE*, ed. Troels Engberg-Pedersen (New York: Cambridge University Press, 2017), 296–321. Jackson Hershbell points out that Plutarch had many Stoics in his circle of friends in his "Plutarch and Stoicism," *Aufstieg und Niedergang der römischen Welt* II.36, no. 5 (1992), 3336–52: 3339.

6. S. V. Stokes, "M. Porcius Cato Uticensis," *Ancient Society* 16 (1986), 19–51: 20. For a critical appraisal of Cato that contends his reputation as a great Roman statesman has been somewhat overstated by historians, see Henriette van der Blom, "Cato and the People," *Bulletin of the Institute of Classical Studies* 55, no. 2 (2012), 39–56.

7. On Cato as a vehicle for recovering classical republican ideals during the eighteenth century, see Frederic M. Litto, "Addison's Cato in the Colonies," *William and Mary Quarterly* 23, no. 3 (1966), 431–49 and Nathaniel Wolloch, "Cato the Younger in the Enlightenment," *Modern Philology* 106, no. 1 (2008), 60–82.

8. Washington even staged a production of the play during the winter of 1788 at Valley Forge. See Forrest McDonald, "Foreword," in Joseph Addison, *Cato: A Tragedy and Selected Essays*, eds. Christine Dunn Henderson and Mark E. Yellin (Indianapolis, IN: Liberty Fund, 2004), vii–x: viii. Washington's high regard for Addison's *Cato* and his efforts to imitate Catonic ideals of enlightened republicanism are further elaborated in Paul K. Longmore, *The Invention of George Washington* (Berkeley, CA: University of California Press, 1988), 173–4, 210.

9. "Cato, Letters V and VII," in *The Essential Antifederalist*, eds. W. B. Allen and Gordon Lloyd (Lanham, MD: Rowman & Littlefield, 2002), 200–4: 202.

10. Reginald Haynes Barrow once noted that "the elder Cato lived again in his grandson" in his *The Romans* (Chicago: Aldine, 1964), 74. The elder Cato's anti-Hellenism is discussed in Erich S. Gruen, *Culture and National Identity in Republican Rome* (Ithaca, NY: Cornell University Press, 1992), 52–83.

11. Plutarch (1906; IV), "Life of Cato the Younger," 370–444: 370. Unless otherwise noted, subsequent parenthetical references in this chapter refer to this writing.

12. After the death of his parents, Cato was raised by his maternal uncle until the latter's assassination when Cato was about five years old.

13. Plutarch (1906; IV), "Life of Phocion," 332.

14. Plutarch notes one instance when Cato refused to whitewash Rome's past mistakes. When Cicero once argued that the notorious Roman politician Clodius "was never legally tribune, and therefore whatever he had done was void, and of no authority," Cato interrupted to say that even though he disapproved of Clodius's proceedings, questioning the validity of his tribuneship was inappropriate: "if he had done ill in his office, he ought to be called to account for it; but the authority of the magistracy ought not to suffer for the faults of the magistrate" (410).

15. Terms such as political corruption and virtue make good sense when working with Cato's civic republicanism. Moreover, such language embeds him within the republican intellectual tradition developed in recent decades by historians of political thought. John Pocock's *The Machiavellian Moment* (Princeton, NJ: Princeton University Press, 1975) is the foundation stone of modern updates on this classical idea, an idea further developed in Quentin Skinner's *The Foundations of Modern Political Thought: The Renaissance* (Cambridge: Cambridge University Press, 1978); "The Idea of Negative Liberty," in *Philosophy in History: Essays on the Historiography of Philosophy*, eds. Richard Rorty, J. B. Schneewind, and Quentin Skinner (Cambridge: Cambridge University Press, 1984); and "The Paradoxes of Political Liberty," in *Liberty*, ed. David Miller (Oxford: Oxford University Press, 1991). A good overview of the concept of corruption and its ongoing resonance in the American political tradition is provided in John Joseph Wallis' "The Concept of Systematic Corruption in American History," in *Corruption and Reform: Lessons from America's Economic History*, eds. Edward L. Glaeser and Claudia Goldin (Chicago, IL: University of Chicago Press, 2006), 23–62.

16. Although on this occasion Cato was unable to show any great valor on account of the ineptitude of his commanding officers, Plutarch writes that "amidst the corruption and disor-

ders of that army, he showed such a love of discipline, so much bravery upon occasion, and so much courage and wisdom in everything, that it appeared he was in no way inferior to the old Cato" (377).

17. So famous was Cato's honesty that "if any very unlikely and incredible thing were asserted," people often remarked "they would not believe it, though Cato himself should affirm it" (389).

18. Plato, *The Republic of Plato*, trans. Allan Bloom, 3rd ed. (Philadelphia: Perseus, 2016), 45. Aristotle's famous dictum that citizenship in a regime among political equals consists in "ruling and being ruled in turn" is found in book seven of his *Politics*, trans. Carnes Lord (Chicago, IL: University of Chicago Press, 1984), 219.

19. Cicero, *On Duties*, eds. M. T. Griffin and E. M. Atkins (New York: Cambridge University Press, 2003), 36.

20. Richard S. Ruderman, "Statesmanship Reconsidered," *Perspectives on Political Science* 41, no. 2 (2012), 86–89: 89.

21. See, e.g., Jeffrey S. Luke, "Character and Conduct in the Public Service: A Review of Historical Perspectives and a Definition of the Twenty-First Century" in *Handbook of Administrative Ethics*, ed. Terry L. Cooper (New York: Marcel Dekker, 1994), 391–412.

22. As Richard Ruderman has argued, cases like Cato show how politics, adversity, and struggle together reveal inner character like nothing else, "bringing to light not only the statesman's modus operandi but also the precise nature of his understanding of and dedication to virtue." See his "Practice and Principles in Ancient Statesmanship," in *Principle and Prudence in Western Political Thought*, ed. Christopher Lynch and Jonathan Marks (Albany, NY: State University of New York Press, 2016), 33–50: 35.

23. A good survey of the predominant view emphasizing the role of Stoicism in Cato's personality is found in Miriam Griffin, "The Intellectual Developments of the Ciceronian Age," in *The Cambridge Ancient History: The Last Age of the Roman Republic, 146–43 B.C.*, 3rd ed., eds. J. A. Crook, Andrew Lintott, and Elizabeth Rawson (New York: Cambridge University Press, 1994), 689–728. For opposing views, consider A. Dragstedt, "Cato's *Politeuma*," *Agon* 3 (1969), 69–96 and Stokes (1986), 39.

24. When Cato inherited the estate of his cousin, Plutarch states that he liquidated the effects and "turned it all into ready money, which he kept by him for any of his friends that should happen to want, to whom he would lend it without interest" (921).

25. According to Plutarch, in his military posts Cato avoided "the terrors of his office," imitating the common soldier rather than the domineering officer and inspiring discipline and the "true love of virtue" among his brothers-in-arms (923).

26. Cato refused his commander's offer of military honors in the form of a crown, pendant, and a golden armband often worn by Rome's most heroic legionnaires. See Barry Strauss, *The Spartacus War* (New York: Simon & Schuster, 2009), 110. There was a touch of condescension in Cato's indifferent reply to Cicero's expression of gratitude upon driving out the "seditious orator" Clodius: "'You must thank the commonwealth,' said he, for whose sake alone he professed to do everything" (928).

27. For elaborations of the change Stoicism underwent in the hands of its Roman practitioners, see Christopher Gill, "The School in the Roman Imperial Period," in *The Cambridge Companion to the Stoics*, ed. Brad Inwood (New York: Cambridge University Press, 2003), 33–59; Gretchen Reydams-Schils, *The Roman Stoics: Self, Responsibility, and Affection* (Chicago: University of Chicago Press, 2005); and Gill (2006).

28. On this point, see Haviland Nelson, "Cato the Younger as a Stoic Orator," *The Classical Weekly* 44, no. 5 (1950), 65–69: 69. For discussions of Stoic oratory, consider George A. Kennedy, *The Art of Persuasion in Greece* (Princeton, NJ: Princeton University Press, 1963), 290–99; Catherine Atherton, "Hand Over Fist: The Failure of Stoic Rhetoric," *The Classical Quarterly* 38, no. 2 (1988), 392–427; and Ned O'Gorman, "Stoic Rhetoric: Prospects of a Problematic," *Advances in the History of Rhetoric* 14, no. 1 (2011), 1–13. Following Cicero, the classicist Rex Stern has referred to the younger Cato as "The First Eloquent Stoic: Cicero on Cato the Younger," *The Classical Journal* 101, no. 1 (2005), 37–49. For an argument that Cato was more verbose than eloquent, see William C. McDermott "Cato the Younger: *loquax* or *eloquens*?" *Classical Bulletin* 46 (1970), 65–75.

29. According to Plutarch, when Cato was once criticized by a colleague for his silence he shot back, "'I will begin to speak, when I have that to say which had not better be unsaid'" (920).

30. Plutarch claims that the other officers present that day gave speeches to the soldiers that were greeted with stony silence. Cato, however, speaking last of all and with a type of "natural passion," galvanized the men to such a pitch that "their officers led them on full of hope and confidence" into combat (949).

31. Cato's combination of Stoic philosophy and public service is discussed in Jakob Wisse, "*De Oratore*: Rhetoric, Philosophy, and the Making of the Ideal Orator," in *Brill's Companion to Cicero: Oratory and Rhetoric*, ed. James M. May (Leiden: Brill, 2002), 375–400; Michael von Albrecht, *Cicero's Style: A Synopsis* (Leiden: Brill, 2003), 219–238; and Stern (2005).

32. In 82 B.C., Sulla had infamously authorized decrees guaranteeing months-long and far-reaching executions of those whom he deemed enemies of the state. Though Plutarch reports the assassins working on behalf of Sulla were hated by everybody "as wicked and polluted wretches," no Roman save Cato dared to call such men to account (927).

33. Cato's reputation for justice was a double-edged sword for ordinary citizens as well as elites, since many "feared to have him one of their judges, yet did not dare to demand his exclusion," lest doing so create an appearance of guilt (946).

34. For example, Cato's campaign for the consulship did not prevent him from reprimanding the people for permitting elections to "become a matter of purchase," going so far as to promise that if victorious he would bring to trial any citizen discovered to be interfering in state affairs unlawfully (929). For their part, Plutarch reports that the people oscillated between resentment and admiration for Cato's "mildness of temper and greatness of spirit" (925).

35. Plutarch (1906; IV) remarks in his "Life of Phocion" that Cato's personality was "little agreeable or acceptable to the people, and he received very slender marks of their favour" (331).

36. Plutarch observes that "the more they considered the excellence of what [Cato] did, the more they were grieved at the difficulty they found to do the like" (922).

37. Cato's at times eccentric conduct did not go unnoticed by Plutarch. When Cato was finally appointed praetor, Plutarch complains that far from doing the office honor and credit, "he disgraced and diminished it by his strange behaviour" (943). In fact Cato sometimes gave too lax an impression to his colleagues, often strolling into court and issuing important judgments without wearing shoes or underwear.

38. For example, Dante placed Cato, "reverend in his bearing and his look," midway between heaven and hell as the warden of Purgatory. See Dante Alighieri, *Purgatory*, trans. Anthony Esolen (New York: Random House, 2003), 5.

39. Edward Gibbon, *The History of the Decline and Fall of the Roman Empire,* ed. David Womersley (Harmondsworth: Penguin, 2005) II: 552. Similarly, Duff (1999) links Cato's inflexibility to his Stoicism while arguing "that Plutarch intended [the "Life of Phocion" and the "Life of Cato Minor"] to be an essay on the dangers of over-rigid adherence to philosophic tenets in general" (131–2, 156).

40. Unlike most Stoic philosophy, Plutarch assigns a positive function to properly regulated *eros*. See H. M. Martin Jr., "Plutarch, Plato, and Eros," *Classical Bulletin* 60, no. 4 (1984), 82–88, and John M. Rist, "Plutarch's *Amatorius*: A Commentary on Plato's Theories of Love," *The Classical Quarterly* 51, no. 2 (2001), 557–75. Yet as the gruff tone of the "Life of Alcibiades" suggests, Plutarch was no hedonist.

41. For a model of statesmanship in this mold, see Bruce Miroff, "Alexander Hamilton: The Aristocrat as Visionary," *International Political Science Review* 9, no. 1 (1988), 43–54.

42. Edmund Burke, "Reflections on the Revolution in France (1790)," in *Reflections on the Revolution in France and Other Writings*, ed. Jesse Norman (New York: Random House, 2015), 425–646: 549.

43. See Patrick J. Buchanan, *A Republic, Not an Empire: Reclaiming America's Destiny* (Washington, DC: Regnery, 1999); Robert Alexander Kraig, *Woodrow Wilson and the Lost World of the Oratorical Statesman* (College Station, TX: Texas A&M University Press, 2014), 44, 81–90; and Greg Weiner, *American Burke: The Uncommon Liberalism of Daniel Patrick Moynihan* (Lawrence, KS: University Press of Kansas, 2016).

44. Erik Hildinger, *Swords Against the Senate: The Rise of the Roman Army and the Fall of the Republic* (Cambridge, MA: Perseus, 2002), ix, 213.

45. Plutarch (1906; IV), "Life of Phocion," 332.

46. T. Corey Brennan credits the Roman constitution's "rough system of informal and formal checks and balances" for working well enough over the span of several centuries to make figures such as Sulla and Caesar "outsized exceptions" to its legal norms. See his "Power and Process Under the Republican 'Constitution,'" in *The Cambridge Companion to the Roman Republic*, ed. Harriet I. Flower (New York: Cambridge University Press, 2004), 31–65: 56. Rome's political institutions and procedures are discussed in greater detail in S. E. Finer, *The History of Government: Ancient Monarchies and Empires* (Oxford: Clarendon Press, 1997), 385–441; Andrew Lintott, *The Constitution of the Roman Republic* (New York: Oxford University Press, 1999), 16–26, 191–255; T. Corey Brennan, *The Praetorship in the Roman Republic*, 2 vols. (New York: Oxford University Press, 2000); Fergus Millar, *The Roman Republic in Political Thought* (Lebanon, NH: University Press of New England, 2002); and Henrik Mouritsen, *Politics in the Roman Republic* (New York: Cambridge University Press, 2017).

47. Plutarch (1906; IV), "Life of Caesar," 256–328: 273.

48. Ibid., 315.

49. Apparently, Caesar's party flung dung and (more dangerous if less odoriferous) darts into the forum at those members who opposed the proposed land reform (402).

50. Caesar, perhaps panged by the sight of Rome's best citizens following Cato "with sad and dejected looks, showing their grief and indignation by their silence," bade one of the men to interpose and obtain his release (404).

51. When the conspirators were brought to trial before the Senate, Caesar—who, in Plutarch's evaluation, saw "all changes and commotions in the state as materials useful for his purposes"—persuaded the senate to be merciful and allow the conspirators a fair trial in accordance with the law before issuing a sentence (392–3). In Cato's only preserved speech, Plutarch states that with "great passion and vehemence" he warned his fellow senators to punish the insurrectionists as well as Caesar, whom he predicted would shortly "ruin the commonwealth by soft words and popular speeches" (393). The most detailed depiction of these events is found in the writings of the Roman historian Sallust, notably *The Jugurthine War/The Conspiracy of Cataline*, trans. S. A. Handford (New York: Penguin, 1963).

52. Pompey and Crassus, fearing the outsized influence Cato might have as consul, deployed every stratagem at their disposal to bribe the people into selecting their preferred candidate. When Cato's "virtue and reputation" seemed to have won him the seat, Pompey shouted out that he heard thunder, dispersing the assembly (Plutarch reports the Romans had long interpreted the sound "as a bad omen, and never concluded any matter after it had thundered") (412). By the time the people had reconvened, new and larger bribes had been distributed and "by these foul means" Cato was defeated.

53. Cato's answer to Pompey's proposal was very much against the wishes not only of Pompey and his family but Cato's nieces as well, and in Plutarch's appraisal "seemed somewhat harsh and haughty" (400).

54. After Cato refused Pompey's entreaties to join together their families, the opportunity to broker an alliance with the commander subsequently fell to Caesar. Pompey happily accepted the hand of Caesar's twenty-four-year-old daughter Julia, a partnership that "well-nigh ruined the Roman Empire, and did destroy the commonwealth" (401). It may never have come to pass, Plutarch speculates, had it not been for Cato's fastidiousness. Had Cato anticipated how his dismissal of Rome's great military commander might have delivered the latter into the hands of one that committed far graver sins, he might have had second thoughts about an arranged marriage.

55. In his "Life of Caesar," Plutarch (1906; IV) maintains that "it was not the quarrel between Pompey and Caesar, as most men imagine, which was the origin of the civil wars, but their union" (268–9). For his part, "Cato, who often foretold what the consequence of this alliance would be, had then the character of a sullen, interfering man, but in the end the reputation of a wise but unsuccessful counsellor" (269).

56. Ibid., 291.

57. When it was proposed that Pompey should be granted emergency powers, Cato had bristled: "The laws ought not to seek protection from Pompey," he said, "but Pompey from the laws" (418). Presently, however, Cato chose to support Pompey's candidacy for the consulship, reasoning that it was better to "freely confer all [authority] on Pompey" rather than "fall into the last extremity," namely, a tyranny led by Caesar. When Pompey was later slain by Caesar's army in Egypt, Cato himself took temporary command of the army, marching the Romans out of Africa before handing the military reins over to the more experienced though volatile Scipio Africanus (427).

58. On suicide as an example of the classical idea of "dying nobly" *pace* Cato's example, see Miriam Griffin, "Philosophy, Cato, and Roman Suicide: II," *Greece & Rome* 33, no. 2 (1986), 192–202: 197.

59. Cato may have had the last laugh on Caesar. Plutarch notes that Cato's daughter, Porcia Catonis, not "inferior to the rest of her family for sober-living and greatness of spirit," wedded Marcus Junius Brutus and was aware of the latter's plot to assassinate Caesar (959).

60. Plutarch relates that the reason for Caesar's dismay is unclear. Though some have argued he had hoped to effect a reconciliation with his longtime antagonist, Plutarch notes that Caesar later authored a polemic, his lost "Anti-Cato," filled with "whatever could be said in derogation" against Cato (886).

61. The posthumous laudation of Cato is summarized in Alexei V. Zadorojnyi, "Cato's Suicide in Plutarch," *The Classical Quarterly* 57, no. 1 (2007), 216–30.

62. Thus opines the Roman historian Marcus Velleius Paterculus in his *Res Gestae Divi Augusti*, trans. Frederick W. Shipley (London and New York: William Heinemann, 1924), 125.

63. Ralph Waldo Emerson, "Self-Reliance" in *Ralph Waldo Emerson: Essays and Lectures*, ed. Joel Porte (New York: Library of America, 1983), 259–82: 265.

64. Jean-Paul Sartre, "Dirty Hands," in *No Exit and Three Other Plays*, trans. Lionel Abel (New York: Vintage, 1989), 125–242. The literature on the concept of "dirty hands," or the tension between principle and expediency in politics, is extensive. See, e.g., Michael Walzer, "Political Action: The Problem of Dirty Hands," *Philosophy & Public Affairs* 2, no. 2 (1973), 160–80; W. Kenneth Howard, "Must Public Hands be Dirty?" *Journal of Value Inquiry* 11, no. 1 (1977), 29–40; Stuart Hampshire, "Public and Private Morality," in *Public and Private Morality*, eds. Stuart Hampshire, T. M. Scanlon, Bernard Williams, Thomas Nagel, and Ronald Dworkin (Cambridge: Cambridge University Press, 1978), 23–54; Dennis F. Thompson, *Political Ethics and Public Office* (Cambridge, MA: Harvard University Press, 1987); C. A. J. Coady, "Politics and the Problem of Dirty Hands," in *A Companion to Ethics*, ed. Peter Singer (Oxford: Wiley-Blackwell, 1993), 373–83; Ruth W. Grant, *Hypocrisy and Integrity: Machiavelli, Rousseau, and the Ethics of Politics* (Chicago, IL: University of Chicago Press, 1997); Max Weber, "Politics as a Vocation," in *The Vocation Lectures: Science as a Vocation, Politics as a Vocation*, eds. Tracy B. Strong, David Owen, and Rodney Livingstone (Indianapolis, IN: Hackett, 2004), 32–94; Neil Levy, "Punishing the Dirty," in *Politics and Morality*, ed. Igor Primoratz (New York: Palgrave Macmillan, 2007), 38–53; John M. Parrish, *Paradoxes of Political Ethics: From Dirty Hands to the Invisible Hand* (Cambridge: Cambridge University Press, 2007); and Michael Walzer, *Just and Unjust Wars: A Moral Argument with Historical Illustrations*, fifth edition (New York: Basic Books, 2015).

65. The point is best and most colorfully made by Niccolò Machiavelli (1998).

66. See Bruno Centrone, "Platonism and Pythagoreanism in the Early Empire," in *The Cambridge History of Greek and Roman Political Thought*, eds. Christopher Rowe and Malcolm Schofield (Cambridge: Cambridge University Press, 2000), 559–83: 577. As Goodman and Soni (2012) put it, Cato "is the kind of man that every statesman aspires to be: physically tough, intellectually brave, unflinchingly principled, beloved despite his warts . . . [d]espite his lost cause, or exactly because of it, Cato succeeded in making himself an icon" (308).

67. Plutarch (1906; IV), "Life of Phocion," 332.

68. Ibid.

69. Unlike bravery or strength, Plutarch believed that justice was an acquired characteristic, a virtue difficult to attain and easy to lose. So valuable should justice be to the political leader, he continues, that its loss is commonly perceived as less excusable and more discrediting than a

decline in natural endowments (416). Cato took very seriously the "entire trust and confidence" Rome placed in his justice—a charge that, as the light of the republic faded, he paid in full.

70. For this point, see Bryan-Paul Frost, "An Interpretation of Plutarch's *Cato the Younger*," *History of Political Thought* 18, no. 1 (1997), 1–23: 12–13.

71. In her "Plutarch's Deterrent Lives: Lessons in Statesmanship," (PhD diss., Columbia University, 2011), Suzanne Said notes that Cato's life illustrates that "in a corrupt political environment, moral virtue is insufficient to serve the common welfare," and that "the statesman, at times, must be willing to relax rigid standards of moral virtue to serve the greater good. Cato, however, lacks willingness to compromise and it is this rigidity that constitutes the flaw at the center of the deterrent message of his Life" (323).

72. Orestes Brownson, "The American Republic," in *The Works of Orestes A. Brownson*, ed. Henry F. Brownson, 20 vols. (Detroit, MI: Thorndike Nourse, 1885), XVIII: 91.

73. In considering Cato's death, Augustine asks: "what can I say but that his own friends, enlightened men as he, prudently dissuaded him, and therefore judged his act to be that of a feeble rather than a strong spirit, and dictated not by honourable feeling forestalling shame, but by weakness shrinking from hardships?" See Saint Augustine, *The City of God*, trans. Marcus Dods, George Wilson, and J. J. Smith, 2 vols. (Edinburgh: T&T Clark, 1871, 1888), I: 34.

74. The classic and best exponent of this view is a fellow theologian and realist, Reinhold Niebuhr. In particular, see his "Augustine's Political Realism" in his *Christian Realism and Political Problems: Essays on Political, Social, Ethical, and Theological Problems* (Fairfield, NJ: Augustus M. Kelley Publishers, 1977), 119–47.

Chapter Three

Humility and Charity in Augustine's *Civitas Dei*

As a rulebook for statesmanship, Augustine's *City of God* (*Civitas Dei*) is a hard read and an even tougher sell.[1] The work is principally concerned with defending Christianity against those critics blaming the faith for the decline of the Roman Empire. Moreover, the book is largely trans-political, by its very title lifting readers' gaze from the crumbling imperial order to the more lasting security found only in the embrace of the Christian God. But the seemingly apolitical cast of *Civitas Dei* should not lull us into thinking Augustine has nothing of note to say about the political or social order of his time or our own. On closer scrutiny, Augustine was very much concerned with changing the way his readers—a readership that perhaps included prospective political leaders—thought about the political realm and how they should conceive their roles as citizens of a secular state.[2] In doing so, he offered up a kind of statesmanship that consciously rejected the models of the past, taking its cues not from the false glint of earthly glory but rooted in the limitations of political life and earthly peace. To the extent that Augustine addressed his writing to thoughtful citizens of all ages, his *Civitas Dei* still speaks to wistful citizens in search of a politics and political leadership based on humility and charity.

Appreciating Augustine's political thought, let alone his theory of statesmanship, presents a formidable challenge for even the most expert reader. Admittedly, interpretive disagreements are likely unavoidable for any author of such prodigious output, especially one of the medieval era in which political views must be unearthed and induced from writing often steeped in recondite theological arguments.[3] Perhaps the most prolific Latin writer of his time, Augustine completed over ninety books and a far greater number of letters, sermons, and retractions, rendering almost any analysis of his political thought necessarily selective and tentative. Focusing on Augustine's fundamentally religious outlook, many scholars throughout the twentieth century portrayed him as negative, pessimistic, or downright apathetic about politics.[4] Others have gone even further, dismissing the presence of any positive political theory at all in his work.[5] Such claims are understandable: surrounded by ruin, impiety, and vice in his travels across Italy, Augustine did not notice much justice in politics. And in the absence of justice, as he famously asks in *Civitas Dei*, "what are kingdoms but great robberies? For what are robberies themselves, but little kingdoms?"[6] In recent years, however, scholars of Augustine spanning the disciplines of theology to political theory have challenged the notion that Augustine wholly divorced himself from political affairs, maintaining that there is a genuine political thinker yet in the Bishop of Hippo.[7] Hence we now witness Augustine's writings applied to topics as varied as political corruption, friendship, and indeed, even leadership.[8] Far from being indifferent or hostile toward politics, these arguments offer Augustine as a salve if not solution for many of the ills afflicting contemporary liberal democracy.[9]

In fact, Augustine's literary motives were both theological and political. Of course, these were two spheres of authority not as divorced in fifth-century Rome as they are in twenty-first century America. Unlike Plutarch, however, Augustine's object had little to do with rescuing the dignity of political life or the glory of service on behalf of one's temporal commonwealth.[10] For Augustine, the care for one's soul was far more serious business than the rise and fall of the political regime one resided in. Pay little mind to the "terrestrial and temporal benefits" that God "grants promiscuously to [the] good and evil," Augustine emphasizes, but focus instead on the "eternal life, everlasting gifts, and . . . the society of the heavenly city itself" (I; 214). For all that, the young Augustine, born in the shadow of the Roman Empire in present-day Algeria in 354, could hardly avoid the enticements of public service and secular acclaim.[11] While a nominal Christian thanks to the solicitude of his doting mother, Monica, Augustine's momentous conversion did not occur until 386. Before that time, he made a name for himself as a public if not overtly political figure, winning accolades for his quick intellect and wit in Carthage, teaching rhetoric to the lawyers and politicians of the future in Rome, and himself taking a turn as court orator in Milan. Such success nourished pride, vanity, and many other vices besides, even as they continued to leave Augustine empty in his personal search for the truth. Eventually tearing himself from secular pursuits and dalliances, Augustine returned to his native Africa in 388 and pledged himself to a life of chastity within the Church following his baptism in Milan the previous year. He settled down on his father's estate in Tagaste, intent on leading a humble life of scholarship and prayer among celibate friends. This time, however, public life sought him out, as he was appointed fellow bishop of the harbor town of

Hippo Regius, a position he held exclusively from 395 until his death in 430 at the age of seventy-six. In the decades following his baptism, his life was one of political conflict, clerical service, and a constant stream of writing and correspondence, resulting in a political theory found scattered throughout his considerable literary legacy during these heady years.[12] Yet his *Civitas Dei* remains arguably the most important, well-known, and conspicuously political of his works. While not the only starting point for beginning a study of Augustine, it is the sprawling setting for his clearest and most vivid commentary on the importance of good leadership against the backdrop of imperial decline.[13]

Contrary to the expectations of his youth, Augustine in time became a reluctant participant in the political affairs of his day. On those occasions when he did involve himself in politics, it was usually to solicit public support for promoting the Christian faith. Sometimes in his official capacity such importunities to civil authorities were carried a step too far, as was the case in his reluctant endorsement of the use of force to bring to heel extremist heretics.[14] Notwithstanding these instances of activism, Augustine's mature political attitude was reserved. Unlike his classical predecessors, he would not permit the city or any other earthly influence to submerge the human soul. Nor would he stand idly by while critics discredited and blamed Christianity for the Roman Empire's decline. Perhaps these two concerns—one by turns intellectual and spiritual, the other political and mundane—were predestined to bump heads. Compressed against each other in the rich Italian soil, Augustine's *Civitas Dei* was the work formed from the warmth kindled by the conflagration of Roman politics, as well as the fire that engulfed his own restless soul.

STATESMANSHIP IN CIVITAS DEI

Augustine's conceit of the two cities is deceptively simple. The cities refer to the City of Man, on the one side, and the City of God, on the other. Their origins and characters refer to humanity's two most ineradicable impulses: the lust for rule after the flesh, and the love of God after the spirit. The cities are not temporally located, nor are their memberships mutually exclusive. The earthly city contains servants of God who are not members of the visible Church, Augustine says, while the Church is populated by "many reprobate mingled with the good, and both are gathered together by the gospel as in a drag net" to be sorted out and separated only on judgment day (II; 281–2).[15] In immediate terms, the objective of Augustine's framework of these two cities was to distinguish the political trajectory of Rome—its rise as well as its fall—from God's plan, which in its stability and purpose is necessarily independent of and superior to secular authority and its fortunes.[16] More generally, however, the sheer transcendence of the divine plan gives the conceit a meaning that reaches beyond Augustine's audience to all human societies.[17] After all, the two cities "are mingled together from the beginning down to the end" of human history and will endure so long as we wait, "made happy by hope" for salvation in the world to come: "our final happiness," as Augustine describes it (II, 292, 307). The City of God which promises perfect justice, happiness, and repose will not and cannot be realized on Earth, the eternal kingdom being, in the words of Jesus Christ, "not of this world" (John 18:36).[18] In its universal application, Augustine issues a reminder to his generation and a warning to future ones that the genesis of the earthly city lies in human sin full-stop, perpetrated through the generations and active or latent in every human heart. Accordingly, in *Civitas Dei* the division between the two cities mirrors the fractures of the soul itself, where sin and salvation, fallen humanity and the spark of the divine are merely opposing sides of the same coin. This "wretched condition" results in a whole host of social problems, where friends are mistaken for enemies, the innocent are punished while the guilty go free, and the criminal is "crowned with honours" while the "blameless man is buried in the darkness of neglect" (II, 311, 347). Given that God's ways are unsearchable and "His ways past finding out," how should the political leader approach his or her task (II, 347–8)?

Unsurprisingly, scholars have provided a variety of answers to this question. Many have pointed to the rarity of admirable political figures in Augustine's time as grounds for concluding that he never expected the arrival of some Christian statesman dedicated to reforming secular politics.[19] Others have argued that the kind of responsibilities and duties such a ruler would confront might make a religious theocracy virtually inescapable.[20] Taking a different approach, still other writers have argued that Augustine favored dialogue between Christian and non-Christian leaders to promote peace, accommodation, and establish common political ground.[21] Following the latter approach, it might be best to conceive the Augustinian political leader as intent on seeking ways to make the discrepancies between the earthly and heavenly cities less severe, a task made easier by not attempting to erase those boundaries. As part of this balancing act, Robert Dodaro has suggested that Augustine's teaching endeavors to harmonize those virtues indispensable to happiness both in heaven and on earth, making possible the practice of "true virtue in government" by closing but not eliminating the gap separating the two cities.[22] Amid these different interpretations of statesmanship in *Civitas Dei*, this much at least is clear: Augustine's ideal ruler would take for his models not the sinful rulers of this world, but seek to approximate the attributes of Christ. Foremost among those qualities, for Augustine, was the willingness to live and lead others in accordance with the simple knowledge that the first shall in time be last (Matt. 20:16).

Turning from scholars of Augustine to his own work, Augustine speculates a good deal on the subject of political leadership in *Civitas Dei*, both indirectly and directly. In his reflections on the vices and virtues of individual rulers, Augustine surveys and evaluates the history of the Roman Empire. But even more to the point, in a chapter entitled "The true felicity of Christian Emperors," Augustine provides a detailed description of his ideal Christian prince, a person capable of moving with ease between the claims and needs of politics as well as those of the soul. In light of its almost superhuman description, it may be that the ruler Augustine describes is evidence for Augustine's anti-political bent, representing a baptized version of the Platonic philosopher-king whose construction is more an exercise in wishful thinking than serious expectation.[23] Even so, ideal models often prove useful in political practice, whether as ways of imagining the political order differently or as benchmarks upon which to judge more incremental reforms. For the time being, however, let us take Augustine at his word.

HUMILITY

As a quality of leadership, humility appears to run counter to the kind of grand statesmanship found in Plutarch, whether grounded in Alcibiadean ambition or Catonic conservatism. As more of a theological than civic virtue, humility is more at home in Thomas Aquinas' *Summa Theologica* than the slash-and-burn world of modern politics.[24] As Plutarch's case studies illustrate, politics is often an arena for assertiveness and confrontation, not a place to downplay one's agency and influence over public affairs. Certainly this belief in one's ability to shape the future has been one of the implied principles of the modern philosophical tradition. Humility is nothing more than a "monkish virtue" as David Hume once described it, or, as Friedrich Nietzsche later described, an outgrowth of the Christian "slave morality" that soothes the suffering and resentment of those weak in mind, body, or spirit.[25] In the United States, Benjamin Franklin was a little less critical of the term, including it in his list of virtues (after being scolded for omitting it) with a characteristically pat and faintly dismissive legend: "Imitate Jesus and Socrates."[26] Nor is the virtue only downplayed among the literary class. While the importance of humility is often paid lip service, in practice it is hard to come by among modern politicians. More often than not, it is the preening showman who wins the election, not the self-effacing public servant. David Bobb states the obvious in noting that "the reality of our fame-addled and power-hungry existence today means that arrogance is rewarded and humility is ignored."[27] Nonetheless, just as many Americans recoil at the absence of moderation in public figures as concealing some deeper character flaw, many citizens take a lack of humility as symptomatic of status-anxiety, insecurity, or some other personal deficiency. Attuned to these misgivings, in recent decades scholars of leadership studies have started praising the virtues of leading from behind, as evidenced by the growth of literature in support of a form of "servant leadership" that underlines the importance of listening, open-mindedness, empathy, cooperation, and compassion in both political and non-political milieux.[28] To counteract poor leadership in society, such arguments suggest, we need more modesty—not ambition.

Humility finds another strong defender in Augustine's *Civitas Dei*, indeed, in Augustine's corpus as a whole.[29] The god-fearing Augustine is himself an embodied lesson in the virtue, given his own efforts to subdue the human tendency toward pride. This was, after all, a figure who spent his last years painstakingly re-reading his work and recanting his past errors. Applying Augustine's personal ethic to politics, Mary Keys has argued that he adduced the sack of Rome as proof positive that human pride "obscures true social and civic vision," blinding people to the sufferings of others and obscuring the healing power of compassion and humility.[30] Yet as he cautions at the beginning of *Civitas Dei*, the virtue of humility is unappealing to most political leaders insofar as it "raises us, not by a quite human arrogance, but by a divine grace, above all earthly dignities that totter on this shifting scene" (I, 1).[31] While a ruler may succeed in subduing foreign and domestic threats, enjoy financial prosperity with high approval ratings, and die a peaceful death after a long life, we should hesitate before calling such a ruler truly happy. After all, Augustine argues, God lavishes "the blessings and privileges of this life" on the wicked as well as the good in order to teach mankind not to desire such a thing as political rule as the highest end (I, 226). Only a humble spirit who keeps before him the fact that the use or abuse of his power will be answerable to God can be called a happy as well as just ruler. As he puts it, happy leaders are those "not lifted up amid the praises of those who pay them sublime honours, and the obsequiousness of those who salute them," but rather those that recall that they are mere mortals whose role on the world stage is but temporary (I, 223). Such rulers serve not out of lust for an "empty glory" but "love of eternal felicity," constantly thinking of the membership in the superior heavenly kingdom granted to those who reign humbly. There is an element of Cato's moderation in Augustine's disavowal of worldly delights, to be sure, but Augustinian humility grows not from a striving after an ever-more severe asceticism nor is it directed toward maintaining the standards of the best earthly regime, Rome or otherwise. Rather, Augustine believed all political aims and secular kingdoms must recognize the basic limits of temporal authority, not as a justification for rebellion but as a means for tempering expectations about what that authority may achieve.[32] While the political leader exercises an indispensible role as "the city's inhabitant, ruler, [and] governor," like even the lowliest member of society he "comes on this condition that he may go, is born on this condition that he may die, entered into the world on this condition that he may pass away."[33] In comparison to the short duration of the life of the statesman, the two cities carry on almost since the beginning of time and will remain in tension until the end of time as mankind knows it.[34] Recognizing this binary reduces or at least relegates politics, along with all other relations and conduct on earth, into a preparatory school "for life eternal," in which both fortunes and misfortunes are of paltry significance (I, 41). For Augustine, this orientation, not the absolutist approach to politics of Alcibiades and Cato, should inform the individual's attitude toward the role, possibilities, and limits of politics.

The Roman Emperor Theodosius Augustus (A.D. 379–395), who briefly reunited the eastern and western halves of the split Empire, is one of Augustine's foremost examples of the humble statesman.[35] Though a fierce opponent of paganism and heresy, Theodosius kept his pride in check during his reign, rejoicing "more to be a member of [the] church than he did to be a king upon the earth" (I, 226). He is praised by Augustine for sharing power as joint emperor with his predecessor's son, Valentinian, guiding and guarding him "with paternal affection, though he might without any difficulty have got rid of him" (I, 224). This solicitude was consistent with Theodosius' desire not for power and wealth but kindness and humanity, as further evidenced by his treatment of prisoners of war whom he handled with respect, refusing to "permit private animosities to affect the treatment of any man after the war" (I, 226).[36] But even more outstanding was what Augustine calls Theodosius' "religious humility." Ruling with faith and piety, Theodosius was willing to admit mistakes and reverse course, recognizing that "the greatest human nobility and loftiness are but vapour." The most prominent instance of his humility took place in 390, when a riot erupted in the port city of Thessalonica leading to the murder of the city's military governor. In a fit of pique, Theodosius directed his army to gather and slaughter some seven thousand inhabitants of the city. Soon perceiving the error in his impulse, he quickly recalled the order.[37] When the reprieve arrived too late to save the people from death, however, not even the Church could stomach supporting him. Led by the Bishop of Milan and Augustine's spiritual mentor, Ambrose, Church officials issued a rare rebuke of the emperor and refused to administer the Eucharist to him until he expressed public remorse for the massacre.[38] The humbled emperor shuffled to the scene of the massacre, laid down his royal insignia, and bowing before "the discipline of the church" begged its forgiveness. When his critics saw such a striking display of "imperial loftiness prostrated," their rage quickly changed to sorrow. On Augustine's telling, this rare display of contrition was not intended to manipulate public opinion or rebuild Theodosius' political stature, but attested to the emperor's genuine repentance for a sin of grave political as well as spiritual consequences.[39] Today, such a scene of remorse by a public official might be viewed skeptically as a sign of weakness or inauthenticity. Yet the surprising humility of the Roman Emperor, particularly his willingness to confess and repent his all-too-human errors in such a public manner, illustrates how such good works may in fact strengthen the political leader's hand with both the general public and the judgment of history. After all, humility certainly performed this service in Theodosius' case. He continued to rule long after his public confession of wrongdoing.[40]

Augustine often contrasts the virtue of humility with the vice of pride, the root of all evil and on his telling a chief cause of the fall of the Roman Empire.[41] Indeed, pride is often related to falling or being struck down in *Civitas Dei*. Pride, leading one downward from God's will to earthly objects and material rewards, causes one to lose sight of one's permanent good. Pride spawned Lucifer and also thwarted his divine schemes, just as the vice has raised up and then struck down many a political leader. Unlike pride, humility exalts the heart and soul, Augustine writes, while pride only debases the spirit. As he puts it, "pious humility enables us to submit to what is above us," pointing upward and beyond the world, while pride, "being a defect of nature," causes one to drop "to a low condition" where pretensions of self-sufficiency are rendered absurd by one's diminished status in relation to the eternal (II, 26, 27).[42] Turning to concrete examples, perhaps no political figure exemplified pride more aggressively than the Mesopotamian king Nimrod—"a 'hunter *against* the Lord'" Augustine calls him, quoting Scripture—at whose feet Augustine lays the grave crime of the infamous Tower of Babylon (II, 108).[43] Though the land upon which the Tower was built enjoyed "a supremacy over other cities as the metropolis and royal residence," Augustine reports, "it did not rise to the grand dimensions designed by its proud and impious founder" (II, 112). As related in the Book of Genesis, the people wished to build edifices high enough to scrape the heavens, primarily out of a wish to make a name for themselves. Nimrod led his "vain and presumptuous" followers in the execution of the design, raising ever higher "this tower against the Lord, and so gave expression to their impious pride" (II, 112, 113). In time, God punished the builders not with physical death but with a confusion of language: "As the tongue is the instrument of domination, in it pride was punished" (II, 113). No longer would the spoken word be capable of uniting the human race, whether to advance pride or for any other purpose. Presently, those who conspired to challenge God would now be misunderstood themselves, God "scattering them from there over all the earth" and "confus[ing] the language of the whole world" (Gen. 11:8–9). Out of this storm was born the city of Babylon (literally, "Confusion"), parent of the Roman Empire (II, 112). For Augustine, the lesson to be inferred from the tale of Babylon's "wonderful construction" and its ill-fated instigator is clear: "The safe and true way to heaven is made by humility, which lifts up the heart to the Lord, not against Him."

To be sure, most things in the earthly city do not remain fixed long enough to become objects of pride or self-aggrandizement. The humble Augustinian statesman recognizes that the world will always be a place of unpredictable change due to the divisions that plague both politics and the human soul. Our affections, Augustine believed, are at a moment's notice subject to alteration, whether our will authorizes such change or not.[44] The soul's passions are simply writ large into human society, passions that work against a sovereign and stable good in a life that "is either subject to accidents, or environed with evils so considerable and grievous" that it could never merit the name of happiness, "if the men who give it this name had condescended to yield to the truth" (II, 306). Indeed, those who do take comfort in earthly joy are not unlike those who take pleasure in "glass in its fragile splendour," constantly in fear that their prized possession may be suddenly shattered (I, 138). For Augustine, the only solid foundation for repose is discovered in the City of God, a counsel that applies to both citizen and statesman, Christian or otherwise. Those charged with positions of authority should never confuse the unbridgeable distance between the two cities, ever mindful of the biblical teaching that those who try to realize heaven on earth will likely learn hard lessons in the virtue of humility.[45]

CHARITY

In addition to Augustine's emphasis on humility, a considerable portion of his political, social, and religious œuvre may be summarized in a single Latin term: *caritas*, which in English may be imperfectly translated as Christian or charitable love.[46] Augustine had in mind more than mere alms-giving when using the word. For him, love is the glue that holds not only the civic state but all of human society together. Spiritually, it is what connects humanity to the divine. Yet like the will itself it is an emotion that can be turned to good or bad ends, assuming ordered or disordered forms in society and thus characterizing regimes to different degrees as virtuous or vicious.[47] On Augustine's account, the best expression of love is the divine love between God and man, a more spiritual and lasting form than transient passions such as *eros* (erotic love) or *cupiditas* (lust).[48] Yet in spite of its religious connotations, *caritas* need not be severed from one's relation to the rest of humanity. Charity has both a religious and secular dimension, and to this extent its orientation is not toward an object or particular action so much as an ongoing disposition toward others—a "habit of the heart," to borrow a phrase from the sociologist Robert Bellah.[49] Nor is this stance necessarily confined to members of the Church, which as Augustine indicates is no different from the wider world itself to the extent that it contains saints and sinners alike.[50] As Eric Gregory has suggested, there is a broader political element implicit in Augustinian charity insofar as it speaks on behalf of "the legitimacy and, at times, the necessity of love for healing politics."[51] Hence *caritas* may serve as a bonding agent that can hold people together on a stronger basis than impersonal attachments to institutions, procedures, and laws. Moreover, its language may offer a more stable and mobilizing vocabulary for reaching agreements than appeals addressed to changing public opinion.[52] Perhaps it is for these reasons that invocations of hope, fellowship, and goodwill have until recently been perennial elements of American political rhetoric, whether in the homilies of the Puritan John Winthrop or the speeches of civil rights leader Martin Luther King, Jr.[53] *Caritas*, it seems, is a non-partisan quality, hardly expected but certainly welcome when discovered among political leaders. Indeed, from conservative stalwarts such as George Will to feminist theorists that emphasize a more "caring" politics, Americans pining for "statecraft as soulcraft" in the twenty-first century constitute a sizable political tent.[54]

Augustine shared the concern for cultivating a kinder, more "soulful" statecraft, as illustrated by his characterization of the charity belonging to his ideal statesman.[55] As he puts it in Book Ten of *Civitas Dei*, the charitable statesman is slow to punish and quick to pardon, desirous that such punishments improve the populace rather than satisfy his wounded pride (I, 223). Pardons for crimes should not be doled out as political favors, as they usually are by most American presidents. Rather, they should have a rehabilitative purpose "with the hope that the transgressor will amend his ways." When issuing orders to subordinates, whatever harshness attends his promulgations should be compensated for by "lenity of mercy and the liberality of benevolence," in recognition of the fact that his subjects will someday be his equals before God. In terms of foreign policy, Augustine's prince is grieved by the necessity of even waging a war that is deemed just, aware of the bloodshed, toil, misery, and finally death attending any violent conflict (II, 311).[56] If, Augustine continues, political leaders conduct themselves in this manner, fulfilling their responsibilities "not through ardent desire of empty glory, but through love of eternal felicity," such persons are made happy in the present time not simply by their political success but through hope and anticipation of eternal reward (I, 223).[57] Charity repays its practitioner with happiness, both in this life and the next.

Of course, few pillars of charity loomed on Rome's terrestrial horizon in Augustine's time.[58] Love may have been in short supply, but there was plenty of enmity to go around. Divided and inflamed "by litigations, wars, quarrels, and such victories as are either life-destroying or short-lived," Augustine skewered leaders and nations that instigated wars on behalf of rapine and vice (II, 53). In particular, the quarrel between the brothers Romulus and Remus portrays how such vice is implicit in and passed down through Roman history, once again issuing from the erroneous view that selfishness and violence rather than charity and dialogue lead to happiness (II, 55). Augustine offers a conciliatory alternative. "The possession of goodness is by no means diminished by being shared with a partner either permanent or temporarily assumed," he argues. On the contrary, the enjoyment of good things increase in proportion "to the concord and charity of each of those who share" rather than hoard their gains. The one most willing to invite others to share in one's bounty, he suggests to both the political leader and ordinary citizen, "will have the greatest abundance to himself." Echoing the Gospel message that those who lose their life will find it, Augustine holds that the more those in society's highest echelons give of themselves and their material belongings the more content they will be. A difficult lesson to understand, and an even more challenging one to obey. But Augustine believed that letting go of attachments to worldly prestige, honors, and power would in turn allow charity to flow into the heart of both the political leader and the community generally. The less that one is attached to, the more one is free. The statesman, of course, sets the example.

Conflict resolution achieved through charity points to a related political good: peace. In *Civitas Dei*, Augustine acknowledges the powerful grip peace exerts on society. For its sake all wars are waged, he claims, and no other earthly good is greeted with more gratitude or in its absence desired more fervently (II, 316). Yet in contrast to many modern political theorists and leaders who rank stability and order as of utmost importance for democratic government, Augustine downplays the advantage of peace in a community if it is not motivated and reinforced by the practice of charity.[59] He believed that peace, like civic glory, was too often misidentified as the highest goal in politics.[60] Whether in the halls of power or the intimacy of the household, Augustine notes that peace often masks sin and corruption, and so it can never be more than a dubious good in Augustine's eyes (II, 308).[61] Nor is it adequate to define peace for humans simply as "the proper arrangements of the body and the satisfaction of appetites," for this desire mankind shares with irrational animals (II, 322). Genuine and lasting peace—peace for the soul, not simply the body—involves more, namely, those preconditions necessary for pursuing knowledge of how to act, live, and (in Augustine's opinion) draw closer to "the perfectly ordered and harmonious enjoyment of God, and of one another in God" (II, 319). Its achievement involves taking a different attitude toward the things of this world, making use of rather than prioritizing the necessaries of this world (II, 326). In practical terms, this concord can be approximated, first, by injuring no one, and second, by "do[ing] good to everyone he can reach," both in the household and society (II, 323). Whether applied to the domestic or political sphere, Augustine hoped that following this code would cultivate relationships based not on a love of power and proud authority, but based on mercy and the duty owed to one's fellows.[62] The effects of charity, Augustine suggests, can permeate political, economic, and other social relationships, joining together the community on a more solid basis than that afforded by mutual interest, a temporary ceasefire, or other tenuous forms of cooperation. [63]

Augustine describes the practice of *caritas* as essential for both political leaders and citizens interested in creating a better, more just political order. Charity orients one away from desires for material goods and vainglory and toward a peace that is more substantive than the absence of conflict. [64] Moreover, Augustine's understanding of the virtue entails not a retreat from society into hermetic isolation, but an understanding of community that unifies humanity amid the divisions created by vice, sin, and material desire. [65] In its concern for others, *caritas* extends beyond the self to one's role as a member of a family, church, community, and human race. In all, it reminds citizens of what they have in common, conceiving politics as more of a shared moral enterprise than a transactional, zero-sum competition. Of course, few if any states or leaders may lay claim to being "a model of Christian charity," to again invoke Winthrop. [66] But one need not perfectly realize the idea to appreciate the importance of the virtue of charity in our political leaders and the problems associated with its evacuation from politics. Whether expressed in the form of a pathological narcissism or easygoing indifference to others, leadership bereft of humility or charity results in a fearful, prideful, and ultimately dangerous reliance on one's own understanding in the discharge of public duties. Down this alley lies dictatorship, not statesmanship.

CONCLUSIONS

In his *Civitas Dei*, Augustine blunts the sharp edges that characterize heroic statesmanship in the fashion of Alcibiadean ambition and, to a lesser degree, Catonic republicanism. To be sure, Augustine does share some qualities with the figures examined so far. Like Alcibiades, Augustine possessed a restless spirit that no political regime or school of philosophy could hope to bridle or satisfy, even as he replaced ambition with heaven as the site of the soul's repose. [67] And similar to the younger Cato, he believed that politics was too important an enterprise to be reduced to a locus for pursuing self-interest and material gain. Ultimately, however, Augustine's antidote to self-striving and the all-too-human vice of pride is found in neither total independence of nor absolute absorption in state affairs. Relying on humility and properly ordered love as the foundations of policy, the Augustinian statesman hopes to oppose and transcend material goods, earthly glory, and pride, and in doing so focus his and the political community's vision on a higher and more lasting kind of human flourishing and community. This is what statesmanship, at its best, seeks to accomplish.

Moreover, for all its emphasis on the superiority of the heavenly city to the earthly one, Augustine does not repudiate the good society. Instead, he presents a form of statesmanship that is humble in attitude, charitable in deed, and governed by hopeful yet tempered expectations about what can be achieved from politics and, for that matter, political leadership. Admirable as this depiction may be, however, the leader hoping to fundamentally transform human character will find Augustine's work a tough pill to swallow. Following the teaching of *Civitas Dei*, one must accept that evil and injustice will never disappear entirely from human affairs.[68] And so the political leader must concede that peace, no matter how perpetual it appears, is a fragile thing in comparison to "the peace which God Himself enjoys," which "passeth all understanding but His own" (II, 535). Perhaps most difficult of all, the statesman must constantly bear before him the fact that he or she is a mere mortal, susceptible to sin, error, and destined one day to perish. Political leaders should picture themselves not as superhuman figures but as pilgrims who use "such advantages of time and of earth as do not fascinate and divert them from God, but rather aid them to endure with greater ease" life's woes and the soul's manifold burdens (II, 326).[69] In light of all these demands made on one's ethical and political outlook, far from being uninterested in statesmanship, Augustine demands more than even the all-too-human exemplars in this book may hope to fulfill.[70]

However difficult Augustine's standards may be for political leaders today, they nonetheless remain instructive for citizens who yearn for a more hopeful political future, if only in reminding us of what has been lost. As we might expect, his ideal ruler is devoted to several virtues one would expect to discover in the work of a medieval theologian: humility, moderation, piety, and solicitousness for the common good are all essential elements of his conduct. Alongside the exercise of these qualities is the leader's recognition that he or she operates on a razor's edge of agency and restraint, making decisions in light of the precarious mutability of human affairs and the overarching inscrutability of God's will. In some way or other, political leaders of the twenty-first century will meet and wrestle with the implicit claims made by Augustine's two cities and his account of statesmanship. So long as the temptations nurtured by pride and self-righteousness reside in the human breast, the moderating influences of humility and charity will be critical elements in the statesman's repertoire.

Linking Augustine's thought to contemporary American politics follows an established scholarly tradition of connecting the United States to late-imperial Rome.[71] In many respects such comparisons are apt. Nonetheless, objections may be raised regarding the applicability of Augustine to our political history. If Cato was better suited for life in Plato's republic than the Roman one, as Cicero argued, does Augustine fit into the American one? As a practical matter, how do we reconcile our principles—be they civic, Christian, or otherwise—with the rough-and-tumble world of politics? Are there in fact limits to a statesmanship split between two kingdoms as opposed to a kind rooted firmly on earth? Moving on from Augustine, we must consider that statesmanship involves not only the acknowledgment of human frailty but also an agency of the hard-swinging kind that would impel victims of injustice toward great acts, such as dumping chests of tea in Boston Harbor. Statesmanship must be humble, but also to some extent exalt human potential and achievement as expressed through the political community. If we hope to rehabilitate and sustain statesmanship, we must venture beyond Augustine's stark horizon and, looking to the United States, ask: what have we here?

NOTES

1. As Eric Gregory notes, many scholars have cast Augustine as "the patron saint of a dour and other-worldly pessimism which emphasizes the radical limits of politics and virtue as compared to a heavenly city." See his "Sympathy and Domination: Adam Smith, Happiness, and the Virtues of Augustinianism," in *Adam Smith as Theologian*, ed. Paul Oslington (New York: Routledge, 2011), 33–45: 34.

2. Describing Augustine's intended readers, John von Heyking notes "the entire *City of God* is directed specifically toward Roman aristocrats who were uncertain as to whether Christianity undermined political virtue, and whether Christian humility undermined their own nobility." See his *Augustine and Politics as Longing in the World* (Columbia, MO: University of Missouri Press, 2001), 158.

3. On the obstacles inherent to any analysis of medieval political philosophy, see Ralph Lerner and Muhsin Mahdi (eds.), *Medieval Political Philosophy: A Sourcebook* (New York: Free Press, 1963), 1–20. As Lerner and Mahdi note, many students of the era "find it hard to see why someone who had a contribution to make to political philosophy did not go about it in a straightforward manner," reflecting an "erroneous view that political philosophy has a typical or normal form of expression" (2).

4. See Reginald Haynes Barrow, *Introduction to St. Augustine* (London: Faber & Faber Ltd., 1950), 249; Theodor E. Mommsen, "St. Augustine and the Christian Idea of Progress: The Background of the City of God," *Journal of the History of Ideas* 12, no. 3 (1951), 346–74; Sheldon S. Wolin, *Politics and Vision: Continuity and Innovation in Western Political Thought* (Boston: Little, Brown, and Company, 1960), 111, 117; Dino Bigongiari, "The Political Ideas of St. Augustine" in *The Political Writings of St. Augustine*, ed. Henry Paolucci (Washington, DC: Regnery, 1962), 343–4; Herbert A. Deane, *The Political and Social Ideas of Saint Augustine* (New York: Columbia University Press, 1966), vii., 29, 56–66, 116–53, 241–3; Rex Martin, "The Two Cities in Augustine's Political Philosophy," *Journal of the History of Ideas* 33, no. 2 (1972), 195–216; Hiram Caton, "St. Augustine's Critique of Politics," *New Scholasticism* 47.4 (1973), 433–57; George J. Lavere, "The Political Realism of Saint Augustine," *Augustinian Studies* 11 (1980), 135–44; Gerhart Niemeyer, "Reason and Faith: The Fallacious Antithesis," in *Essays on Christianity and Political Philosophy*, eds. George W. Carey and James V. Schall (Lanham, MD: University Press of America, 1984), 11–29; James V. Schall, *The Politics of Heaven and Hell* (Lanham, MD: University Press of America, 1984), 51, 57, 60; Oliver O'Donovan, "Augustine's *City of God* XIX and Western Political Thought," *Dionysius* 11 (1987), 89–110; Paul J. Weithman, "Augustine and Aquinas on Original Sin and the Function of Political Authority," *Journal of the History of Philosophy* 30, no. 3 (1992), 353–76; Michael J. White, "Pluralism and Secularism in the Political Order," *University of Dayton Review* 22, no. 3 (1994), 137–53: 144; Gerard O'Daly, *Augustine's City of God: A Reader's Guide* (Oxford: Clarendon, 1999), 209–10; Linda C. Raeder, "Augustine and the Case for Limited Government," *Humanitas* 16, no. 2 (2003), 94–106: 98–99, 104; and John Milbank,

Theology and Social Theory: Beyond Secular Reason, 2nd ed. (Malden, MA: Wiley-Blackwell, 2006).

5. Mommsen (1951); Ernest L. Fortin, "Political Idealism and Christianity in the Thought of St. Augustine" in *Classical Christianity and the Political Order: Reflections on the Theologico-Political Problem*, ed. J. Brian Benestad (Lanham, MD: Rowman & Littlefield, 1996), 31–63; William B. Connolly, *The Augustinian Imperative: A Reflection on the Politics of Morality* (Lanham, MD: Rowman & Littlefield, 2002); B. Hoon Woo, "Pilgrim's Progress in Society: Augustine's Political Thought in *The City of God*," *Political Theology* 16, no. 5 (2015), 421–41: 439; and Michael J. S. Bruno, *Political Augustinianism: Modern Interpretations of Augustine's Political Thought* (Minneapolis, MN: Fortress Press, 2014), 235, 244.

6. Saint Augustine, *The City of God* (1871, 1888), I: 139. With the exception of occasional biblical citations, parenthetical citations in this chapter refer to this edition of Augustine's work.

7. Consider D. J. MacQueen, "The Origin and Dynamics of Society and the State According to St. Augustine," *Augustinian Studies* 4 (1973), 73–101; Robert A. Markus, *Saeculum: History and Society in the Theology of St Augustine*, 2nd ed. (New York and Cambridge: Cambridge University Press, 1989), 173; Peter J. Burnell, "The Status of Politics in St. Augustine's *City of God*," *History of Political Thought* 13, no. 1 (1992), 12–29; John von Heyking, "Soulcraft, Citizenship, and Churchcraft: The View from Hippo," in *Cultivating Citizens: Soulcraft and Citizenship in Contemporary America*, eds. Dwight D. Allman and Michael D. Beaty (Lanham, MD: Lexington, 2002), 29–42: 31–32, 36; Eric Gregory, *Politics and the Order of Love: An Augustinian Ethic of Democratic Citizenship* (Chicago: University of Chicago Press, 2008); John von Heyking, "The Luminous Path of Friendship: Augustine's Account of Friendship and Political Order," in *Friendship & Politics: Essays in Political Thought*, eds. John von Heyking and Richard Avramenko (Notre Dame, IN: University of Notre Dame Press, 2008), 115–38: 116; Luke Bretherton, *Christianity and Contemporary Politics: The Conditions and Possibilities of Faithful Witness* (Malden, MA: Wiley-Blackwell, 2010), 71–125; and R. R. Reno, "Getting Augustine Wrong," *First Things* 272 (2017), 3–4. Between these two interpretive camps pass some scholars who have tried to find some middle ground. See, for instance, Pierre Manent's position that Augustine's perspective is neither that of a political animal nor the devotee of "the theoretical life." Rather, Augustine offers "an intermediary perspective" that in Manent's words adopts "a sorrowful disposition in the face of human miseries." See his *Metamorphoses of the City: On the Western Dynamic*, trans. Marc LePain (Cambridge, MA: Harvard University Press, 2013), 290. Similar shades of nuance are present in Robert Dodaro's *Christ and the Just Society in the Thought of Augustine* (Cambridge: Cambridge University Press, 2004) and Christopher Dawson's *Enquiries into Religion and Culture* (Washington, DC: Catholic University of America Press, 2009), 198, 213.

8. Joseph Clair, *Discerning the Good in the Letters and Sermons of Augustine* (New York: Oxford University Press, 2016), 80, 106.

9. For more extensive overviews of this debate in Augustinian political thought, see Paul Weithman, "Augustine's Political Philosophy," in *The Cambridge Companion to Augustine*, eds. Eleonore Stump and Norman Kretzmann (Cambridge: Cambridge University Press, 2001), 234–52; Robert Dodaro, "Ecclesia and res publica: How Augustinian Are Neo-Augustinian Politics?" in *Augustine and Postmodern Thought. A New Alliance against Modernity?*, eds. Lieven Boeve, Mathijs Lamberigts, and Maarten Wisse (Leuven: Peeters, 2009), 237–272; and Peter Iver Kaufman, "Christian Realism and Augustinian (?) Liberalism," *Journal of Religious Ethics* 38, no. 4 (2010), 699–724.

10. "To him who possesses virtues," writes Augustine, "it is a great virtue to despise glory; for contempt of it is seen by God, but is not manifest to human judgment" (I, 215).

11. Good starting points for Augustine's life include Henry Chadwick, *Augustine* (Oxford: Oxford University Press, 1986) and Garry Wills, *Saint Augustine* (New York: Penguin, 1999). The most valuable biographies of Augustine include Peter Brown, *Augustine of Hippo: A Biography*, revised edition (Berkeley and Los Angeles: University of California Press, 2000); James J. O'Donnell, *Augustine: A New Biography* (New York: Ecco, 2005); Henry Chadwick, *Augustine of Hippo: A Life* (New York: Oxford University Press, 2009); and Miles Hollingworth, *Saint Augustine of Hippo: An Intellectual Biography* (New York: Oxford University

Press, 2013). Perhaps the best scholarly treatment of the *Civitas Dei* is O'Daly's *Augustine's City of God: A Reader's Guide* (1999).

12. Jean Bethke Elshtain, "Why Augustine? Why Now?" in *Augustine and Postmodernism: Confessions and Circumfession*, eds. John D. Caputo and Michael J. Scanlon (Bloomington, IN: Indiana University Press, 2005), 244–56: 244.

13. A more comprehensive analysis of the relationship between politics and ethics in Augustine's body of work would include (among other writings) his written correspondence with Roman politicians such as Marcellinus, Boniface, and Macedonius.

14. The particular episode involved the Church's proclamation to forcefully suppress the heretical teachings (and eventually violent tactics) of the Donatist sect. Augustine quotes and applies Christ's parable to those who refuse to accept the invitation to his grand banquet in the Gospel of Luke: "Go out into the highways and hedges, and whomsoever you find, compel them to come in" (14:23). See his notorious "Epistle 93" in St. Augustine, *Letters*, trans. Wilfrid Parsons (New York: Fathers of the Church, 1953), II: 10.59. Wills (2012) suggests that Augustine was never very comfortable with this stance (166).

15. Augustine notes that both cities "enjoy temporal good things, or are afflicted with temporal evils, but with diverse faith, diverse hope, and diverse love" (II, 292).

16. Following the practice of attributing secular success or failure to divine judgment, many of Augustine's contemporaries had taken Christianity to task as responsible for the Visigoth invasion of Rome in 410.

17. On Augustine as the founder of "metahistory," see Bradley J. Birzer, *Sanctifying the World: The Augustinian Life and Mind of Christopher Dawson* (Fort Royal, VA: Christendom Press, 2007), 73–75.

18. As Miles Hollingsworth describes, "Augustine's contribution to the history of political thought in the West is to be measured, then, in the extent that he amplified St Paul's teachings on the distance between man and God, and on the corresponding rôle and necessity of Grace." See his *Pilgrim City: St. Augustine of Hippo and His Innovation in Political Thought* (London: T&T Clark International, 2010), 208.

19. See Ernest L. Fortin, *Political Idealism and Christianity in the Thought of St. Augustine* (Villanova, PA: Villanova University Press, 1972); Peter Iver Kaufman, "Augustine, Macedonius, and the Courts," *Augustinian Studies* 34, no. 1 (2003), 67–82; and Peter Iver Kaufman, *Incorrectly Political: Augustine and Thomas More* (Notre Dame, IN: University of Notre Dame Press, 2007), 108.

20. Milbank (2006), 380–438.

21. Michael J. Hollerich, "John Milbank, Augustine, and the 'Secular,'" in *History, Apocalypse and the Secular Imagination*, eds. Mark Vessey, Karla Pollmann, and Allan D. Fitzgerald (Bowling Green, OH: Bowling Green State University Press, 1999), 311–26.

22. Robert Dodaro, "Augustine on the Statesman and the Two Cities," in *A Companion to Augustine*, ed. Mark Vessey (Malden, MA: Wiley-Blackwell, 2012), 386–97: 396.

23. See Ernest Fortin, "St. Augustine," in *History of Political Philosophy*, eds. Leo Strauss and Joseph Cropsey, 3rd ed. (Chicago: University of Chicago Press, 1987), 176–205: 196–7.

24. See Michael P. Foley, "Thomas Aquinas' Novel Modesty," *History of Political Thought* 25, no. 3 (2004): 402–23.

25. See David Hume, *An Enquiry Concerning the Principles of Morals*, ed. Tom L. Beauchamp (Oxford: Oxford University Press, 1988), 73; and Friedrich Nietzsche, *Beyond Good and Evil: Prelude to a Philosophy of the Future*, trans. Helen Zimmern (New York: Macmillan, 1907), 227–8.

26. Benjamin Franklin, *The Autobiography & Other Writings* (New York: Bantam, 1982), 84, 77.

27. David J. Bobb, *Humility: An Unlikely Biography of America's Greatest Virtue* (Nashville, TN: Thomas Nelson, 2013), 4. A similar trend is described by the cultural commentator David Brooks, who contends that the United States has undergone "a broad shift from a culture of humility to the culture of what your might call the Big Me, from a culture that encouraged people to think humbly of themselves to a culture that encouraged people to see themselves as the center of the universe." See his *The Road to Character* (New York: Random House, 2015), 6.

28. See, e.g., Robert K. Greenleaf, *Servant Leadership: A Journey into the Nature of Legitimate Power and Greatness* (Mahwah, NJ: Paulist Press, 1977); Larry C. Spears and Michele Lawrence (eds.), *Focus on Leadership: Servant-Leadership for the Twenty-First Century* (New York: John Wiley & Sons, 2002); and James C. Hunter, *The World's Most Powerful Leadership Principle: How to Become a Servant Leader* (New York: Random House, 2004).

29. For studies that describe the importance of humility in Augustine's thought, consider John East, "The Political Relevance of St. Augustine," *The Modern Age* 16, no. 2 (1972), 167–81; Garry Wills, *Confessions of a Conservative* (Garden City, NY: Doubleday, 1979), 202; Phillip Cary, "Study as Love: Augustinian Vision and Catholic Education," in *Augustine and Liberal Education*, eds. Kim Paffenroth and Kevin L. Hughes (Burlington, VT: Ashgate, 2000), 55–80: 66–69; and Joseph J. McInerney, *The Greatness of Humility: St Augustine on Moral Excellence* (Cambridge: James Clarke & Co., 2016).

30. Mary M. Keys, "Augustinian Humility as Natural Right" in *Natural Right and Political Philosophy: Essays in Honor of Catherine Zuckert and Michael Zuckert*, eds. Ann Ward and Lee Ward (Notre Dame, IN: University of Notre Dame Press, 2013), 97–113: 100.

31. Peter Iver Kaufman shows how Augustine attempted to "redeem" the virtue of humility for a post-imperial Rome, hoping to salvage its appeal for a future leader "who prized piety rather than celebrity!" See his *Augustine's Leaders* (Eugene, OR: Wipf and Stock, 2017), 30.

32. This feature is emphasized throughout Jean Bethke Elshtain's *Augustine and the Limits of Politics* (Notre Dame, IN: University of Notre Dame Press, 1995).

33. St. Augustine, "Sermon XXXI," in *St. Augustine: Sermon on the Mount, Harmony of the Gospels, and Homilies on the Gospels*, ed. Philip Schaff (Grand Rapids, MI: Wm. B. Eerdman's, 1956), VI, 748–56: 755.

34. As Augustine puts it in his Commentary on Psalm 142:2: "Know that the origin of the city of God goes back to Abel, as that of the evil one goes back to Cain. It is, therefore, an ancient city, this city of God: always enduring its existence on earth and always sighing for heaven." Quoted in Brown (2000), 314.

35. Theodosius' life and importance in *Civitas Dei* are discussed in greater detail in Kaufman (2017), 23–35.

36. Augustine commends Theodosius' "Christian love" toward his enemies, contrasting his post-war gestures and accommodations with the fierce behavior of consuls like "Cinna, and Marius, and Sylla, and other such men, who wished not to finish civil wars even when they were finished." Theodosius, on the other hand, mourned the fact that such wars had to be waged at all (I, 226).

37. In 390, a riot had erupted in Thessalonica that led to the death of the captain of the provincial garrison.

38. Ambrose authored a private letter to Theodosius outlining the Church's opposition. See his "Ambrose to the Emperor Theodosius I (390)," in *Ambrose of Milan: Political Letters and Speeches*, ed. and trans. J. H. W. G. Liebeschuetz (Liverpool: Liverpool University Press, 2005), 263–69. As Rob Meens points out in his *Penance in Medieval Europe, 600–1200* (Cambridge: Cambridge University Press, 2014), Ambrose's protest was a dangerous if courageous move in light of the emperor's authority over the property of the Church and the lives of its members (21). The availability of such punitive measures at the emperor's disposal lends some evidence to the sincerity of Theodosius' contrition.

39. On this point see Mark J. Doorley, "Limit and Possibility: An Augustinian Counsel to Authority," in Paffenroth and Hughes (2000), 146–62: 150. For Doorley, the episode points to Augustine's teleology concerning "the limited character of human knowledge" and his belief in "a 'beyond' that beckons us to take into account what may be beyond our capacity to know" (159, 161).

40. To put the matter in somewhat transactional terms, the Church got its public act of repentance, while Theodosius was accepted back into the Church and continued to rule until his death in 395.

41. In his early commentaries on the Book of Genesis, Augustine closely links pride to original sin, claiming that Adam and Eve sinned out of pride, i.e., their wish to rule themselves independent of God's will. See Augustine's *Two Books on Genesis: Against the Manichees and*

On the Literal Interpretation of Genesis: An Unfinished Book, trans. Roland J. Teske (Washington, DC: Catholic University of America Press, 1991).

42. Unlike the humble and upfront contrition of Theodosius, the proud cast "about for the shelter of an excuse even in manifest sins" rather than accept blame for wrongdoing (II, 28).

43. Though it is unclear in Genesis whether Nimrod directly ordered the building of the infamous tower, many sources have linked its construction to him directly, i.e., Philo of Alexandria, *Questions and Answers on Genesis*, trans. Ralph Marcus (Cambridge, MA: Harvard University Press, 1953), 172 and Flavius Josepheus, *Jewish Antiquities*, trans. William Whiston (Hertfordshire: Wordsworth, 2006), 16.

44. In his *Pagan Virtue: An Essay In Ethics* (Oxford: Clarendon Press, 1990), John Casey contrasts Greek and Christian understandings of morality and the human soul in the course of arguing that "Christianity rejects the worldliness implicit in the ethic of the virtues, and abhors the values that go with such worldliness" (v). As he puts it, "pride, the desire for honour, and still more wealth and beauty, have nothing to do with Christian goodness."

45. As Marc Guerra has argued, because the distinctions drawn between the two cities resist political absolutes, Augustine "avoids the monadic temptations of ideological totalitarianism and theoretical despotism." The lines he draws "calls attention to the fact that politics is an inherently limited enterprise and that man ultimately longs for a form of wholeness that transcends the political order." See his *Christians as Political Animals: Taking the Measure of Modernity and Modern Democracy* (Wilmington, DE: Intercollegiate Studies Institute Books, 2010), 147.

46. On the challenge of accurately translating *caritas*, see Oliver O'Donovan, *The Problem of Self-Love in St. Augustine* (Eugene, OR: Wipf and Stock, 1980), 11 and William S. Babcock, "*Cupiditas* and *Caritas*: The Early Augustine on Love and Fulfillment," in *Augustine Today*, ed. Richard John Neuhaus (Grand Rapids, MI: William B. Eerdmans, 1993), 1–34: 32.

47. Augustine posits that "the two cities have been formed by two loves: the earthly by the love of self, even to the contempt of God; the heavenly by love of God, even to the contempt of self. The former, in a word, glories in itself, the latter in the Lord" (II, 47).

48. The classic distinction is drawn by Augustine in his *De Doctrina Christianity*, trans. J. F. Shaw (Mineola, NY: Dover, 2009): "I mean by charity that affection of the mind which aims at the enjoyment of God for His own sake, and the enjoyment of one's self and one's neighbor in subordination to God; by lust I mean that affection of the mind which aims at enjoying one's self and one's neighbor, and other corporeal things, without reference to God" (90). Perhaps the most comprehensive analysis of this difficult concept in Augustine's thought can be found in Raymond Canning, *The Unity of Love for God and Neighbour in St. Augustine* (Heverlee, Belgium: Augustinian Historical Institute, 1993), while a more condensed summation is found in David Lyle Jeffrey's entry on "Charity, Cupidity," in his *Dictionary of Biblical Tradition in English Literature* (Grand Rapids, MI: William B. Eerdmans, 1992), 130–7.

49. As Thomas Williams maintains in his discussion of Augustinian charity, "The end of all things, Augustine insists, is God. He alone is to be loved for his own sake—'enjoyed,' in Augustine's terminology. Whatever else is to be loved should be 'used,' that is, loved for the sake of God." See his "Biblical Interpretation" in Stump and Kretzmann (2001), 59–70: 67.

50. At least Augustine does not hide the concept of *caritas* in such a way. In his *Homilies on the First Epistle of John*, trans. Boniface Ramsey (Hyde Park, NY: New City Press, 2008), Augustine reminds his listeners to "spread your charity throughout the world, if you want to love Christ, because Christ's members lie throughout the world" (155).

51. Gregory (2008), 208. But for a gentle critique of Augustine's idea of *caritas* as possibly exercising a de-politicizing role in society, see Hannah Arendt, *Love and St. Augustine*, eds. Joanna Vecchiarelli Scott and Judith Chelius Stark (Chicago, IL: University of Chicago Press, 1996).

52. As Doorley (2000) notes in his discussion of Augustine's approach to leadership, "the transcendent need not be God. It could also be one's country, one's planet, one's universe. However, a recognition of the transcendent does force one, if one is responsible, to question his or her judgments and decisions" as a mere human (160).

53. On this point see Eric Gregory, "Augustinians and the New Liberalism," *Augustinian Studies* 41, no. 4 (2010), 315–32: 327–32.

54. At the risk of collapsing two otherwise very divergent lines of argument, see George F. Will, *Statecraft as Soulcraft: What Government Does* (New York: Simon & Schuster, 1983); David L. Norton, *Democracy and Moral Development: A Politics of Virtue* (Berkeley and Los Angeles: University of California Press, 1991); Robert P. George, *Making Men Moral: Civil Liberties and Public Morality* (New York: Oxford University Press, 1993); Joan C. Tronto, *Moral Boundaries: A Political Argument for an Ethic of Care* (New York: Routledge, 1993); Peter Digeser, *Our Politics, Our Selves? Liberalism, Identity, and Harm* (Princeton, NJ: Princeton University Press, 1995); Allman and Beaty (2002); Virginia Held, *The Ethics of Care: Personal, Political, and Global* (New York: Oxford University Press, 2005); Michael Slote, *The Ethics of Care and Empathy* (New York: Routledge, 2007); and Virginia Held (ed.), *Justice and Care: Essential Readings in Feminist Ethics* (New York: Routledge, 2018).

55. In his analysis of Augustinian *caritas*, James J. O'Donnell summarizes the pervading influence of love over the Christian and Augustinian view of human history as follows: "Love had been disordered by sin in the garden of Eden at the beginning of history and would only be put right at the end of history by the second coming of Christ and the resurrection of bodies. In the meantime . . . sin continues to struggle for and often achieves mastery." See his "Preface" to *Late Have I Loved Thee: Selected Writings of Saint Augustine on Love*, eds. John F. Thornton and Susan B. Varenne (New York: Random House, 2006), xvii–xxvi: xxiii.

56. From the perspective of the heavenly city, any temporal war constitutes a civil war among God's children. Standing in contrast to this discord is the heavenly city, which "calls citizens out of all nations, and gathers together a society of pilgrims of all languages, not scrupling about diversities in the manners, laws, and institutions whereby earthly peace is secured and maintained" (II, 327).

57. Augustine is careful to distinguish domination from glory, contending that praiseworthy glory directs the praises of the crowd "to Him from whom every one receives whatever in him is truly praiseworthy" (I, 215). In contrast, the person who pursues glory "by deceit and artifice, wishing to appear good when is not," surpasses the animal kingdom in duplicity and cruelty.

58. Apart from Theodosius, only one other major figure elicits Augustine's praise for his leadership in *Civitas Dei*. That figure is the Emperor Constantine, whose conversion to Christianity marked a major turning point in the rise of the faith. Yet Constantine is not commended by Augustine for any intrinsic merits—he was "of the true God himself," Augustine remarks somewhat mysteriously—but is introduced mainly as a rebuttal to those who suggest that God bestows kingdoms and worldly success only on pagan demon-worshipers (I, 224, 223). On Augustine's tepid assessment of Constantine as an instrument of divine will, see Kaufman (2017), 14, 18.

59. To give an extreme example, there is no natural injunction in *Civitas Dei* to seek peace and resign nearly all rights and liberty to an earthly sovereign for the sake of physical self-preservation, as we find in Thomas Hobbes' *Leviathan* (1994), 80, 113–4.

60. Peace, Augustine argues, is ultimately ephemeral and should be conceived as "the solace of our misery" that precedes "the positive enjoyment of felicity" based on the cessation of "resistance either from ourselves or from others" (II, 342, 343).

61. In his analysis of Augustine's thought, Andrew Murphy has argued that "although a 'lower' good, and useful purely in instrumental terms, earthly peace and order are to be preserved and nurtured" for the sake of human flourishing and the believer's spiritual progress. See his "Augustine and English Protestants: Authority and Order, Coercion and Dissent in the Earthly City," in Paffenroth and Hughes (2000), 163–76: 163.

62. In *Civitas Dei*, Augustine draws a connection between familial and political peace, maintaining "the well-ordered concord of domestic obedience and domestic rule has a relation to the well-ordered concord of civic obedience and civic rule" (II, 326). Accordingly, he advises the father of a family to frame his domestic rule to align with that of the laws of the city to achieve harmony between the civil and domestic order. For Augustine, the factors contributing to order or disorder in society run deep.

63. As Augustine notes in his dialogue "The Happy Life," if "anyone is determined to be happy, he has to try to get for himself that which lasts forever and cannot be snatched away be any misfortune," in his case God "eternal and everlasting." See Augustine of Hippo, "The

Happy Life" in *Trilogy on Faith and Happiness*, trans. Roland J. Teske (Hyde Park, NY: New City Press, 2010), 23–53: 37.

64. Augustine goes so far as to argue "the dominion of bad men harms themselves far more than their subjects, for they destroy their own souls in their greater license to exercise their lusts" (I, 139). The good man, even if he is a slave to political power, remains free internally; "but the bad man, even if he reigns, is a slave, and that not of one man, but what is far more grievous, of as many masters as he has vices."

65. Mary T. Clark, "Augustine the Christian Thinker," in *From Augustine to Eriugena: Essays on Neoplatonism and Christianity in Honor of John O'Meara*, eds. Francis X. Martin and John A. Richmond (Washington, DC: Catholic University of America Press, 1991), 56–65: 57.

66. See Winthrop's famous sermon, "A Model of Christian Charity," in *The American Puritans: Their Prose and Poetry*, ed. Perry Miller (New York: Columbia University Press, 1956), 79–84.

67. John Figgis once observed a struggle between two personalities in Augustine, i.e., between "a mystic, who could forgo all forms, not only of outward but of inward mechanism, and fly straight . . . [and] a championship of ecclesiastical order, resolute to secure the rights of the Church." See his *The Political Aspects of S. Augustine's "City of God"* (New York: Longmans, Green, and Co., 1921), 7.

68. As Fortin (1987) points out, "God, being all-powerful, could of course do away with evil altogether, but not without the loss of a greater good for mankind. In their own way the evils that he permits contribute to man's spiritual advancement," serving "as a test for the just and a punishment for the wicked" (203).

69. Reflecting on the Augustinian leader's responsibility to navigate between the ideal and the actual, Edgar Brookes has aptly summarized the political dilemma Augustine's thought presents to the would-be leader: "the State can neither be rejected out of hand nor made a final end in itself. We live in this tension: it cannot be otherwise, and we can be thankful for it, because it is a fruitful tension." See his *The City of God and the Politics of Crisis* (London: Oxford University Press, 1960), 83.

70. Kaufman (2017) notes "Augustine wanted something more from his emperors (but would find it in only one), bishops, pastors, and statesmen. He wanted trust in God's sovereignty and divine grace, exemplary humility, compassion, prudence, drams of pessimism about the chances of perfecting righteousness in this world, but a brand of optimism that, he thought, was always in season—optimism about the celestial fate of the faithful" (6).

71. Recent speculations include Cullen Murphy, *Are We Rome? The Fall of an Empire and the Fate of America* (New York: Houghton Mifflin Harcourt, 2007); Vaclav Smil, *Why America Is Not a New Rome* (Cambridge, MA: MIT Press, 2010); Paul Burton, "*Pax Romana/Pax Americana*: Perceptions of Rome in American Political Culture, 2000–2010," *International Journal of the Classical Tradition* 18, no. 1 (2011), 66–104; Geir Lundestad, *The Rise and Decline of the American "Empire": Power and its Limits in Comparative Perspective* (New York: Oxford University Press, 2012); and Maria Wyke, *Caesar in the USA* (Oakland, CA: University of California Press, 2012). Germane to these comparisons is the popular if controversial production of Shakespeare's *Julius Caesar* in New York City's Central Park in 2017, a staging that drew criticism for its graphic portrayal of the assassination of Caesar as President Trump.

Chapter Four

Expedience and Circumspection in John Marshall's *Life of George Washington*

By any conventional measure, Supreme Court Chief Justice John Marshall's *Life of George Washington* was a flop. Intended to be the authoritative biography of the nation's most celebrated general and president of the United States, the work was widely derided at the time of its overdue publication, and since then has been largely forgotten.[1] Surely the sense of personal embarrassment Marshall experienced must have been keen, for he admired no public figure more than Washington. When not busy with Supreme Court duties, he labored for years on the *Life*, digging deep into American military and political history in hopes of etching the memory of the republic's foremost founder in the minds of his fellow citizens and future ones. Yet in spite of his efforts, the work was a failure. At one point, Marshall expressed the desire to publish the work anonymously, and one wonders if his wish was motivated by some faint premonition of the biography's failure.[2] Yet however unfortunate the legacy of the *Life* may be, we should hesitate to dismiss its insights for appreciating the character of American statesmanship as embodied in one of the country's most famous figures—one who continues to be invoked by those seeking to apply his leadership to contemporary American politics.[3]

Even setting aside its famous author, the *Life* is noteworthy for its firsthand analysis of perhaps the most famous American statesman.[4] Throughout Washington's time in the public eye, spanning the battlefields of the American Revolution to his retirement to Mount Vernon, Marshall documents his fellow Virginian's contribution to the development of the constitutional order of the new United States. What emerges from his pen is more than a sober history, but a character sketch of Washington's leadership as detailed by the major challenges and conflicts that helped define American independence. In particular, Marshall dwells at length on Washington's ability to balance active expedience with reserved circumspection, both during war and peacetime. As a work concerned with political leadership, indeed as a work of political theory generally, the *Life* examines a figure that took a different approach to his command than either the heroism of the classical era or the humble form of charity extolled by Augustine and other Christian thinkers. With Marshall's Washington, we enter into a distinctly modern approach to statesmanship.

BACKGROUND OF MARSHALL'S *LIFE*

Writing a book about Washington's public service was never a great goal in John Marshall's life. Truth be told, he was pressured into the enterprise by close friend and fellow Supreme Court justice Bushrod Washington, the President's nephew. Having inherited his uncle's private papers upon his death in 1799, Bushrod approached Marshall with the idea of writing a biography of Washington, apparently out of pecuniary motives, since both men could have used the money.[5] Moreover, Marshall had fought alongside Washington during the American Revolution and greatly admired the nation's first president, and immortalizing his achievements for future generations while earning a profitable return seemed doubly rewarding. Armed with access to the president's private papers, he had good reason to believe he could deliver material that would be both fresh and engaging to the reading public.[6] To top it off, Washington himself had once expressed ample confidence in his brother-in-arms' competence, in words that perhaps now summoned as much apprehension as encouragement. "General Marshall is so capable of making accurate observations," Washington had once observed, "that I am persuaded his information may be relied on with certainty."[7]

So what explains the botched biography? Alas, Marshall underestimated the consuming work of the historian, work that was made all the more challenging as he assumed the taxing duties of Chief Justice of the Supreme Court in 1801. Marshall may have hoped that writing the biography would provide a temporary respite from his bigger project of building the Court's authority through landmark decisions such as *Marbury v. Madison* (1803), *McCulloch v. Maryland* (1819), and *Gibbons v. Ogden* (1824). As it turned out, writing about Washington proved to be more of a chore than a labor of love. Marshall was conscious of the overwhelming task before him even from the beginning. As he acknowledged in a candid letter to Charles Cotesworth Pinckney in 1802, "In march last Mr. Washington placd the papers of our late respected & belovd General in my hands, & requested me to enter, as soon as possible, on the very difficult task of composing the history of his life."[8] As a part-time work, the *Life* was ever hanging over Marshall's head, and in time turned into a plodding and uneven production that flustered the typically calm and composed Chief Justice. Until the end of his life, Marshall would labor painstakingly to revise and edit the biography. He lived to put the final touches on a single-volume version intended for use in schools, perhaps with the wistful hope that if the *Life* was no source of edification for his own generation, future Americans might read the condensed version with greater appreciation.[9] Mostly, they have not read it at all.

Compounding the difficulty of Marshall's efforts was the fact that the *Life* did not sit well with other political leaders of the era. Even before it went to press, Marshall's book was controversial. Its most prominent critic was none other than the Democratic-Republican Thomas Jefferson, a lifelong opponent of the Federalist Marshall who seethed over the mere idea of the work. Despite owning two copies of the five-volume biography, Jefferson condemned the work as nothing more than a "party diatribe" redolent with "libels on one side."[10] Convinced that the book's release was being timed to influence the 1804 presidential election, Jefferson and his supporters maneuvered to diminish the *Life*'s distribution and reception.[11] Scathing reviews were published, deliveries of the work to its subscribers were impeded, and authors were enlisted to write alternative political histories. When the counter-histories Jefferson encouraged failed to materialize, he tried publishing one himself.[12] The backlash against Washington was not confined to Jeffersonians, however. Long before Marshall embarked on the *Life*, John Adams had humorously derided Washington's outsized role in America. "The History of our Revolution will be one continued Lye from one End to the other," he once predicted. "The Essence of the whole will be *that Dr Franklins electrical Rod, Smote the Earth and out Spring General Washington. That Franklin electrified him with his Rod—and thence forward these two conducted all the Policy Negotiations Legislation and War.*"[13] Amid both professional and political distractions and controversy, Marshall was beset by a predicament familiar to many Washington biographers, that is, striking a tone that balances candor with respect for a larger-than-life subject.[14]

In reality, Jefferson and his allies had little cause for concern. From a retail standpoint, the *Life* was a commercial disaster. Other biographies, notably Mason Locke Weems' fanciful *A History of the Life and Death, Virtues and Exploits of General George Washington* (1800), were more popular, and if they were sometimes not as accurate as the *Life* they were certainly more accessible.[15] Nor has its reputation improved with age. The *Life* was "a general disappointment," concluded the historian Edward Corwin.[16] Describing it as "pedantic," "dull," "laborious," and "rambling," Daniel Boorstin dubbed the work the "Marshall fiasco."[17] Helpful "for grasping the nationalistic mood but otherwise without profound historical meaning," Bert James

Loewenberg dismissed it as simply "a bad book."[18] Stylistically, Marcus Cunliffe grouses, the volumes are "prolix, sonorous, and lacking in psychological insight."[19] The biography was far "too long, too formal, and too slowly published" to find any commercial success, adds Gordon Wood.[20] Nor are literary failings the *Life*'s only defect. Other scholars have leveled criticisms at Marshall's "lack of scholarly training," including the fact that some depictions of the battles of the American Revolution appear to have been directly lifted without attribution from contemporaneous histories and published accounts in *The Annual Register*.[21] Surprisingly, among prominent historians, only Charles Beard complimented Marshall's *Life* as "a great work," at least in its portrayal of the economic conflicts that led to the adoption of the Constitution.[22] Such exceptions aside, Albert Beveridge, Marshall's most famous biographer, sums up the scholarly consensus in his description of the "dismal" product as "the least satisfactory of all the labors of Marshall's life."[23]

For all it shortcomings, does Marshall's *Life* still have something to teach the would-be political leader of today? Some think so. Max Lerner, for instance, once described the *Life* as teaching a Burkean lesson in the excesses wrought by political ideas, particularly in those chapters addressing the impact of radical Jacobin ideas on the American people.[24] More to the point, Morton Frisch notes that the work portrays the "ideal of a statesman" steadily pursuing the public interest out of a sense of obligation to his country.[25] Similarly, William Raymond Smith sees "a Homeric quality" in the biography that connects the outcome of events to "the actions of a traditional hero, thus giving the story the dramatic tension of human action instead of the grandeur and sublimity of divine action."[26] For Robert Faulkner, the book achieves Marshall's aims for instructing future statesmen, especially in its portrayal of Washington's willingness to give "duty, honor, and country priority over a concern for his own reputation."[27] Together, these more sympathetic interpretations argue that the *Life*'s strength lies less in its impartiality or accuracy than its philosophic education, and particularly in its treatment of the concept of statesmanship. On this score, the first lesson Marshall's work teaches is that quick thinking and a readiness to act are essential features of good leadership.

EXPEDIENCE

As the life of Alcibiades illustrates, statesmanship is very much a practical skill, and one's principles, no matter how admirable or popular, are not self-executing. Success in public affairs, many scholars of leadership today argue, relies as much on acting with expedience as devotion to a grand code of conduct or ideology.[28] Unlike flexibility, expedience tends to be a more piecemeal and policy-based trait, concerned with weathering the unforeseen contingencies of life with one's integrity intact rather than the great adaptations and re-sets of character. Thus, as Herbert Storing has argued, what counts for many as statesmanship today is not "that kind of statesmanship which had formerly been regarded as its essence: great, 'way of life'-setting, character-forming political leadership."[29] Rather, a more functional notion of statesmanship has emerged, distinguished by a nuts-and-bolts proficiency with "the principles of government structure."[30] Of course, George Washington is not typically proffered as a representative of either the pragmatic or expert-driven models of statesmanship by such scholars.[31] Nonetheless, Marshall's *Life* indicates that Washington was not above deploying a variety of stratagems—sometimes successfully, sometimes not—to advance his larger vision for the nation. Washington would never undergo the vertiginous personal and political transformations that defined Alcibiades. But neither would he adopt a single mode of action that would lead to the ruin of the nation he helped found.

Washington's military acumen, to say nothing of the American commitment to the cause of independence, was first tried by the crucible of combat. The condition of Washington's Continental Army augured poorly for the Americans, given that the latter's army stood inferior to the British in numbers, arms, ammunitions, clothes, and tents.[32] Such embarrassing difficulties required quick thinking and even quicker stealth. Nicknamed the "old fox" by the British commander Lord Cornwallis, General Washington omitted nothing when it came to managing military exigencies and retarding British advances during the American Revolution, whether in terms or battlefield strategy or maintaining order and morale within the Army's ranks.[33] Doing so was no mean task: from the beginning, the ultimate independence of the American colonies appeared doubtful.[34] Needing some advantage to offset the vastly superior British Army, Washington turned to informal tactics to thwart his opponents, most notably the element of surprise. Following the Army's famous crossing of the Delaware River during the bleak winter of 1776—a surprise move in and of itself—the subsequent sallies on the British Army and its Hessian auxiliaries in the battles of Trenton and Princeton were exceptional in Marshall's view for the judicious, bold, and unexpected timing of the engagements (82). Even in more temperate conditions these would be risky moves, as even a casual observer of the disheveled army could see (138).[35] Perhaps it was British General William Howe who was the most startled by the boldness of the American general that winter. As Marshall puts it, "nothing could surpass the astonishment of the British commander at this unexpected display of vigor on the part of the American General" (79). The element of surprise was, naturally, integral to the plan's success. Yet just as significant as the military victory, Washington's daring had a much greater influence on American fortunes than a mere tally of the killed and taken would indicate (82). After a string of losses and setbacks, and facing the prospect of a British capture of the nation's capital, Philadelphia, the "gloomy" prospect of success against the British had sunk the morale of officer and civilian alike "to the lowest point of depression" (73, 79). Yet the surprise attack on the British and the success of the campaign against Hessian forces at the Battle of Trenton had rejuvenated the flagging spirits of the American people, and accelerated military recruiting efforts throughout the nation (82). The episode showed Washington's ability to seize an unexpected opportunity to take advantage of a nodding opponent and rejuvenate the flagging spirits of his countrymen. He had inspired not simply his army, but a nation as well.[36] "To this perfect self-possession under the most desperate circumstances," Marshall avers, "is America, in a great degree, indebted for her independence" (75).

If Washington was at times bold in his wartime maneuvers, he was not foolhardy. When a plan to invade and annex parts of Canada was proposed in 1779 that relied on allied French forces, the General immediately demurred, sensing the strain this would place on the Army's already overstretched resources. While he had been supportive entering the province of Québec in the past, Washington maintained that the major military initiatives against the British should occur within the boundaries of the colonies, not spread throughout North America. Recognizing "the impracticability of executing that part of this magnificent plan," along with "the serious mischief which would result, as well from diverting so large a part of the French force to an object he thought so unpromising," Washington abandoned his support for the invasion (171, 172).[37] Similar restraint was exercised on an even direr occasion. When British General William Howe captured Philadelphia largely unopposed in September 1777, Washington faced immense pressure to launch an immediate counterattack against the British to re-take the capital. As Marshall notes, the views of Congress along with "[p]ublic opinion, which a military chief finds too much difficulty in resisting," urged a counterstrike, yet ignoring the hotheaded appeals of the moment, "Washington came to the wise determination of avoiding one for the present" (98). Combating British forces in the adjoining region, Washington's army was not yet gathered for an all-out battle which if pursued at that time would add loss of life to that of territory. Strategy, not public opinion, should dictate the present course. Washington recognized when to strike and when to hold back, displaying in this instance a deft expediency that refused to be governed by cries for revenge and the emotions of the moment.

Compared to the instances of his military legerdemain, Washington's expedience as president often appears muted in the *Life*. Unaccustomed as were the rest of his peers to the workings of the new national government, he had little opportunity to manipulate the levers of power. Why would he? As the beneficiary of widespread public approval and an absence of political parties during the early part of his administration, the most partisan acrimony Washington encountered was within his own star-crossed cabinet. America's first truly national government was the latest stage in the nation's experiment with independence, and so Washington took into his confidence public servants who might get the job done rather than toe a partisan line. Practicality, not ideology, was Washington's criterion. Thus in selecting his team, Marshall emphasizes the importance Washington gave to the character and competence of an individual rather than merely rewarding his or the Constitution's most vociferous supporters (341). A workable administration rather than purity of political principles was the goal. In selecting Thomas Jefferson to head the Department of State, Marshall remarks with striking generosity that he had chosen a figure that "had been long placed by America among the most eminent of her citizens, and had long been classed by the President with those who were most capable of serving the nation" (337). Edmund Randolph of Virginia, one of the few delegates to the federal convention who declined to add his name to the proposed Constitution, accepted an appointment as the nation's first Attorney General and eventually replaced Jefferson as Secretary of State (338). A plethora of hitherto state-appointed revenue collectors now served at the pleasure of the president of the United States in a federal capacity, and given the truculent behavior of the state governments under the Articles of Confederation, one might excuse the president for cashiering them and appointing more tractable officers. Yet Washington, "uninfluenced by considerations of personal regard," could not be moved "to change men whom he found in place, if worthy of being employed" (340–1). In selecting or retaining individuals on the basis of merit rather than politics, Marshall suggests the president had created an administration so full of talent and character that it could hardly fail to win the affections of the people (341).[38] It did not quite work out that way, as bitter internal power struggles soon erupted within the president's cabinet. Yet few instances attest to Washington's results-oriented expedience more impressively; and fewer such gestures have been made in American government since.

Unsurprisingly, President Washington's expedience was most effective in matters of military planning, a faculty particularly useful in dealing with recalcitrant Native American tribes in the western United States. Land in the Northwest Territory had been ceded to the United States by the British with the Treaty of Paris in 1783, but many tribes living there understandably refused to surrender control of the territory to the national government. At first, the practical Washington preferred negotiation and diplomacy to waging armed conflict on an uncharted frontier. Indeed, as Marshall puts it, Washington had tried earnestly "to give security to the northwestern frontier, by pacific arrangements" for a considerable length of time (354). When hostilities showed no signs of ebbing, however, Washington authorized a number of military expeditions to end the conflict in a more direct manner,

though casualties, desertions, and recruitment failures undermined these efforts. The controversy reached a crisis point in 1791, when the American
army, commanded by Arthur St. Clair, suffered hundreds of casualties in the
"disastrous" Battle of Wabash in the Northwest Territory (262). At last,
Washington laid before Congress a plan to raise a more competent force that
might finally end the resistance, a proposal eventually passed in spite of
partisan squabbling.[39] The move was a dramatic about-face from the president's earlier, nonviolent overtures. But for Marshall, it revealed Washington's resourcefulness in taking an incremental approach to avoid a catas-
trophe the nation could ill afford at the time: "a general war with the Indians"
(415). Ultimately, Washington was unable to solve single-handedly the tensions between Native and non-Native Americans, a relationship that continues to remains strained to the present day. Yet the president's practicality
balanced by patience did not go unnoticed, least of all by Marshall himself
when confronting similar controversies decades later.[40]

Whether in his encounters with British forces or Native American tribes,
Marshall's *Life* portrays Washington's shrewd willingness to take the expedient route to address the circumstances confronting him. As military commander, he kept his options open. On the one hand, he was willing to strike
quickly, as he did at Trenton; on the other hand, he might stay his hand, as he
did in response to proposed expeditions into Canada. As president, he valued
competence over dogma when choosing his cabinet, and was willing to shift
from mediation to coercion when circumstances warranted. On these occasions in the *Life*, Washington evinced a willingness to alter strategy as demanded by the situation, and to exercise force as well as restraint based on
resources in hand and the turn of events. Yet Washington's expedience was
not the only quality that served his leadership. Entwined with his practicality
was a sense of cautious consideration that served him well as he piloted the
nation through the choppy waters of these early years.

CIRCUMSPECTION

It may be somewhat surprising to see a reserved quality such as circumspection listed as a defining feature of statesmanship. After all, many Americans
are predisposed toward the politician who acts with vigor and brio, ready to
make the gutsy call, ruthlessly shooting first and asking questions later. Citizens have little patience for delay when it comes to important matters of
state, often referring to such hesitancy as "waffling" and accusing those who
betray any sign of irresolution of trying to have things both ways. In contrast,
those who act with decision and dispatch are often credited with clear-sighted
resolution. Yet for many who have given serious study to the concept of
political leadership, circumspection and the calm weighing of one's options

proves to be a virtue rather than an insult when applied to political leaders.[41] Something like this idea must have been brewing in the head of many classical thinkers that discussed the concept of prudence (*phronesis*), the virtue that for philosophers such as Aristotle determined the proper means to achieving an end determined through the use of right reason or theoretical wisdom.[42] Similarly, Cato's Roman contemporary, the orator Cicero, also celebrated the leader able to apprehend "the regular curving path through which governments travel, in order that, when you know what direction any commonwealth tends to take, you may be able to hold it back or take measures to meet the change."[43] Together, these classical thinkers stress the importance of forethought and caution as opposed to instinct and speed in the political leader's advancement of the common good. Following this conception, good leadership may at times be disclosed by the measures and actions one refrains from taking, and an approach to confronting sickness in the body politic that, as Morton Frisch and Richard Stevens have counseled, encourages the statesman to play "the nurse if he can and the surgeon if he must."[44] Such an attitude toward statecraft promotes the kind of moderation and farsightedness that is too often absent from government today, forcing the political leader to think a step or two ahead of one's actions lest one's policies be rendered hostage to the next headline, setback, or tweet.

Though certainly capable of quick action, Marshall's Washington nonetheless illustrates how circumspection may be a strength rather than weakness in a military leader. Possessed of manners "rather reserved than free," Washington carried a dignity that in Marshall's estimate derived not from "capricious and ill-examined schemes" but rather a "laborious attention" given to the possible consequences of his actions (465, 466, 469). Useful as this temper was to military planning, it also extended to addressing the legitimate grievances of his fellow soldiers. Although Washington enjoyed great popularity among his men, the *Life* acknowledges that even he could not quell a long-simmering discontent among his soldiers concerning the sustained privations and sufferings of the military (245). For those who served under Washington, pay as well as rest were often in short supply. Thus it was not entirely a shock when Washington, encamped on the Hudson River in the winter of 1781, received word of an alarming mutiny involving several hundred men led by the tired Pennsylvania Continental regiments. The mutineers had declared an intention to march on Philadelphia and demand redress from the government or else resign *en masse*. The situation was grave: Washington could hardly spare the loss of troops at the time and, making matters worse, violence and casualties had occurred in the attempt to suppress the uprising. Marshall notes that Washington, "accustomed as he had been to contemplate hazardous and difficult situations," was unable "under existing circumstances, to resolve instantly on the course it was most prudent to pursue" (246). Initially, his inclination was to report to the mutineers' camp and settle the matter in person. Yet opinions "formed on more mature reflection" prevailed, and he chose to leave negotiations with the regiments to a congressional committee drawn up to accommodate the mutineers, in the meantime preparing his soldiers for dispatch in the event negotiations failed. At first, it seemed the threat had passed when the regiments were granted concessions from the government relating to pay, clothing, and long overdue discharges (247). Soon thereafter, however, a New Jersey brigade issued similar demands, and "the dangerous policy of yielding even to the just demands of soldiers with arms in their hands" was plain for all to see (248). A chain reaction of rebellion seemed to have been ignited, and Washington, "who had been extremely chagrined at the issue of the revolt in the Pennsylvania line," now wasted no time in ordering a detachment of New England troops to "bring [the New Jersey mutineers] to unconditional submission."[45] The uprising was quickly vanquished, and Marshall speculates that Washington's vigorous and prompt measures taken in this instance alerted the attention of the state governments to the necessity of keeping the Continental Army happy. Washington's first attitude toward the conflict between civil and military authority had been one of watchful waiting. But when concessions appeared to have set the stage for additional ultimatums, he refused to back down on defending the military order indispensible to American victory. The incident showed Washington's ability to resist his gut impulse, but only if such a pause and its consequences did not mortally endanger the necessity of a unified military in wartime.

As it turned out, conflict between the state governments and the American military was not quelled so easily. Yet if Washington sought to root out internal dissent among the ranks during the heat of battle, he was nonetheless an ardent advocate of his fellow soldiers in the aftermath of their victory over the British. In 1783, Washington's sympathy for the plight of unpaid war veterans had to be balanced with the best means for achieving their compensation. Browbeating the states seemed unlikely to be effective, as under the Articles of Confederation procuring any funds for national purposes was a tall order indeed. For their part, the disgruntled veterans were tired of excuses: "Soured by their past sufferings, their present wants, and their gloomy prospects," Marshall notes, the men were in a temper that demanded immediate redress (291, 292). A group of veterans resolved to apply pressure directly, dispatching delegations to the Confederation Congress in Philadelphia to obtain in person the "redress of grievances which they seemed to have solicited in vain" (292). Upon learning of the proposed march, Marshall notes, Washington's "characteristic firmness and decision did not forsake him." The situation required not angry indignation directed toward an ungrateful nation, he believed, but measures fit, prudent, and conciliatory. According to Marshall, Washington's "fixed determination" and loyalty to his brothers-in-arms was offset by his opposition to "rash proceedings" that would merely aggravate the antipathy of the states toward national requisitions. Aware that it was easier to prevent than correct "intemperate measures," he sought at first to stop a preparatory meeting of the veterans before it convened. But conscious of their keen injury and sharing their "fear of injustice," Washington resolved to attend the informal gathering and guide the deliberations toward a peaceful resolution, devising measures that would placate the men without unduly inflaming the confederation congress. Of course, Washington was not just any other officer. Exerting every ounce of his influence, he gave a speech that once more praised the "meritorious services and long sufferings" of the men, whose claims he resolved to promote to the public barring any criminal conduct that would betray "the military and national character of America" (292, 293). Think before you take actions that might "open the flood-gates of civil discord, and deluge our rising empire in blood," he warned the men (294). The effort to calm the crisis worked: "the storm, which had been raised so suddenly," now "happily dissipated." Violence between military and civil authority was again averted. As Marshall concludes, it was all that the occasion required (293).

As president, Washington was again called on to mollify anger directed toward the central government, this time issuing from the general public. For many Americans struggling to understand the workings and demands of the new national government, the *bête noire* of their grievances was taxation. One stream of revenue was enough, many believed; a second, national layer imposed by the new federal government was intolerable. In particular, the Whisky Rebellion that occurred in western Pennsylvania beginning in 1791 provided a strong test of the new powers of the national government as well as the commander-in-chief's patience. The furor stemmed from an excise tax levied by Congress on domestic spirits to pay down war debt. Farmers, particularly in the western United States, opposed the tax insofar as it disproportionately affected those living in agricultural regions, where the seasonal operation of whisky stills was an especially profitable sideline.[46] A congressional authorization to create a militia to enforce the collection of the tax heightened tensions, as those hostile to the law began traveling outside Pennsylvania for the purpose of inciting resistance (418). Not wishing to make things worse, Washington initially adopted a diplomatic approach, hoping general public opinion would see the wisdom of the measures. But he drew the line at mob violence, and in September 1794, he issued a proclamation pronouncing his firm determination, "in obedience to the high duty consigned to him by the constitution, to reduce the refractory to obedience" (419). Federal troops marched on Pennsylvania and, meeting no violent resistance from the disaffected, seized and detained for legal prosecution several insurrectionists "who had refused to give assurance of future submission to the laws." The threat of rebellion was quieted—at least for the time being.[47] Once again, Washington had terminated without bloodshed "an insurrection which, at one time, threatened to shake the government to its foundations" as Shays' Rebellion had some seven years before (420).[48] For Marshall, the episode illustrated the "prudent vigor" of the president, motivated not by rashness but a measured assessment of the best means to ensure both the safety of the Union and the execution of its laws.

One final example of Washington's patience occurs at the end of the *Life*, when he had finally retired to his beloved and long-neglected Mount Vernon in the summer of 1798. By then, public outrage toward his administration concerning the controversial Neutrality Proclamation was history, and Marshall reports he was inundated with a daily stream of testimonials "of the grateful and ardent affection universally felt by his fellow-citizens" (301). No longer was the Francophilia that motivated past attacks on his character a concern. On the contrary, with French cruisers routinely seizing American vessels with impunity, war with France seemed more likely than not (458). Congress had passed measures for "retaliating [against] the injuries which had been sustained, and for repelling those which were threatened," including a law authorizing the formation of a regular army (459). At the sound of war drums, the nation once again turned to Washington, hoping once more he might lead the American army, plan strategy, and "induce the utmost exertion of its physical strength" against the French. Stories of Washington's willingness to leave behind the comforts of home to serve his country were the stuff of legend in Marshall's time as much as our own. But Washington's attitude on this occasion proved to be different. In June, President John Adams and his Secretary of War James McHenry separately sent letters entreating Washington to once again lead the nation in its hour of need. And as he had so often in the past, he assented—but tentatively, and with important preconditions. Of course, he wrote to McHenry, he would not "withhold any services I could render when required by my country" (460). Moreover, he responded to Adams, if a war with France was truly imminent, any delay in preparations "may be dangerous, improper, and not to be justified by prudence." But two stipulations attended his assurances: that he, personally, would be permitted to choose the highest-ranking officers under his command and that he should not be called out of his long-awaited retirement until France had actually invaded the United States. In fact, he correctly predicted that the French Directory would soon collapse under its own divisions and corruption, allowing the two nations to reconcile their differences.[49] It was a clever move on Washington's part, and one that deserves a bit more levity than is found in Marshall's praise of his fellow Virginian's ability to balance "the cares and attentions of office with his agricultural pursuits" (461). Gladly would America's foremost general answer the call of his country once more—but only if it really needed him.

As both military commander and president, the *Life* portrays Washington's circumspection as a core characteristic of his statesmanship. Indeed, at times it appears to be his wisdom that stood out most in Marshall's remembrance of the man. Washington's career, he observes, provided "ample and repeated proofs" of the "practical good sense, and of that sound judgment, which is perhaps the most rare, and is certainly the most valuable quality of the human mind" (467). His character aimed at "no object distinct from the public good," and contemplated "at a distance those situations in which the United States might probably be placed; and digest[ed], before the occasion required action, the line of conduct which it would be proper to observe." On Marshall's account, Washington understood the difference between efforts to accommodate and persuade, on the one hand, and the use of compulsion and force, on the other, preferring the former to the latter whenever possible. But he would not allow hopes for a peaceful resolution of conflict to endanger larger commitments to military discipline or public safety. Even to the time of Washington's death in December 1799, the *Life* shows that he applied due diligence to matters large and small, in the public arena as well as in his private affairs: the prospect of war, however probable, should not unduly jeopardize the long-awaited comforts of domestic tranquility.

CONCLUSIONS

Marshall's *Life of George Washington* is the story of a statesman as told by a statesman. But in Marshall's time, it was George Washington who was the nation's undoubted cynosure, a matter that surely dictated the countless revisions of the biography long after agreeing to its production. In the end, the *Life* solidifies the notion that Washington's success was, to a considerable degree, bound and conducive to that of the United States. As Marshall reflects in his conclusion to the *Life*, "It is impossible to contemplate the great events which have occurred in the United States, under the auspices of Washington, without ascribing them, in some measure, to him" (468). But his celebrated status in the hearts and minds of his fellow Americans did not mean that his example and deeds should be frozen in the past, incapable of emulation for future generations of Americans. Despite its rocky path to publication and its widespread criticism, Marshall held out hope someday people might read and profit from the *Life*, with its "ample and repeated proofs" of Washington's conduct serving as a model "of that practical good sense, and of that sound judgment, which is perhaps the most rare, and is certainly the most valuable quality of the human mind" (467). He intended the *Life* to live on not merely as a work of history or biography, but as primer in statesmanship, providing "a lesson well meriting the attention of those who are candidates for political fame" (468).[50]

Marshall's message in the *Life* continues to resonate today. While broadly favorable, Marshall's assessment of Washington is nonetheless human rather than hagiographic. Though Marshall does not hesitate to praise Washington's willingness to stand up for what he believed was right against the prevailing "gusts of passion"—his defense of the Neutrality Proclamation between Great Britain and France as well as his Farewell Address of 1796 are particularly notable examples of this independence—he is no demigod able to govern military or political circumstances beyond his control (469). Taken as a whole, the picture that emerges is that of a Washington more expedient and circumspect than he is often portrayed in the popular imagination, as he was compelled to balanced attachment to principle with the particular demands of place and time. It was not Washington's ability to conquer fortune and completely determine the course of national events that wins Marshall's admiration, for this he was incapable of doing. Rather, Marshall's esteem for Washington lies in his ability to lead the nation in a way that was practical without compromising himself, expedient but not rash. Washington embodied qualities of statesmanship that transcend even his admirable accomplishments, forging a link between his life and those of future political leaders. Were he alive today, Marshall might be dismayed that his *Life* never was or will be a bestseller. But in a time when models of statesmanship are needed more than ever, his work might well be dusted off for a new generation of readers.

Even if his *Life* remains a clunker, however, John Marshall's pride of place in American jurisprudence is secure. In time, his judicial opinions did much to shape the political, economic, and legal landscape of the founding generation as well as those that have followed in its wake.[51] Washington's example no doubt loomed large in his mind as he, in his own right, grew into the nation's prototypical "judicial statesman," defining and defending the rule of law and the authority of the Supreme Court.[52] As we turn to the twentieth century, Marshall's trajectory signals an increasing trend as statesmanship ramifies into contexts that break with the traditional molds of the past. From Washington, we at last turn to Addams—and not the one you might expect.

NOTES

1. C. V. Ridgely's verdict resonates as strongly today as it did when he reviewed the *Life* in 1931: "Marshall's fame as a judge is still growing, but, as a biographer, he has long since been forgotten." See his "The Life of George Washington, by John Marshall," *Indiana Law Journal* 6, no. 4 (1931), 277–88: 287.

2. Marshall wished to remain anonymous more or less from the moment he began writing the *Life*, motivated perhaps as much by faint premonition of its failure as his characteristic self-effacement. See, for instance, his letter to his friend Charles Cotesworth Pinckney in 1802, in which he declares he does "knot [sic] wish to be known" as the author of the biography. See "To Charles Cotesworth Pinckney, November 21, 1802," in *John Marshall: Writings*, ed. Charles F. Hobson (New York: Penguin, 2010), 225–7: 225.

3. See, e.g., James Rees and Stephen J. Spignesi, *George Washington's Leadership Lessons: What the Father of Our Country Can Teach Us About Effective Leadership and Charac-*

ter (Hoboken, NJ: Wiley, 2007); Richard Brookhiser, *George Washington on Leadership* (New York: Perseus, 2008); Gerald M. Carbone, *Washington: Lessons in Leadership* (New York: St. Martin's Press, 2010); and John Avlon, *Washington's Farewell: The Founding Father's Warning to Future Generations* (New York: Simon & Schuster, 2017).

4. Though Marshall often drew on the statesman's vocabulary of duty and responsibility in his Supreme Court opinions, these instances transpired in judicial contexts, applying more often than not to the Supreme Court's responsibility to elevate law above politics.

5. Marshall, who did not join the Supreme Court until 1801, stood in need of money to pay his brother, James, for a land purchase in Virginia. See Marcus Cunliffe, "John Marshall's George Washington," in *In Search of America: Transatlantic Essays, 1951–1990* (Westport, CT: Greenwood Press, 1991), 141–51: 142.

6. Marshall's *Life* was one of a handful of Washington biographies (with remarkably similar titles) released in the years following the American Revolution, including David Humphreys' *The Life of General Washington* (1789), Mason Locke Weems' *Life and Memorable Actions of George Washington* (1800), John Corry's *Life of Washington* (1801), and David Ramsay's *Life of George Washington* (1807).

7. Quoted in W. B. Allen, *George Washington: America's First Progressive* (New York: Peter Lang, 2008), 196.

8. See "To Charles Cotesworth Pinckney," in Hobson (2010), 225.

9. As Marshall lamented in a letter to the newspaper publisher Caleb P. Wayne, "Having, Heaven knows how reluctantly, consented against my judgement, to be known as the author of the work in question I cannot be insensible to the opinions entertaind of it, but I am much more sollicitous to hear the strictures upon it than to know what parts may be thought exempt from censure . . . I wish to correct obvious imperfections & the animadversions of others woud aid me very much in doing so." See "To Caleb P. Wayne, July 20, 1804," in Hobson (2010), 263–64: 264.

10. See Cunliffe (1991), 144 and "Jefferson to Adams, 15 June 1813," quoted in Albert Beveridge, *The Life of John Marshall* (Boston and New York: Houghton Mifflin, 1919), III: 266.

11. Jefferson's trepidation was unfounded. In fact, only the first two volumes of the *Life* had been released by the time of the election. See Jean Edward Smith, *John Marshall: Definer of a Nation* (New York: Henry Holt and Co., 1996), 333.

12. Cunliffe (1991), 146. The product of Jefferson's efforts was his unpublished *Anas*, a political history based on state papers, notes, and reports amassed during his tenure as the nation's first Secretary of State. See Joanne B. Freeman, "Slander, Poison, Whispers, and Fame: Jefferson's 'Anas' and Political Gossip in the Early Republic," *Journal of the Early Republic* 15, no. 1 (1995), 25–57.

13. Quoted in Robert Ferguson, "The American Enlightenment, 1750–1820," in *The Cambridge History of American Literature*, ed. Sacvan Bercovitch (Cambridge: Cambridge University Press, 1994), 347–537: 348. In a letter to Thomas Jefferson in 1813, Adams ridiculed the *Life* as "a Mausolaeum, 100 feet square at the base, and 200 feet high" (quoted in Cunliffe 1991, 143).

14. As Curtis Nettels once lamented, "the tradition of Washington as a semi-sacred character is still so strong that one is not likely to undertake lightly the task of criticizing the hero symbol. The modern historian has thus become involved in a dilemma. He has hesitated to be caught in a cross fire of demands of sacred tradition on the one side and the exacting requirements of historical methods on the other." See his "The Washington Theme in American History," *Proceedings of the Massachusetts Historical Society* 68 (1952), 171–98: 178–79.

15. See Christopher Harris, "Mason Locke Weems's *Life of Washington*: The Making of a Bestseller," *The Southern Literary Journal* 19, no. 2 (1987), 92–101. Contrasting Weems' work to Marshall's *Life*, Gordon Wood notes, "Weems's fast-paced and fanciful biography sold thousands of copies and went through twenty-nine editions in two decades and a half following its publication in 1800. The public wanted Weems's human interest stories, even if they were fabricated." See his *Empire of Liberty: A History of the Early Republic, 1789–1815* (New York: Oxford, 2009), 566.

16. Edward S. Corwin, *John Marshall and the Constitution* (New Haven, CT: Yale University Press, 1919), 208.

17. Daniel J. Boorstin, *The Americans: The National Experience* (New York: Random House, 1965), 342.

18. Bert James Loewenberg, *American History in American Thought: Christopher Columbus to Henry Adams* (New York: Simon and Schuster, 1972), 216, 215.

19. Cunliffe (1991), 145.

20. Wood (2009), 565.

21. See William A. Foran, "John Marshall as Historian," *American Historical Review* 43, no. 1 (1937), 51–64 and Saul K. Padover, "The Political Ideas of John Marshall," *Social Research* 26, no. 1 (1959), 47–70: 50.

22. Charles A. Beard, *Economic Origins of Jeffersonian Democracy* (New York: Macmillan, 1915), 242. In addition to Beard, Washington Irving and Jared Sparks round out the notable historians defending the *Life*'s historical credentials. See Allan B. Magruder, *John Marshall: American Statesman* (Boston and New York: Houghton, Mifflin and Co., 1885), 238, and Jared Sparks (ed.), *The Writings of George Washington: Life of Washington* (New York: Harper & Brothers, 1852), xii.

23. Beveridge (1919), III: 239, 223.

24. Max Lerner, "John Marshall and the Campaign of History," *Columbia Law Review* 39, no. 3 (1939), 396–431: 397–8.

25. Morton J. Frisch, "John Marshall's Philosophy of Constitutional Republicanism," *Review of Politics* 20, no. 1 (1958), 34–45: 38.

26. William Raymond Smith, *History as Argument: Three Patriot Historians of the American Revolution* (The Hague: Mouton & Co., 1966), 121. Similarly, Thomas Shevory argues that the *Life* represents Marshall's engagement in "what Friedrich Nietzsche called 'monumental history.' It is the celebration of political character and the exposition of political morality," made sharper in contrast to "the enthusiastic temperament of the nonvirtuous many." See his "John Marshall as Republican," in *John Marshall's Achievement: Law, Politics, and Constitutional Interpretations*, ed. Thomas C. Shevory (New York: Greenwood Press, 1989), 75–93: 79, 80.

27. Robert K. Faulkner, "John Marshall and the 'False Glare' of Fame," in *The Noblest Minds: Fame, Honor, and the American Founding*, ed. Peter McNamara (Lanham, MD: Rowman & Littlefield, 1999), 163–86: 163–4.

28. See, e.g., Michael D. Mumford and Judy R. Van Doom, "The Leadership of Pragmatism: Reconsidering Franklin in the Age of Charisma," *Leadership Quarterly* 12, no. 3 (2001), 279–309; Michael D. Mumford, Jazmine Espejo, Samuel T. Hunter, Katrina Bedell-Avers, Dawn L. Eubanks, and Shane Connelly, "The Sources of Leader Violence: A Comparison of Ideological and Non-ideological Leaders," *Leadership Quarterly* 18, no. 3 (2007), 217–35; and Katrina Bedell-Avers, Samuel T. Hunter, Amanda D. Angie, Dawn L. Eubanks, and Michael D. Mumford, "Charismatic, Ideological, and Pragmatic Leaders: An Examination of Leader–Leader Interactions," *Leadership Quarterly* 20, no. 3 (2009), 299–315.

29. Storing (1995), 413.

30. Ibid.

31. Paul Carrese, for example, has said that Washington's "consistent dedication to liberty, constitutionalism, and moderation" represents a formidable alternative to "the Machiavellianism" of modern political thought. See his "George Washington's Greatness and Aristotelian Virtue: Enduring Lessons for Constitutional Democracy," in Holloway (2008), 145–69: 161. Similarities between Washington's political philosophy and Greek and Roman thought are further detailed in Garry Wills, *Cincinnatus: George Washington and the Enlightenment* (Garden City, NY: Doubleday, 1984), and Jeffry H. Morrison, *The Political Philosophy of George Washington* (Baltimore, MD: Johns Hopkins University Press, 2009), 62–106.

32. John Marshall, *The Life of George Washington: Special Edition for Schools*, eds. Robert Faulkner and Paul Carrese (Indianapolis, IN: Liberty Fund, 2000), 47. First published in 1838, this single-volume edition of the *Life* was Marshall's final revision of the work in addition to being the most commercially successful. Subsequent parenthetical references in this chapter refer to this edition of the *Life*.

33. Assessments of Washington's generalship often differ on the question of whether Washington was an aggressive or defensive-minded strategist. Compare, e.g., Dave R. Palmer, *The Way of the Fox: American Strategy in the War for America* (Westport, CT: Greenwood Press, 1975) with Russell F. Weigley, "American Strategy: A Call for Strategic History," in *Reconsiderations on the Revolutionary War: Selected Essays*, ed. Don Higginbotham (Westport, CT: Greenwood Press, 1978), 32–53.

34. The Americans tasted an early defeat when British troops seized New York City as a result of the Battle of Long Island in August 1776.

35. Dr. Benjamin Rush, who treated the American army at Valley Forge, did not mince words in his diagnosis of the Army: "The troops dirty, undisciplined, and ragged" manned "pickets left 5 days and sentries, 24 hours, without relief . . . [there reigned] bad bread; no order; universal disgust." Quoted in Esmond Wright (ed.), *The Fire of Liberty* (London: Folio Society, 1983), 118.

36. John Colville (1979) has described "a statesman's most distinguishing characteristic" as "his ability to inspire. He must also have courage, persistence, imagination, and a thick skin," as well as "the tenacity never to give up, never to be deflected from his objective—however many detours he makes in order to attain it—and never to despair" (3). These characteristics form an apt summary of Marshall's depiction of Washington's conduct during the Revolution.

37. Congress chose to table the planned expedition, but its supporters refused to let the scheme die. After it was again proposed, Washington was compelled to repeat his disapproval of the plan and demand clearer instructions about its execution (172). Eventually the invasion of Canada was reluctantly given up.

38. Later in the *Life*, Marshall does not gloss over the acrimony that beset Washington's Cabinet, nor does he heap blame for the drama solely on Thomas Jefferson. For Marshall, the split within the administration was symptomatic of the political animosity affecting the nation at large (364, 367).

39. By 1791, partisanship had begun to rear its head in Congress. Nonetheless, Marshall remarks with some surprise that even this action encountered strenuous opposition (363).

40. That is, in the famous "Marshall Trilogy" comprising his opinions in the cases of *Johnson v. M'Intosh* (1823), *Cherokee Nation v. Georgia* (1831), and *Worcester v. Georgia* (1832).

41. For example, Coats (1995) argues that the activity of statesmanship deals not only with bold, life-or-death decisions but also involves "the daily stream of contingencies facing a body politic," which require reflection on the means for achieving the general good through persuasion, coercion, and prudential judgment (35, 21).

42. Politically speaking, Aristotle said, prudence is the virtue that distinguished the statesman from the citizen, for such leaders "have the capacity of seeing what is good for themselves and for mankind," a farsightedness that renders "men capable of managing households and states." See Aristotle, *Nicomachean Ethics*, trans. Martin Ostwald (Upper Saddle River, NJ: Prentice Hall, 1999), 153. For Aristotle, statesmanship was the highest expression of prudence, a practical virtue that concerned the knowledge of both universals and particulars at the political level. On this point, see Terry Hoy's "The Idea of Prudential Wisdom in Politics," *The Western Political Quarterly* 11, no. 2 (1958), 243–50: 243–4.

43. Cicero, *De Res Publica*, trans. Clinton Walker Keyes (Cambridge, MA: Harvard University Press, 1994), 161, 155. On the role of prudential statesmanship in Cicero's thought, see Walter Nicgorski, "Cicero's Focus: From the Best Regime to the Model Statesman," *Political Theory* 19, no. 2 (1991), 230–51.

44. Morton J. Frisch and Richard G. Stevens, "Introduction," in *American Political Thought: The Philosophic Dimensions of American Statesmanship*, eds. Morton J. Frisch and Richard G. Stevens (New York: Scribner's Sons, 1971), 3–21: 8.

45. Even more striking, Marshall recounts, the surrender was to be followed by an immediate execution of the most prominent insubordinates (247).

46. See William Hogeland, *The Whisky Rebellion: George Washington, Alexander Hamilton, and the Frontier Rebels who Challenged America's Newfound Sovereignty* (New York: Simon & Schuster, 2010), 65–68.

47. Marshall describes a recalcitrant temper that stubbornly persisted in Pennsylvania toward national policy, ready to rise again should the army be recalled (419).

48. There was a warning implicit in Washington's success. That such a spirit of opposition could emerge and grow so quickly in conditions of prosperity was an ominous sign (420). For Marshall, the episode illustrated the fickleness of human nature and mutability of public opinion, two variables "which the statesman can never safely disregard."

49. Eventually, diplomatic overtures did resolve the differences between the countries, culminating in the Treaty of Mortefontaine in 1800 (461).

50. As Marshall once wrote to his grandson, "History is among the essential departments of knowledge; and, to an American, the histories of England and of the United States are most instructive. Every man ought to be intimately acquainted with the history of his own country." See his letter "To John Marshall, Jr., November 7, 1834," in Hobson (2010), 847–8: 847.

51. On the significance of Marshall's tenure as Chief Justice, see Smith (1996); Charles F. Hobson, "Defining the Office: John Marshall as Chief Justice," *University of Pennsylvania Law Review* 154, no. 6 (2006), 1421–61; R. Kent Newmyer, *John Marshall and the Heroic Age of the Supreme Court* (Baton Rouge, LA: Louisiana State University Press, 2007); Joel Richard Paul, *Without Precedent: Chief Justice John Marshall and His Times* (New York: Random House, 2018); and Clyde H. Ray, *John Marshall's Constitutionalism* (Albany, NY: State University of New York Press, 2019).

52. The concept of judicial statesmanship is elaborated in Gary J. Jacobsohn, *Pragmatism, Statesmanship, and the Supreme Court* (Ithaca, NY: Cornell University Press, 1977); Anirudh Prasad, "Imprints of Marshallian Judicial Statesmanship," *Journal of Indian Law Institute* 22, no. 2 (1980), 240–58; Harry M. Clor, "Judicial Statesmanship and Constitutional Interpretation," *South Texas Law Journal* 26, no. 3 (1985), 397–433; Paul O. Carrese, "Judicial Statesmanship, the Jurisprudence of Individualism, and Tocqueville's Common Law Spirit," *Review of Politics* 60, no. 3 (1998), 465–95; and Neil S. Siegel, "The Virtue of Judicial Statesmanship," *Texas Law Review* 86, no. 5 (2008), 959–1032. The particular contours of Marshall's judicial statesmanship—which I think include the concepts of expedience and circumspection we find in his description of Washington—merit more careful analysis than can be afforded here.

Chapter Five

Mobilization and Struggle in Jane Addams' *Twenty Years at Hull-House*

Hurtling toward the wind-swept, rapidly modernizing, and poverty-stricken Chicago of the late-nineteenth century, Laura Jane Addams' task is simple and soon stated: she has her work cut out for her. Amid urban decay and city streets piled high with unholy refuse, Hull House was an unlikely beacon of hope tucked in the city's northwest corner. Yet Addams' leadership and legacy are arguably incidental to Chicago and perhaps America itself, for the significance of her work transcends time and place. Since her death in 1935, Addams' dedication to mobilizing and empowering society's most vulnerable individuals has become an inspiration for the many social reformers that have followed in her path. Thus while she is not as well-known as some of the other figures that line the corridor of great political leaders, her first-person narrative of the role she played in developing, instituting, and administering Hull House has a claim on the consideration of all who seek in great or small ways to establish and effect political change. Out of all of the figures we have examined, it is Addams that comes closest to articulating the elusive idea of modern democratic leadership.

The importance of Addams' work is often overshadowed by her relative obscurity, her somewhat subdued personal character mirroring the type of leadership she embodied. Like Washington, Addams often found herself cast into the public spotlight despite rarely courting either popularity or political office.[1] Nor did she have much experience at all in public administration before her trial by fire at Hull House. In that capacity she worked tirelessly to alleviate physical, mental, and spiritual poverty, even as her efforts took place off the political stage and on the frontlines of everyday economic distress. As a result, her greatest mark was left in the realm of civil society. This orientation did not reflect an antipathy on Addams' part toward conven-

91

tional politics *per se*: on the contrary, she was game to assume public office and take on entrenched political forces when getting results required a more direct engagement in politics. But rather than a single-minded focus on climbing the political ladder, Addams largely took a more informal and unorthodox path in her leadership role. To put matters simply, when she saw a vacuum of leadership at the local level she addressed its absence not by railing against an impersonal "system" or trying to beat corrupt politicians at their own game. Rather, she sought to build ideas of equality, citizenship, and social harmony from the bottom up, all the while mindful that change often occurs slowly, as reforms needed to wind their way through political structures, layers of bureaucracy, and the informal power brokers who had a vested interest in maintaining the status quo. Radical and practical describe her approach; citizenship grounded in both rights and responsibilities characterize its object.

Like many figures in American history, Addams' life has been combed over by a cottage industry of devotees. Sometimes she is portrayed as a kind of super-heroine, an inspiring figure who single-handedly raised Chicago's poor and immigrant classes out of the depths of despair.[2] Others contend that Addams' work was much more haphazard, fortuitous, and impetuous than her more numerous admirers are willing to concede.[3] Most biographies, however, have situated her squarely within the Progressive Era as a stalwart representative of an intellectual movement emphasizing social reform, economic justice, and resistance to elitism in all its myriad expressions.[4] But while historians differ on their attitude toward Addams, her life and work have by and large earned praise across the political aisle. Indeed, both the political left and the right have long esteemed Addams as a model of good leadership. Some have painted Addams' approach in conservative colors, pointing to her emphasis on ameliorative as opposed to revolutionary measures and on the value of local and small-scale relief of poverty.[5] More recently, some scholars have applied Addams' thought to contemporary democratic theory, highlighting the value of her writing for current debates surrounding citizen responsibility, civic engagement, populism, and humane labor.[6] Taking an even wider view, others have mined Addams' writings for their application to global politics, with her activism on behalf of new immigrants to the United States serving as a model for contemporary ideas of transnational friendship, hospitality, and peace.[7] Yet for all the work that has been done on Addams, few scholars have turned to her approach to leadership as plainly articulated in her most well-known book, *Twenty Years at Hull-House* (1910).

Addams is the only woman in addition to being the only quasi-political figure in this book. Like the Chicago of her time, statesmanship has historically been a man's world. Does this mean that women can play the role of "stateswoman" only in informal ways? No. It doesn't. Her challenge from society's periphery should only deepen our appreciation of what she was able to accomplish, precisely because Addams challenged existing forms of exclusion from both within and without, working both through as well as against entrenched sites of authority. Perhaps being legally barred from voting or holding major political offices strengthened her perception that democracy encompassed not only a political but also a social dimension.[8] It certainly did not dilute her accomplishments, which have proven more lasting than the mark left by many of her male contemporaries that populated the halls of political power. Her example and success at Hull House invites readers to look at the concept of statesmanship from a different perspective than the vantage point employed so far, showing how opportunities for effective political leadership may occur in inconspicuous places and times, even where we least expect.

JANE ADDAMS' "SPIRITUAL STRUGGLE"

Like the younger Cato, Jane Addams realized from an early age that she had big shoes to fill in life. Judging by its title, *Twenty Years* would appear to cover just Addams' life in Chicago. In fact, the work spans a much longer time in order to develop the picture of leadership that came into its own on Halsted Street. In detailing her journey toward social reformer, Addams reveals that she never believed herself to be marked for great things. Rather, she thought that early influences and yearnings gradually shaped the person "upon whom various social and industrial movements" later reacted, a formation that makes her personal history inseparable from that of her mission at Hull House (ix).[9] She did not start out as a city girl. A child of the pleasant open frontier of Cedarville, Illinois, the natural world permeated her life from the time of her birth in 1860. A village "set in a scene of rural beauty," Cedarville represented a kind of adolescent playground for her and her siblings as they gathered walnuts, chased rainbows, and sacrificed dead snakes under rolling pine-shadowed skies (16). Hovering over Addams' life was the "dominant influence" of her father, John H. Addams, a noted bank president, Republican state senator, and forever object of emulation for young Jane, to whose memory she dedicated *Twenty Years* (1).[10] While financially secure, Addams reveals that her upbringing was not without difficulties. When Addams' maternal mother as well as several other siblings and friends died while Addams was still a young girl, she recalls being pierced with the "sharp worry" of mortal dread that quickened her toward "the great world of moral enterprise and serious undertakings" (20, 21).[11] With the help of her older sisters—Addams was grateful to be part of a large, supportive, and pious family—she raised a growing family while continuing to come to terms with the responsibilities of adulthood.[12] In the still-wild Midwestern prairie, she honed the skills of cultivating and preserving cohesion amid the strife, economic hardship, and adversity she would encounter years later in Chicago.

Second only to Alcibiades in her wanderlust, Addams too had to leave her place of birth in order to find her vocation as a political reformer. Following in the footsteps of her older sisters, at the age of seventeen Addams enrolled in religious studies at the Rockford Female Seminary and graduated in 1881, the year her father suddenly died (43).[13] She then completed courses at the Women's Medical College in Philadelphia with financial assistance from her late father's estate, but her studies were cut short by a recurrent "spinal difficulty" exacerbated by nervous afflictions that afflicted her throughout life (65).[14] During her extended convalescence—a period during which she was "literally bound to a bed in my sister's house for six months"—she expressed a desire to travel to Europe to take a long, close look at the world. So she did. "In pursuit of cultivation," she sailed across the Atlantic with the hope that she might discover what her purpose in life should be (71).[15] There she discovered not only the challenge of urban poverty, but also the movements toward social and economic reform that would play such an inspirational role when she finally returned to her Illinois roots.

Unlike many contemporary study abroad trips, Addams was forever changed by her visits to Europe. Her medical background led her to investigate and inventory the conditions of public health and sanitation in the great cities of Europe, and her observations of poverty and deprivation informed her efforts toward reforming social injustices at home. One such encounter was determinative on this score, shaping her leadership ever after.[16] Addams had familiarized herself with the principles of Settlement philosophy during a trip to Oxford, England, learning how volunteer workers that lived in housing settlements with society's urban poor might in cooperation promote the social, physical, educational, and political betterment of the least advantaged. But at the famed Toynbee Hall in 1888, a college settlement in London's East End, she finally witnessed firsthand the practical application of the idea.[17] As she stood on its doorsteps, she held in her hands a notice of introduction and in her heart the "high expectations and a certain belief that whatever perplexities and discouragement concerning the life of the poor were in store for me," the solace of daily work on their behalf would steel her against the difficulties inherent in her vocation (87–88). Working with and alongside the poor, Addams had found an escape from "the snare of preparation" in which so many young people found themselves trapped, unable or unwilling to make any effort to improve the lot of humanity (89).

Once back in the United States, Addams wasted no time in getting to work. She attended a gathering comprised of like-minded social reformers outside Plymouth, Massachusetts in 1892 (113). At the meeting, she spoke at length on the matters she had witnessed in the past several years, namely, the "motives and strivings" of those on the frontlines of reforming injustices inherent to and stemming from social and political structures. Pointing out the many contradictions she saw between democratic ideas and practice, Addams and her fellow reformers affirmed a shared commitment to improving American democracy in economic, social, and political terms. The stakes were high, and the transformation she envisioned extended far beyond the relief of material want. As she declared, "there is nothing after disease, indigence and a sense of guilt, so fatal to health and to life itself as the want of a proper outlet for active faculties" (118). Central to this endeavor were not simply legal changes but also services and facilities that would cultivate and nourish these faculties among both wealthy and poor Americans, for in truth civic helplessness afflicted both groups: while poverty quickly smothered civic cooperation among the poor, parents and schoolteachers of the wealthy as often neglected instilling the responsibilities of citizenship in their children (119–21). Keeping alight the spark of human creativity on behalf of a better world—an impulse essential to the "Intimations of Immortality" that Addams believed were latent in all human souls as well as her own—was a key motive of the Settlement movement as she saw it, which embraced all strata of society: men and women, educated and ignorant, religious and secular (117). What she described as a "very simple plan" was in fact never guaranteed to work: Addams, echoing the language of America's founding fathers, often described the Settlement movement as an "experiment" (85). But that uncertainty did not mean her efforts at Hull House were not earnest. Believing that democratic ideals were hollow unless applied to practical problems, she would no longer wait for "the system" to catch up to her and her fellow reformers' strivings.[18]

Hull House was perhaps the most famous achievement of this Settlement impulse in America, with Addams' *Twenty Years at Hull-House* its literary fruit.[19] In few instances were the values as well as aspirations of the movement given more concrete expression as they were at Hull House.[20] Resting beneath the blue-glass colonnades shimmering across the city skyline, the "fine old house" on Halsted Street opened its doors in 1889 thanks to the efforts of Addams and her fellow social reformer Ellen Gates Starr (93).[21] Its charter invoked many of the larger motives of the Settlement movement: "To provide a center for a higher civic and social life; to institute and maintain educational and philanthropic enterprises, and to investigate and improve the conditions in the industrial districts of Chicago" (112). Addams planned the settlement as a refuge from the storm "in a part of the city where many primitive and actual needs" of immigrants and the destitute might be met by a team of volunteers that would "learn of life from life itself" (85). The population of the house included about twenty young, well-educated men and women that, when not otherwise employed, volunteered their time at the Settlement alongside Addams, the Settlement's sole full-time volunteer. Addams says her memory of the frenetic first few years is "more or less blurred with fatigue," as the house encountered a number of challenges in terms of start-up costs (147). As is the case for many non-profits, funding was always uncertain, forcing Addams like Washington to frequently weigh principle with expedience, whether in the form of accepting "tainted money" from outside donors, voting up or down "one golden scheme after another" proposed by supporters, or petitioning local politicians on issues ranging from child labor laws to overdue pension payments (138, 140, 150). Finally, after hard years spent tilling the "soil of a community life," the center began to build a reputation as a gathering point where "the companionship of mutual interests" flourished among Chicago's immigrant population (151).

Hull House represented the defining moment of Addams' life work, but it was certainly not the last word on her leadership. As the success of Hull House grew, so did the reputation of its founders. Many of those who helped administer the house later became charter members of the International League for Labor Education, legitimating the belief among many residents that they were engaged in "a movement of world-wide significance and manifold manifestation" (230). Using peace as a calling card, Addams waded further and further into American politics, even as she endeavored to shield the operations of Hull House from partisan attacks.[22] She took part in the women's suffrage and civil rights movements as an extension of the Settlement's goal of socializing democracy (453).[23] When World War I broke out in Europe in 1914, Addams assumed a significant leadership role in organizing the Women's Peace Party—an organization still active today—as well as other national and international pacifist movements. To be sure, she still had a knack for making adversaries, even among her fellow travellers in the Progressive Party.[24] Yet her star continued to rise, and in 1931 she became the first American woman to receive the Nobel Peace Prize for her contributions advancing the cause of "peace and fraternity among nations."[25] Reflecting on the trajectory of her life in *Twenty Years*, Addams expressed hope that the lessons she had learned in Chicago might one day be profitably applied to international politics, believing that the feeling of "internationalism engendered in the immigrant quarters of American cities might be recognized as an effective instrument in the cause of peace" (308). An unlikely idea, perhaps, but one that reveals just how far Addams' goals had grown from her humble Cedarville beginnings.

Yet for all her efforts on the world stage, Hull House remains Jane Addams' signature achievement, and the book that documents its development may itself be seen as a product of her reformist impulse. Solving "the social and industrial problems" created by modern industrial life required "an experimental effort," which included recording for posterity what worked and what failed in relieving the "overaccumulation at one end of society and the destitution at the other" (125, 126). Righting the economic scales was not to be expected from the often tortoise-like pace of municipal, state, and federal legislation. Instead, she believed that democratic reforms might be realized through mobilizing, empowering, and channeling civic energies in the direction of reforms contributing to a better future for all Chicagoans. The first step in this process was to flip on the power.

MOBILIZATION

As much as the individual is important to any account of political statesmanship, history teaches that political actors can start as well as put out fires, and many times the most effective leader is one who refuses to shoulder civic responsibilities belonging to all members of the community.[26] The mobilization of dispersed resources, notably the scattered energies of one's fellow citizens, is key to such an understanding of such leadership. As Cheryl Mabey once put it, the explanation for modern crises of leadership "may not lie in the caliber of our current leaders, but rather in our failure to mobilize group resources to solve the group's problems."[27] The fault of many social ills, on such accounts, belongs not to weak and uninspiring politicians so much as a lack of organization, empowerment, and proper channeling of the civic resources left dormant in the body politic. Here is a different standard of leadership success, one based on mobilizing citizens to act on their own initiatives rather than cultivating exceptional figures who will do so on their behalf. In keeping with this focus on civic empowerment, many scholars of leadership have in recent years articulated a theory of citizen-leadership that emphasizes the virtues of local participation, civic education, and decentralized decision-making authority.[28] The best form of statesmanship, such accounts suggest, leaves one's fellow citizens a little more organized, informed, and active than he or she found them.

At Hull House, mobilization and empowerment of those on society's margins was at the epicenter of Addams' leadership. Working day in and day out to mitigate the centrifugal forces of urban life, she learned firsthand the nuts and bolts of building cohesion and collective action out of social fragmentation and political indifference. The challenges she faced included more than just acclimating recent immigrants to new environmental, cultural, and political institutions. She realized these immigrants would form a part of the wider labor force in Chicago, in which great ideological differences existed separating those who believed "business is business" from political radicals "who claimed that nothing could be done to really moralize the industrial situation until society should be reorganized" (184). Directly or indirectly, both positions downplayed the individual's role in creating a more equitable future, preferring to wait out squalid conditions in the hope of a better tomorrow. However well-intentioned some individuals might have been, Addams considered many committed social reformers to be either overly radical or too far removed from the everyday plight of the working class and conditions of poor, instead complacently giving "themselves over to discussion of general principles" and causes rather focusing on practical measures of reform (158, 184).[29] Thus Addams perceived that if the condition of the average worker was ever to improve, better organization was needed on multiple fronts: within the immigrant communities themselves; across the formal boundaries separating immigrant from non-immigrant; and the creation of a political platform on behalf of the working underclass that eschewed the radical stances of the intellectual advocates or opponents of social reform. No matter one's place of birth or background, Addams wanted people to stop sitting on their hands and roll up their sleeves to begin building the stronger bonds of cohesion necessary to effect social change.

For Addams, the key to creating such social change was education, a distinctive feature of Hull House as well as recent theories of "democratic statesmanship."[30] Addams gave education the broadest possible interpretation, including formal and informal as well as structured and spontaneous learning for members of the community.[31] In purely infrastructural terms, Hull House's earliest efforts included establishing the first public playground and kindergarten in the city (101).[32] Yet Addams wanted Hull House to be more than a children's daycare or place of remedial instruction.[33] Opportunities for enlightenment extended throughout daily life in the house: in its open kitchen, library, gymnasium, art gallery, and even a little theater where both international stories and timeless tragedies and comedies were performed (389). In a kind of reproach to the reigning utilitarian calculus of the day, art for art's sake was encouraged in studios lined with paintings, etchings, and lithographs (373).[34] The doors of the house's drawing rooms were flung open like "the warm welcome of an inn," Addams recalls, to provide a meeting place of minds, an early and successful instance of the sort of deliberative democracy political theorists extol but have a hard time instantiating (126).[35] What an oasis amid the smoke-filled rooms of Chicago politics! Creeds from Christianity to atheism and social theories spanning capitalist individualism to communism were parsed, discussed, compared, and critiqued, as Hull House became a place where, in Addams' characterization, discussants were interested in getting "to the root of things" (179).[36] In its emphasis on conversation carried on "both with the radical and the conservative" and refusing to "limit its friends to any one political party or economic school," Hull House quickly earned a somewhat dubious reputation as "a place for enthusiasms" that elicited suspicion from liberals and conservatives alike (452, 184).[37] But any publicity for the house was to the good, and indeed public intellectuals and scholars from diverse areas of study soon flocked to the house to edify "the mind of the worker," lifting her by "the effort of thought" from "the monotony of manual labor" to the larger world

(435).[38] Regardless of what outsiders said, Addams believed that such dialogue was instrumental to creating the mobilization, cohesion, and simple neighborliness essential to addressing problems with a collective voice.[39] After all, she claimed, humanity's good sense was "finer and better" than the facts of life that often drove them apart, and so she worked to ensure that core similarities were not overpowered by the apparent differences of language, race, and religion (111–12). Participants tested political and social philosophies against everyday life, and over time became "solidly united," both on the basis of their "mutual experience in an industrial quarter" as well as the need for some "social control and protective legislation" to ameliorate economic hardship (196).[40] Sorting through their differences and finding some common ground, the apathy bred by extremist hand-wringing was diminished, and it would not be too much of an exaggeration to suggest that the residents of Hull House developed a kind of political moderation that even a Cato or Augustine could admire.[41]

In addition to feeding the mind and spirit of workers, Addams states that active participation in the intellectual and social clubs of Hull House empowered new immigrants politically. Alongside groups devoted to literature, philosophy, and the arts were meetings regarding more practical and quotidian subjects. Weekly organizational and financial meetings gave residents practice in being participants in deliberative assemblies and seeing the importance of "full discussion and understanding" before taking political action (204). Such assemblies pointed to the value of social clubs not simply as outlets for recreation, but as instruments of fellowship that, in Addams' words, lead individuals "from a sense of isolation to one of civic responsibility" (365). It is true that Addams refused to micromanage any of these meetings as part of her facilitative approach to the general operations of Hull House, declaring that "the entire organization of the social life at Hull-House, while it has been fostered and directed by residents and others, has been largely pushed and vitalized from within by the club members themselves."[42] But by providing the setting and tools for effective citizenship, by seeing that "friendly relations with individuals" could be a prerequisite for improving "the industrial and social problems challenging the moral resources of our contemporary life," Addams was the impetus behind the movement toward a better appreciation of the possibilities and obligations of democratic citizenship (366).

It was not enough, however, that an individual had a sense of his or her potential as an agent of political change. The energies of the residents needed to be directed in a particular direction as well, lest one merely fall back into the idle theorizing Addams disliked.[43] Consequently, for Addams education and empowerment always invited the additional question: education to what end? Learning at Hull House was not simply an attempt to grow a natural *aristoi* within the migrant and worker community, but was intended as a practical conductor for good citizenship and cultivation of the "moral sensibility" that Addams believed to be inseparable from social progress (357). As she put it, people must be brought into direct contact with social problems to better understand and address "the compulsions and hardships, the stupidities and cruelties of life" in the industrial sector (366). Thus informal investigations were organized and conducted on phenomena deemed harmful to the general welfare, guided by a spirit of "scientific patience" and self-restraint during the slow, piecemeal "accumulation of facts" (302–4, 126).[44] Analyses of the causes of an epidemic of typhoid fever on Halsted Street; testing a supposed link between worker fatigue and tuberculosis; and determinations of how to include city newsboys (numbering in the thousands) under the state's new child labor laws were only some of the social and civic ends that education in Hull House served (296–7, 301–3). In dealing with such problems, Addams and others tried to steer a course between top-down "definite rules and regulations" and any overly idiosyncratic approach based on "some knowledge of . . . life and habits as a whole" (162). A spirit of experimentation and boundless patience, guided by the steady accumulation and impartial evaluation of empirical evidence, was the recipe that Addams believed might produce this middle ground, and from that basis the chances for more efficient and successful reforms could be maximized. Leading the Settlement "along from the concrete to the abstract," Addams concludes, such efforts productively directed the energies of mobilized residents in the direction of practical political reforms (306).[45]

The triad of organization, empowerment, and direction form the pillars on which rested Addams' political leadership. Throughout her time at Hull House, she concentrated not on the great political statesman of the past and how they had mobilized their people—although she did admire such figures, Abraham Lincoln in particular—but on ways to work in concert with others to allay the "general spirit of bitterness and strife" prevalent in her day (434).[46] Her hopes were not simply economic; as we have seen, she possessed a social, intellectual, and civic vision for all Chicagoans. Informing this vision was her immense faith in the educability and power of the residents. Where such education was successful, she believed "the differences of training and cultivation" evident in the strongest and weakest voices of the people became "lost in the unity of purpose and in the fact that they are all human voices lifted by a high motive" (125). To achieve this harmony, residents would need to be have their minds expanded by an appreciation for the pleasures of the intellectual life. They would need to learn about their own power through dialogue and critical engagement concerning social ills. Finally, they would have to aim their newfound agency toward a higher civic purpose, namely, those reforms that would build a better community for themselves, others, and future generations of Americans.[47] Yet as Addams was fully aware, great social and economic change seldom emerges easily, and her work at Hull House was not without conflict.

THE STATESWOMAN'S CHALLENGE

A life in politics is not typically one of down comforters and carpet slippers. That was certainly not the case for Jane Addams, whose consistent readiness to challenge the status quo points to a broader antagonistic element in many modern theories of statesmanship. Indeed, a range of arguments have insisted that statesmanship demands clamor, controversy, adversity, or even violent crises in order to fully unveil itself. Speaking to the Hamilton Club in Chicago in 1899, future President Theodore Roosevelt waxed poetic about the virtues of "the strenuous life" based on "toil and effort, of labor and strife," praising the "high success" that comes "to the man who does not shrink from danger, from hardship, or from bitter toil."[48] "It is only through strife," Roosevelt concluded, "through hard and dangerous endeavor, that we shall ultimately win the goal of true national greatness."[49] Among political theorists, Werner Dannhauser once described difficulty as essential to statesmanship, portraying the statesman's vocation as one that necessarily involves surmounting obstacles.[50] More recently, Jeffrey Tulis has suggested that moments of crisis sharpen the political leader's decision-making abilities, arguing that it is a challenge to think of any well-known statesmen whose reputation does not owe something to "exceptional political circumstances."[51] As the presidential historian Doris Kearns Goodwin has recently pointed out, growth in political leadership requires the ability to keep one's bearings and find meaning in the face of adversity and setbacks.[52] Such challenges need not be formulated in terms of great events or watershed moments. In order to test their mettle and mature as military commanders or political figures, Alcibiades needed his Nicias; Cato, his Caesar; Augustine, pagan philosophy; and Washington, his Cornwallis. The particular antagonist is not as important as the opportunities such conflict affords, both to stiffen one's spine and develop leadership abilities that, when effective, rejuvenate the flagging spirits of leader and citizen alike.[53]

Willful or not, public ignorance was a major challenge to even setting up an establishment like Hull House. Finding a proper location for the settlement, no minor difficulty, turned out to be the least of Addams' worries. Funding for Hull House itself was paltry and uncertain, due partly to a vexing and "unfounded optimism that there was no real poverty among us" (158).[54] The absence of basic regulations on business practices and and environmental safety paint an ugly picture, with roadways "inexpressibly dirty, the number of schools inadequate, sanitary legislation unenforced, the street lighting bad, the paving miserable and altogether lacking in the alleys and smaller streets, and the stables foul beyond description" (98). Making matters worse, most newly arrived immigrants to America were largely unaware of their surroundings, and after "long and exhausting hours of work" they had little energy to befriend their neighbors or learn about resources for assistance (204). Addams describes how she and her colleagues were forced to take the lead in defending members of the community from those that would prey on such ignorance, describing the short-term relationship between Hull House and the individual worker as "the big brother whose mere presence on the playground protects the little one from bullies" (167). Over time, Hull House functioned as "an information and interpretation bureau," directing individuals to institutions ranging from law offices and county agencies to hospitals and asylums. With the diffusion of such knowledge, Addams found that greater attention was given to the plight of the city's poor. In overcoming apathy to poverty and neglect in these early, heady years, Addams further appreciated the importance of public pressure in changing the status quo. Left to their own devices, public authorities adopt the policy of "never taking an initiative, and always waiting to be urged to do their duty," an indifference that may prove fatal "in a neighborhood where there is little initiative among the citizens" (98).

In addition to ignorance and apathy, Addams also had to confront rampant pessimism among the poor working class. A good many of those who frequented Hull House buckled not simply under the weight of physical necessity but also dashed ambitions. Several residents had been so browbeaten by economic hardship that, as Addams puts it, they were now "caricatures of what they meant to be" in life, simply roaming the halls as "hollow ghosts" (100). "Poverty itself" was at times blamed as the cause of many ills, becoming yet another generalization that threatened to undermine efforts toward piecemeal reform (158). Among the ways Addams attempted to change this mindset was by building a bridge between the past, present, and a yet-undetermined future, notably in her creation of the Hull House Labor Museum. The little museum displayed products, instruments, and photographs illustrating technical advancement in methods of spinning, weaving, and other crafts, depicting the forward progress from crude tools and grueling drudgery to sophisticated machinery and timesaving technology (237, 240). Before its visitors' eyes was a dramatic and tangible representation of the "orderly evolution" of industry, proceeding "similarly and peacefully year by year among the workers of each nation, heedless of differences in language, religion, and political experiences" (237). Of course, the march toward ever-greater technique, efficiency, and human progress was attended with much cruelty besides (240). Yet for those resigned to their economic lot in life, the manifestations of industrial progress pricked the mind to the possibility of further reform.[55] As Addams puts it, the worker could take comfort from the fact that others had lived through more primitive periods of industrial history, and that future practices making work less exploitative might be accelerated by creativity and reforms on the part of those willing to act and experiment. The museum motivated as it educated, inspiring workers to imagine and work toward a better, more humane economic future.

When the situation called for it, Addams did not flinch from a direct challenge to the city's political machinery and centers of power. One malodorous instance will suffice for illustration. Addams and her friends never got used to seeing (or smelling) the many huge wooden boxes overflowing with trash on Halsted Street. The boxes and their debris were more than mere eyesores: rags, food, and other products cleaned and sold by the merchants and street peddlers residing near Hull House added to the refuse and foul odors (281, 283).[56] As Addams recounts, toddlers climbed on the boxes; older children pretended the receptacles were missile shields; and in time, the containers became makeshift benches on which lovers sat and "held enchanted converse" (281). The situation was both at once a public health crisis as well as a collective action problem.[57] As the mountains of garbage continued to rise, Addams finally decided to take matters into her own hands, placing a bid for the ward contract for garbage removal. Despite some grousing by city officials, Addams eventually obtained the job and, as it turned out, more than she had bargained for. The garbage inspector was no sinecure position on her watch but required constant requests for new supplies and diligent supervision, including daily oversight of the removal and transfer of the ward's refuse.[58] Indeed, so meticulous was Addams in her work that the position was eliminated by the mayor of Chicago, who transferred its responsibilities to an office—"ward superintendent"—that only men could fill (289). Yet Addams had made her point. Believing that people "credit most easily that which we see," her results had delivered a message to those who had witnessed her overcome the challenge of unsanitary streets and an inefficient bureaucracy (288).[59] Cleaning up the neighborhood proved to be an instance of leadership with ripple effects: Halsted Street breathed a little easier, the extant political system suffered a glancing blow, and the confidence of her fellow citizens was strengthened having now witnessed a tangible improvement in public health that might inspire future efforts.

Throughout *Twenty Years*, Addams overcomes challenges within and without Hull House. But perhaps the most significant misgivings she faced down were her own self-doubts, hesitations and insecurities that she struggled with long before ever embarking on the Settlement experiment. Looking back on her youth, she invoked Matthew Arnold to describe herself as "Weary of myself and sick of asking / What I am and what I ought to be," and surely the answers to such tormented questions were not always obvious during the gray harmony of Chicago winters (78).[60] At Hull House, difficulties were endless, rewards were few, and its staff "were often bitterly pressed for money and worried by the prospect of unpaid bills" (150). The constant vacillations between hope and despair during these heady years would have tested anyone's patience and commitment.[61] Rather than lamenting her situation, however, Addams suggests that setbacks were a source of learning, with her struggles making it somewhat easier for her to meet and understand the plight of others. She had no patience for those of her "pampered" peers that, having "taken their learning too quickly" retreated self-satisfied "from the active, emotional life" without having acquired the "old healthful reaction resulting in activity from the mere presence of suffering or of helplessness" (71). For Addams as well as social reformers today, encounters with failure are inevitable—a part of the job one must expect when living among the indigent. Yet suffering can also serve as the grit in the political leader's oyster. Through her experiences, including failures, Addams learned that leadership, social change, and life itself was not unidirectional in its trajectory but marked by fits and starts doused with a great deal of loss and bitter defeat.[62] When later she reflected on the "deep depression" and at times overwhelming "sense of failure" that afflicted her early in life, it made the perseverance and the personal progress she had made seem all the more remarkable (66).[63]

Whether challenging public indifference toward the indigent, cynicism toward change, a corrupt political system, or her own perceived shortcomings, Addams' travails at Hull House illustrate that doubts, obstacles, and conflict need not form a permanent block to the political leader's success. Time and again, she made the best of the less-than-ideal situations, often using impediments as opportunities for further experimentation and reform. To some extent, Addams represents an alternative to the Catonic statecraft of resistance to change, showing how subversion and innovation, too, can be a source of effective statesmanship.[64] More importantly, however, Addams' life shows how setbacks may enhance both political leadership and a life well-lived—an important lesson, for political leaders and ordinary citizens alike.

CONCLUSIONS

Unlike the overtly political leaders examined so far, Addams' success at Hull House illustrates how effective leadership is not consigned to the soaring public speeches or the backroom wheeling and dealing often associated with contemporary politics. Although later in her career Addams did move into city, state, and eventually international politics, much of the heavy lifting that went into making the dream of Hull House a reality proceeded in an indirect, non-political manner, as Addams along with Hull House's rotating cast of volunteers and residents devised and implemented solutions to social problems that local office-holders proved unable or unwilling to address. Her success should be an education in and of itself for men, women, and all those occupying society's margins regarding their individual and collective potential as engines of political reform and change. After all, as many political theorists and commentators have long argued, dramatic political change and reforms often happens in ways that do not conform to the typical constitutional blueprint.[65] On many occasions in American history, social, political, and legal aspirations have been pressured into reality by the American people themselves.[66] Such was the case for Jane Addams; such was the legacy of Hull House.

Addams' leadership may be seen as an early contribution to the contemporary emphasis on service learning and civic engagement, giving her form of leadership a horizontal and democratic structure that, like the humble statesman we find in Saint Augustine, eschews an authoritative leader-follower dichotomy.[67] That Addams would seek to challenge old models of leadership is unsurprising, given the difficult issues of cultural and ethnic diversity she was forced to navigate. As she emphasized, "the only thing to dread in the Settlement" is that it might somehow lose "its flexibility, its power of quick adaptation, its readiness to change its methods as its environment may demand" (126). In her willingness to experiment in all aspects of her leadership, Addams modeled the idea of a citizen leader who recognizes when to lead and when to follow, when to listen and when to act. Moreover, in making available the possibility of political leadership to a wider swath of the general public—in a phrase, by democratizing statesmanship—Addams gave expression to a more expansive and protean understanding of leadership, one that involved the strivings of elected officials but also union officers, private charities, faith-based organizations, and other kinds of voluntary organizations. While cognizant of the powerful forces working against any change, Addams never denied the possibility of a kind of leadership that, if done well, could leave the world, the nation, or at least the city street a better place than it was before.

There was one challenge, however, that Addams could not overcome: time. Of course, any leader as well as any person is at the mercy of that, to endure or struggle helplessly against. Yet the statesman or stateswoman, riding along easy in the reins of power, often forgets how easily the years unwind and upend even seemingly permanent political accomplishments. Good leadership is in some way a Sisiphyian task, wherein one educates and appeals to a people's better angels only to have to renew such calls with each subsequent generation. Wander down Halsted Street in Chicago today and while much urban squalor has been removed, you will find the Settlement that Addams helped build alive only in fading memory: Hull House shuttered permanently in 2012 due to bankruptcy.[68] Hull House became an extraordinary presence in the city's nineteenth ward, and then it died. This event is mentioned not to devalue the significance of Addams' deeds for the immigrant community or her contributions to better, more humane public policy, for which citizens today should be grateful. To point out time's influence is rather to signify a larger critique of the concept we have been examining. As Shakespeare's Mark Antony famously lamented, "The evil that men do lives after them," while "the good is oft interred with their bones."[69] Statesmen and stateswomen are temporary phenomena, momentous yet short-lived, whose feats are not guaranteed to outlast even the next generation. Where does that leave the rest of us?

NOTES

1. Jean Bethke Elshtain notes that Addams "lived a quintessentially public life; there are no mysterious lost periods in her story." Apart from a months-long recuperation from back surgery, "her whereabouts and her actions are well documented." See her *Jane Addams and the Dream of American Democracy* (New York: Basic Books, 2002), 15.

2. See the examples of Addams' popularity prior to World War I as discussed by Elshtain (2002), 198–200. Other mostly hagiographic accounts include her nephew James Weber Linn's *Jane Addams: A Biography* (New York: Appleton-Century, 1935); Margaret Tims, *Jane Addams of Hull-House, 1860–1935* (London: George Allen & Unwin, 1961); and John C. Farrell, *Beloved Lady: A History of Jane Addams' Ideas on Reform and Peace* (Baltimore, MD: Johns Hopkins University Press, 1967). In fact, one is hard pressed to find a book-length treatment of Addams that is not generally adulatory.

3. See, e.g., Jill Conway, "Jane Addams: An American Heroine," *Daedalus* 93, no. 2 (1964), 761–80; Rivka Shpak Lissak, *Pluralism and Progressives: Hull House and the New Immigrants, 1890–1919* (Chicago: University of Chicago Press, 1989); and Tom Lutz, *American Nervousness, 1903: An Anecdotal History* (Ithaca, NY: Cornell University Press, 1991).

4. Prominent biographies that emphasize these contributions include Elshtain (2002); Victoria Bissell Brown, *The Education of Jane Addams* (Philadelphia: University of Pennsylvania Press, 2004); and Louise W. Knight, *Citizen: Jane Addams and the Struggle for Democracy* (Chicago: University of Chicago Press, 2005). Philosophical analyses include Charlene Haddock Seigfried, *Feminism and Pragmatism: Reweaving the Social Fabric* (Chicago: University of Chicago Press, 1996), 67–89, and Maurice Hamington, *Embodied Care, Jane Addams, Maurice Merleau-Ponty, and Feminist Ethics* (Urbana: University of Illinois Press, 2004).

5. James T. Kloppenberg, *The Virtues of Liberalism* (New York: Oxford University Press, 1998), 127–8. Addams' realist bent is elaborated by Jean Bethke Elshtain in her *Real Politics: At the Center of Everyday Life* (Baltimore, MD, Johns Hopkins University Press, 2000), 4–7.

6. See, e.g., Nora Hanagan, "Democratizing Responsibility: Jane Addams's Pragmatist Ethics," *Polity* 45, no. 3 (2013), 347–71 and Joel Winkelman, "A Working Democracy: Jane Addams on the Meaning of Work," *Review of Politics* 75, no. 3 (2013), 357–82.

7. See Judith Green, "Social Democracy, Cosmopolitan Hospitality, and Intercivilizational Peace: Lessons from Jane Addams," in *Feminist Interpretations of Jane Addams*, ed. Maurice Hamington (University Park, PA: Pennsylvania State University Press, 2010), 223–254; Patricia M. Shields, "Building the Fabric of Peace: Jane Addams and Peaceweaving," *Global Virtue Ethics Review* 7, no. 3 (2016), 21–33; and Wynne Walker Moskop, "Jane Addams and Possibilities for Transnational Political Friendship," *American Political Thought* 7, no. 3 (2018), 400–31.

8. For the claim that democracy implies social in addition to political relationships, see James T. Kloppenberg, *Uncertain Victory: Social Democracy and Progressivism in European and American Thought, 1870–1920* (New York: Oxford University Press, 1986).

9. Parenthetical references in this chapter are to Addams' *Twenty Years at Hull-House with Autobiographical Notes* (New York: Macmillan, 1912).

10. Elshtain (2002) notes that Addams would rise every morning at 3:00 because that was the time her father awakened (33).

11. In addition to the death of her parents, several of Addams' siblings passed away shortly after childbirth.

12. Reflecting on the period between her mother and father's death, Addams once noted "a household of children, whose mother is dead . . . perform unaccustomed offices for each other and awkwardly exchange consolations." Quoted in Brown (2004), 24.

13. In terms of intellectual interests, Addams had a penchant for history and the works she read tie nicely to the statesmen examined here. She recollects her father paid her five cents "a 'Life' for each Plutarch hero I could intelligently report to him and twenty-five cents for every volume of [Washington] Irving's 'Life of Washington'" (47). Somewhere, John Marshall sighed.

14. Addams confesses that her "long illness left me in a state of nervous exhaustion with which I struggled for years, traces of it remaining long after Hull-House was opened in 1889" (66).

15. Later, Addams would lament the time wasted during this period of "passive receptivity" when she, like many of her peers, was hopelessly mired in a state of curious inactivity at the very point in life she wished to change the world for the better (88).

16. In fact, Toynbee Hall inspired many pioneers of social reform to carry out similar projects in the United States, Hull House included. But see Knight (1991) for a discussion of the changes that Settlement philosophy underwent during its transatlantic voyage (127–31).

17. East End bared the face of the city's "hideous human need and suffering," and Addams doubtless had little trouble drawing parallels between its relationship to London and the dilapidated nineteenth ward to the rest of Chicago (68).

18. Hanagan (2013), 349.

19. Of course, *Twenty Years at Hull-House* is not a comprehensive autobiography of Addams' life. One would need to examine Addams' other written works, including her many articles, books, correspondence, and other primary source materials to arrive at a total picture of her leadership. On Addams' tendency toward literary embellishment (a trait she shares with Plutarch), see Brown (2004), 50 and Knight (2005), 41.

20. Indeed, the book bearing its name reflects the cooperative trademark of the house. While Addams was the author, the book's illustrations, cover design, and index were compiled by different residents of Hull House (ix).

21. Originally the homestead of one of Chicago's foremost citizens, Charles J. Hull, the house's "gracious aspect" had long suffered from neglect and required considerable refurbishing by Addams and Starr before it was habitable (93).

22. In 1912, Addams publicly endorsed Theodore Roosevelt and the Progressive Party platform. Elshtain (2002) notes that her support hurt her efforts to preserve Hull House as a place that remained above everyday politics (189).

23. Louise W. Knight, *Jane Addams: Spirit in Action* (New York: W.W. Norton, 2010), 151 and Elizabeth Agnew, "Meeting Needs, Promoting Peace: Jane Addams and Her 21st Century Counterparts," *Soundings* 90, no. 3–4 (2007), 207–42: 209. On Addams' support for participatory democracy, see Daniel Levine, *Jane Addams and the Liberal Tradition* (Madison: State Historical Society of Wisconsin, 1971), 29, 184.

24. Illustrating Addams' knack for finding sparring partners on both sides of the political aisle, in 1917 her anti-war stance involved her in a public spat with *The New Republic* magazine and her fellow Progressive thinker and sometime visitor to Hull House, John Dewey. The contretemps is recapitulated by Louise W. Knight in her "John Dewey and Jane Addams Debate War," in *Trained Capacities: John Dewey, Rhetoric, and Democratic Practice*, eds. Brian Jackson and Gregory Clark (Columbia, SC: University of South Carolina Press, 2014), 106–24.

25. Presentation Speech by Halvdan Koht, member of the Nobel Committee, on December 10, 1931. Quoted in "Jane Addams and Nicholas Murray Butler," *Nobel Lectures: Peace, 1926–1950*, ed. Frederick W. Haberman (Amsterdam: Elsevier, 1972), 125–42: 127. In 1907, Addams spoke at the First National Peace Congress and helped organize the Second National Peace Congress convened in Chicago two years later (Knight 2010, 156).

26. See, e.g., Robert Nozick's libertarian argument that the material prosperity of society waxes as centralized political authority wanes in his *Anarchy, State, and Utopia* (New York: Basic Books, 1974). A more recent if less philosophic restatement of such leadership (or lack thereof) is articulated in Joseph L. Badaracco Jr.'s *Leading Quietly: An Unorthodox Guide to Doing the Right Thing* (Boston, MA: Harvard Business School Press, 2002).

27. Cheryl Mabey, "The Making of a Citizen Leader," in *The Leader's Companion: Insights on Leadership Through the Ages*, ed. J. Thomas Wren (New York: Free Press, 1995), 310–17: 312.

28. Consider, for example, Harry C. Boyte, *Commonwealth: A Return to Citizen Politics* (New York: Free Press, 1989) as well as his *Everyday Politics: Reconnecting Citizens and the Public Life* (Philadelphia, PA: University of Pennsylvania Press, 2004); Andrew J. Perrin, *Citizen Speak: The Democratic Imagination in American Life* (Chicago: University of Chicago Press, 2006); and Kelly Louise Anders and Maria Cisaltina da Silveira Nunes Dinis, "Demonstrating Citizen Leadership: A Case Study of Jane Addams," *The International Journal of Interdisciplinary Civic and Political Studies* 10, no. 1 (2015), 13–19.

29. In a critical appraisal of the young educated class of her day, Addams laments the fact that in the United States there was "a shock of inaction" as "a fast-growing number of cultivated young people who have no recognized outlet for their active faculties. They hear constantly of the great social maladjustment, but no way is provided for them to change it, and their uselessness hangs about them heavily" (120).

30. Marc Landy and Sidney Milkis (2000) have argued that citizen education is an essential criterion of presidential greatness, holding that "just as a parent is held responsible for the moral and practical education of his children, so a president bears a large share of responsibility for the public's civic education. A democratic leader is one who takes the public to school. By these criteria, the great presidents did indeed provide meaningful democratic leadership" (4). On the relationship between statesmanship and education, see also Ceaser (2007), 267.

31. Regular courses in English and citizenship were among the more formal examples of education at Hull House. Addams believed that effective political participation depended on a basic civic, linguistic, and intellectual threshold of knowledge, and made Hull House a place for such instruction. Moreover, she characterized a working understanding of English as "a desperate need" for the newly arrived immigrant: "[A] meager knowledge of English may mean an opportunity to work in a factory versus nonemployment," she pointed out, or even "a question of life or death when a sharp command must be understood in order to avoid the danger of a descending crane" (438).

32. Addams made sure that the dozens of children who came to the house were carefully organized into groups that would arouse the "higher imagination" of the individual, with activities that emphasized self-initiative as well as "the deep-seated craving for social intercourse" felt by all individuals (105, 109).

33. Bob Pepperman Taylor has argued that while Addams may initially have conceived the Settlement's role in purely philanthropic terms, her tenure at Hull House "taught her the beauty of building a democratic community, and the ugliness of demeaning the poor through a condescending philanthropy." See his "Jane Addams and Democratic Citizenship," in *Friends and Citizens: Essays in Honor of Wilson Carey McWilliams*, eds. Peter Dennis Bathory and Nancy L. Schwartz (Lanham, MD: Rowman and Littlefield, 2001), 130–48: 130.

34. Addams notes that she threw her support behind the "visionaries and enthusiasts, unsuccessful artists, writers, and reformers" who sought some creative outlet to relieve the suffering caused by material want (176). As a result, Hull House grew into a popular artistic hub as well as an economic refuge, where the human soul could sing of its resilience even though deprived of the "tawdry goods and chattels" of life (176).

35. For a particularly Quixotic example, see Bruce Ackerman and James S. Fishkin's proposed *Deliberation Day* (New Haven, CT: Yale University Press, 2004), esp. 221–8. Discussion groups at Hull House emphasized values of listening, deliberation, reciprocity, and tolerance—in short, the healthy fruits of free speech.

36. Sandra Opdycke puts it this way: "Addams was convinced that in any democratic society, people of all shades of opinion needed to hear and understand each others' views . . . [therefore an emphasis on diverse views] became an important part of the Hull-House mis-

sion." See her *Jane Addams and Her Vision for America* (Upper Saddle River, NJ: Prentice Hall, 2012), 66.

37. Addams, a believer in "the extraordinary pliability of human nature," thought that the clash of divergent political and social opinions would facilitate political moderation (452). As she argued, "fanaticism is engendered only when men, finding no contradiction to their theories, at last believe that the very universe lends itself as an exemplification of one point of view"—an apt description of some of our partisan echo chambers today (179). For a scholarly application of Addams' argument, consider Cass R. Sunstein, *Going to Extremes: How Like Minds Unite and Divide* (New York: Oxford University Press, 2009).

38. Addams and her fellow attendees naturally grew restless during overly pedantic lectures. To Addams, it seemed as though professional scholars were prone "to leave to the charlatan [sic] the teaching of those things which deeply concern the welfare of mankind," with the result "that the mass of men get their intellectual food from the outcasts of scholarship, who provide millions of books, pictures, and shows, not to instruct and guide, but for the sake of their own financial profit" (431).

39. Such settings also provided the occasion for a good deal of local self-rule (342). The clubs were frequently run autonomously, forming a model of associational cohesion long before the idea of "social capital" was ever a twinkle in the sociologist Robert Putnam's eye.

40. Through shared commiseration emerged fellowship. As noted above, Addams often criticized modes of instruction that sheltered pupils from the outside world, leading individuals to believe that their lives had "nothing to do with the bitter poverty and the social maladjustment" surrounding them (73).

41. Addams compares these conversations to "the changing of swords in Hamlet," as abstract philosophies became less dogmatic, "while the concrete minds, dealing constantly with daily affairs, in the end demonstrate the reality of abstract notions" (193). On Addams' insistence that citizens be led "from the concrete to the more abstract" in political affairs, see Elshtain (2002), 172.

42. As her fellow social reformer Emily Balch put it, Addams "incorporated [Hull House] and helped it to be itself." Quoted in Louise W. Knight, "Jane Addams and Hull House: Historical Lessons on Nonprofit Leadership," *Nonprofit Management & Leadership* 2, no. 2 (1991), 125–41: 134.

43. Such helplessness only fueled the worst impulses of humanity. Like Augustine, Addams recognized that the human will was a frail thing when faced with the world's temptations, and animalistic demands only expanded with the rise of industrial society. As she acknowledged, "long and exhausting hours of work are almost sure to be followed by lurid and exciting pleasures" (204). Harried and exhausted, self-indulgence and hedonistic recreation is what most laborers searched for, particularly the city's youth who were perpetually "impatient of control" (348, 350).

44. Mary Jo Deegan, *Jane Addams and the Men of the Chicago School, 1892–1918* (New Brunswick, NJ: Transaction, 1988), 39. Deegan comments that Addams considered the gathering of empirical data to be essential to documenting the severity of poverty (50).

45. Conversely, Addams deplored the "spirit of generalization and lack of organization" that excused idleness and impeded efforts toward alleviating poverty (159).

46. Lincoln was a contemporary of Addams' father, John, who moved in some of the same Illinois political circles as the future president. Addams describes herself in *Twenty Years* as a great admirer of "the martyred President," always feeling "a thrill" when she heard his name spoken (31). Yet there was also a practical dimension to her esteem for Lincoln, tied to the democratic and pragmatic ethos she believed informed his political creed. She celebrated the "invigorating and clarifying power" that infused Lincoln's political vision of a more free and humane nation, confirming her belief that the "tremendous experiment" of self-government depended above all on the common people for its success (37). At Hull House, Addams' esteem for Lincoln was so great that notwithstanding "exigent demands upon my slender purse" at Christmastime she purchased and distributed copies of Carl Schurz's *Appreciation of Abraham Lincoln* to a club of young men (36).

47. As Camilla Stivers has argued, Addams "knew poor immigrants as individuals and families, not merely as statistics," allowing her to see an individual's contributions to civic life

and the benefits accruing to a government that tapped into rather than tried to snuff out cultural diversity. See her "A Civic Machinery for Democratic Expression: Jane Addams on Public Administration," in *Jane Addams and the Practice of Democracy*, eds. Marilyn Fischer, Carol Nackenoff, and Wendy Chmielewski (Urbana and Chicago: University of Illinois Press, 2009), 86–97.

48. Theodore Roosevelt, "The Strenuous Life," in *The Strenuous Life: Essays and Addresses* (New York: Century, 1906), 1–21: 1.

49. Ibid., 21.

50. Werner J. Dannhauser, "Reflections on Statesmanship and Bureaucracy," in *Bureaucrats, Policy Analysts, Statesmen: Who Leads?*, ed. Robert A. Goldwin (Washington, DC: American Enterprise Institute Press, 1980), 114–32: 118.

51. Tulis (2010), 114. On the relationship between conflict and statesmanship, consider also Newell (2012), 187 and Overeem and Bakker (2016), 7.

52. Doris Kearns Goodwin, *Leadership in Turbulent Times* (New York: Simon & Schuster, 2018), 97.

53. James MacGregor Burns has called transformational leadership as that which raises "the level of human conduct and ethical aspiration of both leader and led, and thus it has a transforming effect on both." Using Gandhi's influence as a modern example, he describes his leadership as one in which "leaders throw themselves into a relationship with followers who will feel 'elevated' by it and often become more active themselves, thereby creating new cadres of leaders." See his "The Power of Leadership," in *Political Leadership in Democratic Societies*, eds. Anthony Mughan and S. C. Patterson (Chicago: Nelson-Hall, 1992), 17–28: 26.

54. In Hull House's early years, Addams recalls, there existed "no Charity Organization Society in Chicago and the Visiting Nurse Association had not yet begun its beneficial work," while "relief societies, although conscientiously administered, were inadequate in extent and antiquated in method" (158).

55. In fact, the museum served multiple purposes insofar as it evinced the march of industrial progress, connected workers across generations, and gave greater meaning to the contributions older émigrés made to the cultural and educational environment of the Settlement. Addams recounts showing a group of older Russian women the spinning wheel, an invention that many of them had never encountered but whose appearance called to mind their practice of hand spinning using spindles. The labor museum having made "a direct appeal to former experiences," Addams remarks, "the immigrant visitors were able for the moment to instruct their American hostesses in an old and honored craft, as was indeed becoming to their age and experience" (242).

56. Addams cites as examples of the effluvia "the decayed fruit and vegetables discarded by the Italian and Greek fruit peddlers," and the "residuum" of cleaning rags "fished out of the city dumps and brought to the homes of the rag pickers for further sorting and washing" (281).

57. Many of those who lived on Halsted Street diligently swept their own doorsteps but remained blithely ignorant of the broader health effects of poor public sanitation. Addams and her colleagues repeatedly pointed out to members of the general public that personal cleanliness "in a crowded city quarter" would not protect against the spread of disease if individuals did not also encourage the authorities to keep the city's common spaces clean (283).

58. Addams ensured that her crew was ready to collect the garbage and made sure to follow them "to their dreary destination at the dump" (286–7). She also made few friends in suing negligent landlords for not supplying adequate garbage receptacles (287).

59. Other women were especially affected by Addams' position. She notes that many foreign-born women were "much shocked by this abrupt departure into the ways of men, and it took a great deal of explanation to convey the idea even remotely that if it were a womanly task to go about in tenement houses in order to nurse the sick, it might be quite as womanly to go through the same district in order to prevent the breeding of so-called 'filth diseases'" (287). Some women were sold on the connection; others remained skeptical.

60. One episode suffices to illustrate Addams' soul-searching. During a trip to Europe in 1896, she visited the home of the famous Russian author Leo Tolstoy, whose dogged insistence on living alongside the poor rather than patronizing them at arm's length was the kind of leadership she at the time admired: "The prospect of seeing Tolstoy filled me with the hope of

finding a clue to the tangled affairs of city poverty," she remembers (262). However, the brief meeting that occurred showed her the risk of meeting one's heroes: insulted by an irritable Tolstoy, she left jarred, curious "as to why he was so regarded as sage and saint," and compelled to look ever deeper within herself to discern the type of leadership she might offer the world (269). This meeting between the two famous social reformers is parsed by James Cracraft in his *Two Shining Souls: Jane Addams, Leo Tolstoy, and the Quest for Global Peace* (Lanham, MD: Lexington, 2012).

61. Addams suffered from nervous exhaustion and depression throughout her life, though she refused to dwell on these episodes in *Twenty Years*. In general, she refused to feel much pity for herself. During the bout of illness that occurred shortly after her father's passing, Addams was administered milk and electric shock treatments as therapy, though she recognized the inanity of her physicians' measures. "To be put to bed and fed on milk is not what [a patient] requires," she once wrote. "What she needs is simple, health-giving activity, which, involving the use of all her faculties, shall be a response to all the claims which she so keenly feels." See her *Democracy and Social Ethics* (New York: Macmillan, 1905), 87.

62. As she once put it, "In his own way each man must struggle, lest the moral law become a far-off abstraction utterly separated from his active life" (66).

63. The challenges Addams endured while growing up also seemed to influence her mature view on the value of struggle and toil. In Hull House's early days, she writes, "we at times believed that the very [economic and social] struggle itself might become a source of strength. The devotion of the mothers to their children, the dread of the men lest they fail to provide for the family dependent upon their daily exertions, at moments seemed to us the secret stores of strength from which society is fed" (133).

64. Richard Ruderman (2012) has described statesmanship as attempting to strike a balance between conservation and innovation in any given regime (89).

65. For arguments that invoke this kind of constitutional populism, see Edmund S. Morgan, *Inventing the People: The Rise of Popular Sovereignty in England and America* (New York: Norton, 1988), 13–14; Bruce Ackerman, *We the People: Foundations* (Cambridge, MA: Harvard University Press, 1991); Bruce Ackerman, *We the People: Transformations* (Cambridge, MA: Harvard University Press, 1998); Jason Frank, *Constituent Moments: Enacting the People in Postrevolutionary America* (Durham, NC: Duke University Press, 2010), 3–4, 31–33, 250–1; and Bruce Ackerman, *We the People: The Civil Rights Revolution* (Cambridge, MA: Harvard University Press, 2014).

66. Arguments on behalf of this idea are elaborated in various forms by Richard D. Parker, *"Here, the People Rule": A Constitutional Populist Manifesto* (Cambridge, MA: Harvard University Press, 1994); Wayne D. Moore, *Constitutional Rights and Powers of the People* (Princeton, NJ: Princeton University Press, 1996), 13–65, 275–86; Cass R. Sunstein, *The Partial Constitution* (Cambridge, MA: Harvard University Press, 1998); Mark Tushnet, *Taking the Constitution Away from the Courts* (Princeton, NJ: Princeton University Press, 1999), 33–53, 177–94; Jeremy Waldron, *Law and Disagreement* (New York: Oxford University Press, 1999); Larry D. Kramer, "Popular Constitutionalism, circa 2004," *California Law Review* 92, no. 4 (2004), 959–1010; Larry D. Kramer, *The People Themselves: Popular Constitutionalism and Judicial Review* (New York: Oxford University Press, 2004); Doni Gewirtzman, "Glory Days: Popular Constitutionalism, Nostalgia, and the True Nature of Constitutional Culture," *Georgetown Law Review* 93 (2005), 897–938; and Sheldom Nahmod, "Constitutional Education for *The People Themselves*," *Chicago-Kent Law Review* 81, no. 3 (2006), 1091–1107.

67. For arguments that draw connections between Addams, education, and more egalitarian forms of leadership, consider Ira Harkavy and John Puckett, "Lessons from Hull House for the Contemporary Urban University," *Social Science Review* 68, no. 3 (1994), 299–321; Keith Morton and John Saltmarsh, "Addams, Day, and Dewey: The Emergence of Community Service in American Culture," *Michigan Journal of Community Service Learning* 4, no. 1 (1997), 137–149; Gary Daynes and Nicholas V. Longo, "Jane Addams and the Origins of Service-Learning Practice in the United States," *Michigan Journal of Community Service Learning* 11, no. 1 (2004), 5–13; Nicholas V. Longo, *Why Community Matters: Connecting Education with Civic Life* (Albany, NY: State University of New York Press, 2007), 45–66; Carol Nackenoff, "New Politics for New Selves: Jane Addams's Legacy for Democratic Citizenship in the

Twenty-First Century," in Fischer, Nackenoff, and Chmielewski (2009), 119–42; and Mary Jo Deegan, "Jane Addams, Feminist Pragmatism, and Service Learning," in *The Cambridge Handbook of Service Learning and Community Engagement*, eds. Corey Dolgon, Tania D. Mitchell, and Timothy K. Eatman (New York: Cambridge University Press, 2017), 51–63.

68. Kate Thayer, "Hull House closing Friday," *The Chicago Tribune*, January 25, 2012, https://www.chicagotribune.com/news/ct-xpm-2012-01-25-ct-met-hull-house-20120126-story.html.

69. William Shakespeare, *Julius Caesar*, ed. Louis B. Wright (New York: Washington Square Press, 1969), 56.

Conclusion

Statesmanship in the Twenty-First Century

Statesmanship is a concept both timeless and timely in politics, ephemeral yet recurrent throughout history, spanning diverse political regimes, positions of authority, and populations. It is a word that seems beguilingly clear yet proves frustratingly hard to pin down. Now, in the era of President Trump, understanding the concept is as important as ever. His stunning victory continues to provide fodder for debate for all those concerned with the topic of political leadership and its place in democratic government. One may argue that the president's larger-than-life personality and insistence on an "America-first" approach to governance shows that Americans retain some hope that effective individual leadership can improve the lives of citizens. Without denying the importance of competent elected officials, others contend that hopes for its realization are misplaced in a figure such as Trump. Still others resist on grounds of principle the promises of any figure peddling political salvation. After all, the Constitution's preamble begins with "We the People," not "I the Statesman." In spite of these differences, what unites all these arguments is a concern with statesmanship, its qualities, and its proper role in American government in the twenty-first century.

The persons and arguments we have surveyed contribute to but do not exhaust an ongoing dialogue about statesmanship that will likely span the past, present, and future of politics. Plutarch's *Lives* provides perhaps the best portrayals of the great political players of the classical era, and few figures embody the qualities of ambition and flexibility more than the Greek military and political leader Alcibiades. Impressive in both armed and political conflict, Alcibiades was driven by a passion for distinction unmatched by his fellow countrymen, coupled with a nigh-instinctive flexibility that proved indispensible for eluding both domestic rivals and foreign enemies. In contrast, what Plutarch's younger Cato lacked in flexibility he made up for in discipline and self-government, traits that went hand-in-hand with an un-yielding resistance to any corruption of the legal, social, and political order that had made the Roman Republic a superpower. Pointedly repudiating Rome, the work of Saint Augustine represents a radical departure from the emphasis on civic fulfillment and glory so integral to ancient politics. In his *Civitas Dei*, he advances a more compassionate understanding of leadership, defined by humility and charity toward friends, fellow citizens, and enemies alike. Yet Augustine's more conciliatory approach is itself tested by John Marshall's *Life of George Washington*, a work that illustrates how a success-ful military and political leader may have to balance pragmatic expedience with considered circumspection. Finally, Jane Addams shows how political community might flourish even in seemingly hopeless environments, as her *Twenty Years at Hull-House* describes the mobilization, empowerment, and courage required for democratic leadership in her time as well as our own. In their strengths and weaknesses, these figures shed some much-needed light on the shadowy concept of statesmanship.

This much may be expected in light of the foregoing discussion: those individuals who navigate the political landscape with all its accidents and contingencies using a single *modus operandi* are likely short-lived public stewards. Indeed, excessive ambition, resistance, humility, expedience, or iconoclasm is more likely to result in ever-more shortsighted leaders and public policies. As Bruce Ackerman warns, "statesmen who make a fetish of some particular strategic formula" are a recipe for disaster.[1] Going forward, statesmanship in the twenty-first century must resist ready-made categories and fixed definitions, while still learning and drawing from past incarnations. It is the task of the statesmen and stateswomen of the future to choose the combination of faculties that allow them to best articulate and chart their own community's future.

The resistance of statesmanship to a single, fixed attribute begs the ques-tion: if the qualities examined here can be used well or poorly depending on whether they are put to good or bad ends, how can one ultimately distinguish the statesman from the demagogue, autocrat, or other unsavory political ac-tor? What common characteristic can we use to tell the difference between these forms of authority? To address this issue very provisionally, we should bear in mind that the object of the statesman or stateswoman is ultimately statecraft, which in general terms can be conceived as the promotion or defense of the common good or welfare of the political community. Absent some idea of the public good that lies outside one's own will, the political leader soon grows beholden to his own itching ego and its demand for ever-greater power. Specification of this good, and the extent that it too is liable to corruptive influence, involve questions of political theory that go beyond the scope of this work. But wedded to the qualities explored here, this frame permits us to distinguish the statesman from the partisan, lobbyist, or other political actor intent on advancing the partial interest of his or her favored ideology or group.[2]

Another complication related to the aspects of statesmanship gathered here relates to their potential incommensurability. It may be insisted that when read together, these figures form less of a unity than a great debate. It is true that many of the personalities described here exist in some friction with one another, particularly when applied to cold, hard reality.[3] Certainly it is difficult to conceive what, for example, humble ambition or flexible resistance would look like in theory, let alone as a practice. Indeed, perhaps no individual can hope to copy all the qualities examined here. Thus a more extensive analysis of the concept of statesmanship might venture answers to a host of questions related to the sheer variety of characters examined here: can these avatars of statesmanship be woven into a unified whole? Should they be? Need they be?

Settled answers to these good questions, if such answers do exist, should be part of a broader civic dialogue about the character of political leadership, one that is more granular than the sweeping generalizations we often trade in when discussing leadership today. Moreover, such analyses may in fact empower rather than vitiate the responsibilities of democratic citizenship. By striving for more specificity about the types of qualities we are missing in political leaders, we build a richer and more precise vocabulary for evaluating leadership than responses to poll questions such as whether the nation is generally on the right or wrong track. At the very least, further refinements of the concept result in clearer definitions of the qualities we should look for in political representatives in the future. Call it Orwellian, but we do well not to underestimate the importance of clear definitions in politics. Consider this analysis a starting point, meant to fire our political imagination about an idea made up of various and frequently discordant elements. As leaders worldwide continue to gain positions of power based on promises to deliver solutions to seemingly ineluctable global challenges, now is the time to bring statesmanship into clearer focus, not lob the concept down the memory hole.

Nor should a better understanding of statesmanship be a project limited only to the great gaggle. On the contrary, it is a subject that must be given more serious consideration among political theorists. In recent years, study of the concept has been the province of a small cadre of (usually conservative) scholars. To some extent, the neglect is understandable, if regrettable. At the risk of sounding too much like an antiperspirant ad, statesmanship traditionally has an odor of aristocratic masculinity. Yet the figures we have parsed go some way toward laying the groundwork for further inquiry into a topic that should not be relegated to one sex, historical era, or particular nation. In a time when political theorists are under pressure to think outside the traditional Western canon and apply their work directly to everyday politics, one could do worse than build on the notion of comparative statesmanship begun here. This book cracks open that door. Now, at this critical moment in our politics, is the time to kick it wide open.

In the aftermath of the 2016 election, we would be wise to no longer ridicule or discount the importance that a single individual can exercise over our political system. Political leadership has played an important role in human history, and its influence will continue to be felt in the United States, whether through its presence or absence. Ultimately, improving the quality of political leadership will require more from citizens than periodic trips to the ballot box. As Americans continue charting an uncertain course toward the republic's future, let us be vigilant for political candidates that reflect the qualities brought to light here. Let us also be mindful that, like the novel figures examined in these pages, the statesman or stateswoman of the future may be a character such as we have never seen before.

NOTES

1. Bruce A. Ackerman, *Social Justice in the Liberal State* (New Haven, CT: Yale University Press, 1980), 303.
2. Joseph R. Fornieri, *Abraham Lincoln, Philosopher Statesman* (Carbondale, IL: Southern Illinois University Press, 2014), 10.
3. It must also be acknowledged, however, that areas of commonality also exist among these political leaders. To give just a single example, a readiness to defy the political odds distinguishes Alcibiades, the younger Cato, Washington, and Addams to different degrees.

References

Aalders, G. J. D. *Plutarch's Political Thought*. Translated by A. M. Manekofsky. Amsterdam, Oxford, and New York: North Holland Publishing Co., 1982.

Ackerman, Bruce A. *Social Justice in the Liberal State*. New Haven, CT: Yale University Press, 1980.

———. *We the People: Foundations*. Cambridge, MA: Harvard University Press, 1991

———. *We the People: Transformations*. Cambridge, MA: Harvard University Press, 1998.

———. *We the People: The Civil Rights Revolution*. Cambridge, MA: Harvard University Press, 2014.

Ackerman, Bruce and James S. Fishkin. *Deliberation Day*. New Haven, CT: Yale University Press, 2004.

Addams, Jane. *Democracy and Social Ethics*. New York: Macmillan, 1905.

———. *Twenty Years at Hull-House with Autobiographical Notes*. New York: Macmillan, 1912.

Agnew, Elizabeth. "Meeting Needs, Promoting Peace: Jane Addams and Her 21st Century Counterparts," *Soundings* 90, no. 3–4 (2007): 207–42.

Aitken, Jonathan. *Margaret Thatcher: Power and Personality*. London: Bloomsbury, 2013.

Albrecht, Michael von. *Cicero's Style: A Synopsis*. Leiden: Brill, 2003.

Alexandria, Philo of. *Questions and Answers on Genesis*. Translated by Ralph Marcus. Cambridge, MA: Harvard University Press, 1953.

Allen, W. B. *George Washington: America's First Progressive*. New York: Peter Lang, 2008.

Allen, W. B. and Gordon Lloyd, eds. *The Essential Antifederalist*. Lanham, MD: Rowman & Littlefield, 2002.

Allman, Dwight D. and Michael D. Beaty, eds. *Cultivating Citizens: Soulcraft and Citizenship in Contemporary America*. Lanham, MD: Lexington, 2002.

Anders, Kelly Louise and Maria Cisaltina da Silveira Nunes Dinis. "Demonstrating Citizen Leadership: A Case Study of Jane Addams," *The International Journal of Interdisciplinary Civic and Political Studies* 10, no. 1 (2015): 13–19.

Aquinas, Thomas. *On Law, Morality, and Politics*. 2nd ed. Translated by Richard J. Regan. Indianapolis, IN: Hackett, 2002.

Arendt, Hannah. *Love and St. Augustine*. Edited by Joanna Vecchiarelli Scott and Judith Chelius Stark. Chicago, IL: University of Chicago Press, 1996.

Aristotle. *The Politics*. Translated by Carnes Lord. Chicago: University of Chicago Press, 1984.

———. *Nicomachean Ethics*. Translated by Martin Ostwald. Upper Saddle River, NJ: Prentice Hall, 1999.

Atherton, Catherine. "Hand Over Fist: The Failure of Stoic Rhetoric," *The Classical Quarterly* 38, no. 2 (1988): 392–427.

Atkins, Jed W. *Cicero on Politics and the Limits of Reason*. New York: Cambridge University Press, 2013.

———. *Roman Political Thought*. New York: Cambridge University Press, 2018.

Augustine, Saint. *The City of God*. Translated by Marcus Dods, George Wilson, and J.J. Smith. 2 vols. Edinburgh: T&T Clark, 1871, 1888.

———. *Letters*. Translated by Wilfrid Parsons. 6 vols. New York: Fathers of the Church, 1953.

———. *Two Books on Genesis: Against the Manichees and On the Literal Interpretation of Genesis: An Unfinished Book*. Translated by Roland J. Teske. Washington, DC: Catholic University of America Press, 1991.

———. *Homilies on the First Epistle of John*. Translated by Boniface Ramsey. Hyde Park, NY: New City Press, 2008.

———. *On Christian Doctrine*. Translated by J.F. Shaw. Mineola, NY: Dover, 2009.

———. *Trilogy on Faith and Happiness*. Translated by Roland J. Teske. Hyde Park, NY: New City Press, 2010.

Avlon, John. *Washington's Farewell: The Founding Father's Warning to Future Generations*. New York: Simon & Schuster, 2017.

Badaracco, Jr., Joseph L. *Leading Quietly: An Unorthodox Guide to Doing the Right Thing*. Boston, MA: Harvard Business School Press, 2002.

Baldwin, Christopher E. "Franklin's Classical American Statesmanship," *Perspectives on Political Science* 41, no. 2 (2012): 67–74.

Barber, Benjamin R. *An Aristocracy of Everyone: The Politics of Education and the Future of America*. New York: Ballantine Books, 1992.

———. *A Passion for Democracy: American Essays*. Princeton, NJ: Princeton University Press, 1998.

Barkalow, Jordan. "American *Paideia*: Public and Private Leadership and the Cultivation of Civic Virtue," *Expositions* 8, no. 2 (2014): 131–54.

Barrow, Reginald Haynes. *Introduction to St. Augustine*. London: Faber & Faber Ltd., 1950.

———. *The Romans*. Chicago: Aldine, 1964.

———. *Plutarch and His Times*. Bloomington, IN and London: Indiana University Press, 1967.

Bathory, Peter Dennis and Nancy L. Schwartz, eds. *Friends and Citizens: Essays in Honor of Wilson Carey McWilliams*. Lanham, MD: Rowman and Littlefield, 2001.

Baudelaire, Charles. *The Painter of Modern Life and Other Essays*. Translated by Jonathan Mayne. London: Phaidon, 1995.

Beard, Charles A. *Economic Origins of Jeffersonian Democracy*. New York: Macmillan, 1915.

Becker, Jeffrey A. "Statesmanship and Power: A Biography of Ambition in America." PhD diss., Rutgers University, 2004.

———. *Ambition in America: Political Power and the Collapse of Citizenship*. Lexington, KY: University Press of Kentucky, 2014.

Bedell-Avers, Katrina, Samuel T. Hunter, Amanda D. Angie, Dawn L. Eubanks, and Michael D. Mumford, "Charismatic, Ideological, and Pragmatic Leaders: An Examination of Leader Leader Interactions," *Leadership Quarterly* 20, no. 3 (2009): 299–315.

Beneker, Jeffrey. *The Passionate Statesman: Erōs and Politics in Plutarch's Lives*. New York: Oxford University Press, 2012.

Benestad, J. Brian, ed. *Classical Christianity and the Political Order: Reflections on the Theologico-Political Problem*. Lanham, MD: Rowman & Littlefield, 1996.

Bercovitch, Sacvan, ed. *The Cambridge History of American Literature*. Cambridge: Cambridge University Press, 1994.

Beveridge, Albert. *The Life of John Marshall*. 4 vols. Boston and New York: Houghton, Mifflin, and Co., 1919.

Birzer, Bradley J. *Sanctifying the World: The Augustinian Life and Mind of Christopher Dawson*. Fort Royal, VA: Christendom Press, 2007.

Blois, Lukas de, Jeroen Bons, Ton Kessels, and Dirk M. Schenkeveld, eds. *The Statesman in Plutarch's Works*. Leiden and Boston, MA: BRILL, 2005.

Blom, Henriette van der. "Cato and the People," *Bulletin of the Institute of Classical Studies* 55, no. 2 (2012): 39–56.

Bobb, David J. *Humility: An Unlikely Biography of America's Greatest Virtue.* Nashville, TN: Thomas Nelson, 2013.

Boeve, Lieven, Mathijis Lamberigts, and Maarten Wisse, eds. *Augustine and Postmodern Thought. A New Alliance against Modernity?* Leuven: Peeters, 2009.

Boorstin, Daniel J. *The Americans: The National Experience.* New York: Random House, 1965.

Boyte, Harry C. *Commonwealth: A Return to Citizen Politics.* New York: Free Press, 1989.

———. *Everyday Politics: Reconnecting Citizens and the Public Life.* Philadelphia, PA: University of Pennsylvania Press, 2004.

Brennan, T. Corey. *The Praetorship in the Roman Republic.* 2 vols. New York: Oxford University Press, 2000.

Bretherton, Luke. *Christianity and Contemporary Politics: The Conditions and Possibilities of Faithful Witness.* Malden, MA: Wiley-Blackwell, 2010.

Brookes, Edgar. *The City of God and the Politics of Crisis.* London: Oxford University Press, 1960.

Brookhiser, Richard. *George Washington on Leadership.* New York: Perseus, 2008.

Brooks, David. *The Road to Character.* New York: Random House, 2015.

Brown, Peter. *Augustine of Hippo: A Biography.* Revised edition. Berkeley and Los Angeles: University of California Press, 2000.

Brown, Victoria Bissell. *The Education of Jane Addams.* Philadelphia: University of Pennsylvania Press, 2004.

Brownson, Orestes. *The Works of Orestes A. Brownson.* Edited by Henry F. Brownson. 20 vols. Detroit, MI: Thorndike Nourse, 1882–5.

Bruno, Michael J. S. *Political Augustinianism: Modern Interpretations of Augustine's Political Thought.* Minneapolis, MN: Fortress Press, 2014.

Buchanan, Patrick J. *A Republic, Not an Empire: Reclaiming America's Destiny.* Washington, DC: Regenry, 1999.

Burke, Edmund. *Reflections on the Revolution in France and Other Writings.* Edited by Jesse Norman. New York: Random House, 2015.

Burnell, Peter J. "The Status of Politics in St. Augustine's *City of God*," *History of Political Thought* 13, no. 1 (1992): 12–29.

Burns, James McGregor. *Leadership.* New York: Harper and Row, 1978.

Burton, Paul. "*Pax Romana/Pax Americana*: Perceptions of Rome in American Political Culture, 2000–2010," *International Journal of the Classical Tradition* 18, no. 1 (2011): 66–104.

Caldwell, Dan and Timothy J. McKeown, eds. *Diplomacy, Force, and Leadership: Essays in Honor of Alexander L. George.* Boulder, CO: Westview, 1993.

Canning, Raymond. *The Unity of Love for God and Neighbour in St. Augustine.* Heverlee, Belgium: Augustinian Historical Institute, 1993.

Caputo, John D. and Michael J. Scanlon, eds. *Augustine and Postmodernism: Confessions and Circumfession.* Bloomington, IN: Indiana University Press, 2005.

Carbone, Gerald M. *Washington: Lessons in Leadership.* New York: St. Martin's Press, 2010.

Carey, George W. and James V. Schall, eds. *Essays on Christianity and Political Philosophy.* Lanham, MD: University Press of America, 1984.

Carrese, Paul O. "Judicial Statesmanship, the Jurisprudence of Individualism, and Tocqueville's Common Law Spirit," *Review of Politics* 60, no. 3 (1998): 465–95.

Casey, John. *Pagan Virtue: An Essay In Ethics.* Oxford: Clarendon Press, 1990.

Caton, Hiram. "St. Augustine's Critique of Politics," *New Scholasticism* 47, no. 4 (1973): 433–57.

Ceaser, James W. "Demagoguery, Statesmanship, and the American Presidency," *Critical Review* 19, no. 2 (2007): 257–98.

Chadwick, Henry. *Augustine.* Oxford: Oxford University Press, 1986.

———. *Augustine of Hippo: A Life.* New York: Oxford University Press, 2009.

Churchill, Winston S. *The Second World War: The Gathering Storm.* Boston, MA: Houghton, Mifflin, and Co., 1948.

Cicero. *Letters to Atticus.* Translated by D. R. Shackleton Bailey. 7 vols. Cambridge: Cambridge University Press, 1965–70.

——. *De Res Publica*. Translated by Clinton Walker Keyes. Cambridge, MA: Harvard University Press, 2004.

——. *On Duties*. Edited by M. T. Griffin and E. M. Atkins. New York: Cambridge University Press, 2003.

Clair, Joseph. *Discerning the Good in the Letters and Sermons of Augustine*. New York: Oxford University Press, 2016.

Clor, Harry M. "Judicial Statesmanship and Constitutional Interpretation," *South Texas Law Journal* 26, no. 3 (1985): 397–433.

Coats, Jr., John Wendell. *Statesmanship: Six Modern Illustrations of a Modified Ancient Ideal*. Selinsgrove, PA: Susquehanna University Press, 1995.

Colburn, Trevor, ed. *Fame and the Founding Fathers: Essays by Douglass Adair*. New York: W.W. Norton and Co., 1974.

Coleman, Janet, ed. *The Individual in Political Theory and Practice*. New York: Oxford University Press, 1996.

Colville, John. "The Qualities of a Statesman," *Schweizer Monatshefte: Zeitschrift fur Politik, Wirtschaft, Kultur* 59, no. 2 (1979): 1–11.

Connolly, William B. *The Augustinian Imperative: A Reflection on the Politics of Morality*. Lanham, MD: Rowman & Littlefield, 2002.

Constant, Benjamin. *Constant: Political Writings*. Edited and translated by Biancamaria Fontana. New York: Cambridge University Press, 1988.

Conway, Jill. "Jane Addams: An American Heroine," *Daedalus* 93, no. 2 (1964): 761–80.

Cooper, Terry L., ed. *Handbook of Administrative Ethics*. New York: Marcel Dekker, 1994.

Corwin, Edward S. *John Marshall and the Constitution*. New Haven, CT: Yale University Press, 1919.

Cracraft, James. *Two Shining Souls: Jane Addams, Leo Tolstoy, and the Quest for Global Peace*. Lanham, MD: Lexington, 2012.

Craig, Gordon A. *Germany: 1866–1945*. New York: Oxford University Press, 1978.

Croly, Herbert. *The Promise of American Life*. Princeton, NJ: Princeton University Press, 2014.

Crook, J. A., Andrew Lintott, and Elizabeth Rawson, eds. *The Cambridge Ancient History: The Last Age of the Roman Republic, 146–43 B.C.* 3rd ed. New York: Cambridge University Press, 1994.

Cunliffe, Marcus. *In Search of America: Transatlantic Essays, 1951–1990*. Westport, CT: Greenwood Press, 1991.

Dahl, Robert A. *Democracy and Its Critics*. New Haven, CT: Yale University Press, 1989.

Dante, Alighieri. *Purgatory*. Translated by Anthony Esolen. New York: Random House, 2003.

Dawson, Christopher. *Enquiries into Religion and Culture*. Washington, DC: Catholic University of America Press, 2009.

Daynes, Gary and Nicholas V. Longo. "Jane Addams and the Origins of Service-Learning Practice in the United States," *Michigan Journal of Community Service Learning* 11, no. 1 (2004), 5–13.

Deane, Herbert A. *The Political and Social Ideas of Saint Augustine*. New York: Columbia University Press, 1966.

Deegan, Mary Jo. *Jane Addams and the Men of the Chicago School, 1892–1918*. New Brunswick, NJ: Transaction, 1988.

Digeser, Peter. *Our Politics, Our Selves? Liberalism, Identity, and Harm*. Princeton, NJ: Princeton University Press, 1995.

Dodaro, Robert. *Christ and the Just Society in the Thought of Augustine*. Cambridge: Cambridge University Press, 2004.

Dolgon, Corey, Tania D. Mitchell, and Timothy K. Eatman, eds. *The Cambridge Handbook of Service Learning and Community Engagement*. New York: Cambridge University Press, 2017.

Dragstedt, A. "Cato's *Politeuma*," *Agon*, 3 (1969): 69–96.

Duff, Tim. *Plutarch's Lives: Exploring Virtue and Vice*. Oxford: Clarendon Press, 1999.

——. "Models of Education in Plutarch," *Journal of Hellenic Studies* 128 (2008): 1–26.

East, John. "The Political Relevance of St. Augustine," *The Modern Age* 16, no. 2 (1972): 167–81.

Edmunds, Lowell. *Chance and Intelligence in Thucydides*. Cambridge, MA: Harvard University Press, 1975.

Elshtain, Jean Bethke. *Augustine and the Limits of Politics*. Notre Dame, IN: University of Notre Dame Press, 1995.

———. *Real Politics: At the Center of Everyday Life*. Baltimore, MD, Johns Hopkins University Press, 2000.

———. *Jane Addams and the Dream of American Democracy*. New York: Basic Books, 2002.

Emerson, Ralph Waldo. *Ralph Waldo Emerson: Essays and Lectures*. Edited by Joel Porte. New York: Library of America, 1983.

Engberg-Pedersen, Troels, ed. *From Stoicism to Platonism: The Development of Philosophy, 100 BCE–100 CE*. New York: Cambridge University Press, 2017.

Erasmus, Desiderius. *The Education of a Christian Prince*. Edited and translated by Lisa Jardine. New York: Cambridge University Press, 1997.

Farrell, John C. *Beloved Lady: A History of Jane Addams' Ideas on Reform and Peace*. Baltimore, MD: Johns Hopkins University Press, 1967.

Faulkner, Robert K. *The Case for Greatness: Honorable Ambition and Its Critics*. New Haven, CT: Yale University Press, 2007.

Fetter, James T. "The Great Man in Politics: Magnanimity in the History of Western Political Thought." PhD diss., University of Notre Dame, 2012.

Fiedler, Fred. *A Theory of Leadership Effectiveness*. New York: McGraw-Hill, 1967.

Figgis, John. *The Political Aspects of S. Augustine's "City of God."* New York: Longmans, Green, and Co., 1921.

Finer, S. E. *The History of Government: Ancient Monarchies and Empires*. Oxford: Clarendon Press, 1997.

Finlay, John. "The Night of Alcibiades," *The Hudson Review* 47, no. 1 (1994): 57–79.

Fischer, Marilyn, Carol Nackenoff, and Wendy Chmielewski, eds. *Jane Addams and the Practice of Democracy*. Urbana and Chicago: University of Illinois Press, 2009.

Flacelière, Robert. *Daily Life in Greece at the Time of Pericles*. Translated by Peter Green. London: Phoenix Press, 2002.

Flower, Harriet I., ed. *The Cambridge Companion to the Roman Republic*. New York: Cambridge University Press, 2004.

Foley, Michael P. "Thomas Aquinas' Novel Modesty," *History of Political Thought* 25, no. 3 (2004): 402–23.

Foran, William A. "John Marshall as Historian," *American Historical Review* 43, no. 1 (1937): 51–64.

Forde, Steven. *The Ambition to Rule: Alcibiades and the Politics of Imperialism in Thucydides*. Ithaca, NY: Cornell University Press, 1989.

Fornieri, Joseph R. *Abraham Lincoln, Philosopher Statesman*. Carbondale, IL: Southern Illinois University Press, 2014.

Fortin, Ernest L. *Political Idealism and Christianity in the Thought of St. Augustine*. Villanova, PA: Villanova University Press, 1972.

Frank, Jason. *Constituent Moments: Enacting the People in Postrevolutionary America.* Durham, NC: Duke University Press, 2010.

Franklin, Benjamin. *The Autobiography & Other Writings*. New York: Bantam, 1982.

Freeman, Joanne B. "Slander, Poison, Whispers, and Fame: Jefferson's 'Anas' and Political Gossip in the Early Republic," *Journal of the Early Republic* 15, no. 1 (1995): 25–57.

Frisch, Morton J. "John Marshall's Philosophy of Constitutional Republicanism," *Review of Politics* 20, no. 1 (1958): 34–45.

Frisch, Morton J. and Richard G. Stevens. "Introduction." In *American Political Thought: The Philosophic Dimensions of American Statesmanship*, 3–21, edited by Morton J. Frisch and Richard G. Stevens. New York: Scribner's Sons, 1971.

Frost, Bryan-Paul. "An Interpretation of Plutarch's *Cato the Younger*," *History of Political Thought* 18, no. 1 (1997): 1–23.

Fulkerson, Laurel. "Plutarch on the Statesman: Stability, Change, and Regret," *Illinois Classical Studies* 37 (2012): 51–74.

———. *No Regrets: Remorse in Classical Antiquity*. Oxford: Oxford University Press, 2013.

George, Robert Lloyd. *A Modern Plutarch: Comparisons of the Most Influential Modern Statesmen*. New York: Overlook Duckworth, 2016.

George, Robert P. *Making Men Moral: Civil Liberties and Public Morality*. New York: Oxford University Press, 1993.

Geuss, Raymond. *Philosophy and Real Politics*. Princeton, NJ: Princeton University Press, 2008.

Gewirtzman, Doni. "Glory Days: Popular Constitutionalism, Nostalgia, and the True Nature of Constitutional Culture," *Georgetown Law Review* 93 (2005): 897–938.

Gianakaris, C. J. "The Legacy of Plutarch," *Western Humanities Review* 22, no. 3 (1968): 207–13.

Gibbon, Edward. *The History of the Decline and Fall of the Roman Empire*. Edited by David Womersley. 3 vols. Harmondsworth: Penguin, 2005.

Gill, Christopher. *The Structured Self in Hellenistic and Roman Thought*. New York: Oxford University Press, 2006.

Glaeser, Edward L. and Claudia Goldin, eds. *Corruption and Reform: Lessons from America's Economic History*. Chicago, IL: University of Chicago Press, 2006.

Goldwin, Robert A., ed. *Bureaucrats, Policy Analysts, Statesmen: Who Leads?* Washington, DC: American Enterprise Institute Press, 1980.

Goodman, Rob and Jimmy Soni. *Rome's Last Citizen: The Life and Legacy of Cato, Mortal Enemy of Caesar*. New York: St. Martin's Press, 2012.

Goodwin, Doris Kearns. *Leadership in Turbulent Times*. New York: Simon & Schuster, 2018.

Goodwin, William W., ed. *Plutarch's Morals*. 5 vols. Boston, MA: Little, Brown, and Co., 1878.

Grant, Ruth W. *Hypocrisy and Integrity: Machiavelli, Rousseau, and the Ethics of Politics*. Chicago, IL: University of Chicago Press, 1997.

Greenleaf, Robert K. *Servant Leadership: A Journey into the Nature of Legitimate Power and Greatness*. Mahwah, NJ: Paulist Press, 1977.

Greenstein, Fred I. "The Impact of Personality on Politics: An Attempt to Clear Away the Underbrush," *American Political Science Review* 61, no. 3 (1967): 629–41.

———. *Personality and Politics: Problems of Evidence, Inference, and Conceptualization*. Chicago: Markham, 1969.

Gregory, Eric. *Politics and the Order of Love: An Augustinian Ethic of Democratic Citizenship*. Chicago: University of Chicago Press, 2008.

———. "Augustinians and the New Liberalism," *Augustinian Studies* 41, no. 4 (2010): 315–32.

Gribble, David. *Alcibiades and Athens: A Study in Literary Presentation*. Oxford: Clarendon Press, 1999.

Griffin, Miriam. "Philosophy, Cato, and Roman Suicide: II," *Greece & Rome*, 33, no. 2 (1986): 192–202.

Gruen, Erich S. *Culture and National Identity in Republican Rome*. Ithaca, NY: Cornell University Press, 1992.

Gueguen, John A. "Reflections on the Presidency," *Presidential Studies Quarterly* 12, no. 4 (1982): 470–84.

Guerra, Marc. *Christians as Political Animals: Taking the Measure of Modernity and Modern Democracy*. Wilmington, DE: Intercollegiate Studies Institute Books, 2010.

Haberman, Frederick W., ed. *Nobel Lectures: Peace, 1926–1950*. Amsterdam: Elsevier, 1972.

Hall, Gene E. and Shirley M. Hord. *Change in Schools: Facilitating the Process*. Albany, NY: State University of New York Press, 1987.

Hamilton, Alexander, John Jay, and James Madison. *The Federalist*. Edited by George W. Carey and James McClellan. Indianapolis, IN: Liberty Fund, 2001.

Hamington, Maurice. *Embodied Care, Jane Addams, Maurice Merleau-Ponty, and Feminist Ethics*. Urbana: University of Illinois Press, 2004.

——— (ed.). *Feminist Interpretations of Jane Addams*. University Park, PA: Pennsylvania State University Press, 2010.

Hammer, Dean. *Roman Political Thought: From Cicero to Augustine*. New York: Cambridge University Press, 2014.

Hampshire, Stuart, T. M. Scanlon, Bernard Williams, Thomas Nagel, and Ronald Dworkin, eds. *Public and Private Morality*. Cambridge: Cambridge University Press, 1978.

Hanagan, Nora. "Democratizing Responsibility: Jane Addams's Pragmatist Ethics," *Polity* 45, no. 3 (2013): 347–71.

Harkavy, Ira and John Puckett. "Lessons from Hull House for the Contemporary Urban University," *Social Science Review* 68, no. 3 (1994): 299–321.

Harris, Christopher. "Mason Locke Weems's *Life of Washington*: The Making of a Bestseller," *The Southern Literary Journal* 19, no. 2 (1987): 92–101.

Heifetz, Ronald, Alexander Grashow, and Marty Linsky, *The Practice of Adaptive Leadership*. Boston, MA: Harvard Business Press, 2009.

Heifetz, Ronald A. and Donald L. Laurie. "The Work of Leadership," *Harvard Business Review* 75, no. 1 (1997): 124–34.

Held, Virginia. *The Ethics of Care: Personal, Political, and Global*. New York: Oxford University Press, 2005.

——— (ed.). *Justice and Care: Essential Readings in Feminist Ethics*. New York: Routledge, 2018.

Helfer, Ariel. *Socrates and Alcibiades: Plato's Drama of Political Ambition and Philosophy*. Philadelphia: University of Pennsylvania Press, 2017.

Henderson, Christine Dunn and Mark E. Yellin, eds. *Joseph Addison's Cato: A Tragedy and Selected Essays*. Indianapolis, IN: Liberty Fund, 2004.

Hersey, Paul. *The Situational Leader*. New York: Warner, 1985.

Hershbell, Jackson. "Plutarch and Stoicism," *Aufstieg und Niedergang der römischen Welt* II.36, no. 5 (1992): 3336–52.

Heyking, John von. *Augustine and Politics as Longing in the World*. Columbia, MO: University of Missouri Press, 2001.

Heyking, John von and Richard Avramenko, eds. *Friendship & Politics: Essays in Political Thought*. Notre Dame, IN: University of Notre Dame Press, 2008.

Higginbotham, Don, ed. *Reconsiderations on the Revolutionary War: Selected Essays*. Westport, CT: Greenwood Press, 1978.

Hildinger, Erik. *Swords Against the Senate: The Rise of the Roman Army and the Fall of the Republic*. Cambridge, MA: Perseus, 2002.

Hobbes, Thomas. *Leviathan*. Edited by Edwin Curley. Indianapolis, IN: Hackett, 1994.

Hobson, Charles F. "Defining the Office: John Marshall as Chief Justice," *University of Pennsylvania Law Review* 154, no. 6 (2006): 1421–61.

Hogeland, William. *The Whisky Rebellion: George Washington, Alexander Hamilton, and the Frontier Rebels who Challenged America's Newfound Sovereignty*. New York: Simon & Schuster, 2010.

Hollingworth, Miles. *Pilgrim City: St. Augustine of Hippo and His Innovation in Political Thought*. London: T&T Clark International, 2010.

———. *Saint Augustine of Hippo: An Intellectual Biography*. New York: Oxford University Press, 2013.

Holloway, Carson, ed. *Magnanimity and Statesmanship*. Lanham, MD: Rowman & Littlefeld, 2008.

Howard, W. Kenneth. "Must Public Hands be Dirty?" *Journal of Value Inquiry* 11, no. 1 (1977): 29–40.

Hoy, Terry. "The Idea of Prudential Wisdom in Politics," *The Western Political Quarterly* 11, no. 2 (1958): 243–50.

Hoyer, Eric. "Alcibiades' Challenge to Democratic Politics." PhD diss., University of Pennsylvania, 2011.

Hughes-Hallett, Lucy. *Heroes: Saviors, Traitors, and Supermen: A History of Hero Worship*. New York: Knopf, 2004.

Humble, Noreen, ed. *Plutarch's Lives: Parallelism and Purpose*. Swansea: Classical Press of Wales, 2010.

Hume, David. *An Enquiry Concerning the Principles of Morals*. Edited by Tom L. Beauchamp. Oxford: Oxford University Press, 1998.

124 *References*

Hunter, James C. *The World's Most Powerful Leadership Principle: How to Become a Servant Leader*. New York: Random House, 2004.

Inwood, Brad, ed. *The Cambridge Companion to the Stoics*. New York: Cambridge University Press, 2003.

Jackson, Brian and Gregory Clark, eds. *Trained Capacities: John Dewey, Rhetoric, and Democratic Practice*. Columbia, SC: University of South Carolina Press, 2014.

Jacobsohn, Gary J. *Pragmatism, Statesmanship, and the Supreme Court*. Ithaca, NY: Cornell University Press, 1977.

Jaffa, Harry V., ed. *Statesmanship: Essays in Honor of Sir Winston Spencer Churchill*. Durham, NC: Carolina Academic Press, 1981.

Jeffrey, David Lyle. *A Dictionary of Biblical Tradition in English Literature*. Grand Rapids, MI: William B. Eerdmans, 1992.

Jones, Christopher P. *Plutarch and Rome*. Oxford: Clarendon Press, 1971.

Josepheus, Flavius. *Jewish Antiquities*. Translated by William Whiston. Hertfordshire: Wordsworth, 2006.

Kagan, Donald, ed. *Studies in the Greek Historians: In Memory of Adam Parry*. New York: Cambridge University Press, 1975.

Kapust, Daniel J. *Republicanism, Rhetoric, and Roman Political Thought: Sallust, Livy, and Tacitus*. New York: Cambridge University Press, 2011.

Kaufman, Peter. "Augustine, Macedonius, and the Courts," *Augustinian Studies* 34, no. 1 (2003): 67–82.

———. *Incorrectly Political: Augustine and Thomas More*. Notre Dame, IN: University of Notre Dame Press, 2007.

———. "Christian Realism and Augustinian (?) Liberalism," *Journal of Religious Ethics* 38, no. 4 (2010): 699–724.

———. *Augustine's Leaders*. Eugene, OR: Wipf and Stock, 2017.

Kennedy, George A. *The Art of Persuasion in Greece*. Princeton, NJ: Princeton University Press, 1963.

Kloppenberg, James T. *Uncertain Victory: Social Democracy and Progressivism in European and American Thought, 1870–1920*. New York: Oxford University Press, 1986.

———. *The Virtues of Liberalism*. New York: Oxford University Press, 1998.

Knight, Louise W. "Jane Addams and Hull House: Historical Lessons on Nonprofit Leadership," *Nonprofit Management & Leadership* 2, no. 2 (1991): 125–41.

———. *Citizen: Jane Addams and the Struggle for Democracy*. Chicago: University of Chicago Press, 2005.

———. *Jane Addams: Spirit in Action*. New York: W.W. Norton, 2010.

Kraig, Robert Alexander. *Woodrow Wilson and the Lost World of the Oratorical Statesman*. College Station, TX: Texas A&M University Press, 2014.

Kramer, Larry D. "Popular Constitutionalism, circa 2004," *California Law Review* 92, no. 4 (2004): 959–1010.

———. *The People Themselves: Popular Constitutionalism and Judicial Review*. New York: Oxford University Press, 2004.

Lamberton, Robert. *Plutarch*. New Haven, CT: Yale University Press, 2001.

Landy, Marc and Sidney M. Milkis. *Presidential Greatness*. Lawrence: University Press of Kansas, 2000.

Lavere, George J. "The Political Realism of Saint Augustine," *Augustinian Studies* 11 (1980): 135–44.

Lerner, Max. "John Marshall and the Campaign of History," *Columbia Law Review* 39, no. 3 (1939): 396–431.

Lerner, Ralph. *Naïve Readings: Reveilles Political and Philosophic*. Chicago: University of Chicago Press, 2016.

Lerner, Ralph and Muhsin Mahdi, eds. *Medieval Political Philosophy: A Sourcebook*. New York: Free Press, 1963.

Levine, Daniel. *Jane Addams and the Liberal Tradition*. Madison: State Historical Society of Wisconsin, 1971.

Liebert, Hugh. *Plutarch's Politics: Between City and Empire*. New York: Cambridge University Press, 2016.

Liebeschuetz, J.H.W.G., ed. *Ambrose of Milan: Political Letters and Speeches*. Liverpool: Liverpool University Press, 2005.

Linn, James Weber. *Jane Addams: A Biography*. New York: Appleton-Century, 1935.

Lintott, Andrew. *The Constitution of the Roman Republic*. New York: Oxford University Press, 1999.

Lissak, Rivka Shpak. *Pluralism and Progressives: Hull House and the New Immigrants, 1890–1919*. Chicago: University of Chicago Press, 1989.

Litto, Frederic M. "Addison's Cato in the Colonies," *William and Mary Quarterly* 23, no. 3 (1966): 431–49.

Loewenberg, Bert James. *American History in American Thought: Christopher Columbus to Henry Adams*. New York: Simon and Schuster, 1972.

Longmore, Paul K. *The Invention of George Washington*. Berkeley, CA: University of California Press, 1988.

Longo, Nicholas V. *Why Community Matters: Connecting Education with Civic Life*. Albany, NY: State University of New York Press, 2007.

Lorde, Carnes. *The Modern Prince: What Leaders Need to Know Now*. New Haven, CT: Yale University Press, 2003.

Lundestad, Geir. *The Rise and Decline of the American "Empire": Power and its Limits in Comparative Perspective*. New York: Oxford University Press, 2012.

Lutz, Tom. *American Nervousness, 1903: An Anecdotal History*. Ithaca, NY: Cornell University Press, 1991.

Lynch, Christopher and Jonathan Marks, eds. *Principle and Prudence in Western Political Thought*. Albany, NY: State University of New York Press, 2016.

Lyotard, Jean-François. *The Postmodern Condition*. Minneapolis, MN: University of Minnesota Press, 1984.

Machiavelli, Niccolò. *The Prince*. Translated by Harvey C. Mansfield. 2nd ed. Chicago: University of Chicago Press, 1998.

MacQueen, D. J. "The Origin and Dynamics of Society and the State According to St. Augustine," *Augustinian Studies* 4 (1973): 73–101.

Macurdy, Grace Harriet. "Alcibiades: A Study of a Greek Statesman from the Pages of His Contemporaries," *The Classical Weekly* 2, no. 18 (1909): 138–40.

Magruder, Allan B. *John Marshall: American Statesman*. Boston and New York: Houghton, Mifflin, and Co., 1885.

Mahoney, Daniel J. *De Gaulle: Statesmanship, Grandeur, and Modern Democracy*. New York: Routledge, 2017.

Mandeville, Bernard. *The Fable of the Bees, or Private Vices, Publick Benefits*. Edited by F. B. Kaye. Indianapolis, IN: Liberty Fund, 1988.

Manent, Pierre. *Metamorphoses of the City: On the Western Dynamic*. Translated by Marc LePain. Cambridge, MA: Harvard University Press, 2013.

Markus, Robert A. *Saeculum: History and Society in the Theology of St Augustine*. 2nd ed. New York and Cambridge: Cambridge University Press, 1989.

Marshall, John. *John Marshall: Writings*. Edited by Charles F. Hobson. New York: Penguin, 2010.

———. *The Life of George Washington: Special Edition for Schools*. Edited by Robert Faulkner and Paul Carrese. Indianapolis, IN: Liberty Fund, 2000.

Martin, Francis X and John A. Richmond, eds. *From Augustine to Eriugena: Essays on Neoplatonism and Christianity in Honor of John O'Meara*. Washington, DC: Catholic University of America Press, 1991.

Martin, Hubert M. "Moral Failure Without Vice in Plutarch's Athenian *Lives*," *Ploutarchos* 12, no. 1 (1995): 13–18.

Martin, Jr., H. M. "Plutarch, Plato, and Eros," *Classical Bulletin* 60, no. 4 (1984): 82–88.

Martin, Rex. "The Two Cities in Augustine's Political Philosophy," *Journal of the History of Ideas* 33, no. 2 (1972): 195–216.

Martin, Thomas F. *Our Restless Heart: The Augustinian Tradition.* Maryknoll, NY: Orbis, 2003.

May, James M., ed. *Brill's Companion to Cicero: Oratory and Rhetoric.* Leiden: Brill, 2002.

McClay, Wilfred M. "Response to Papers by Major, Baldwin, and Bailey: Democratic Statesmanship and the Blue Guitar," *Perspectives on Political Science* 41, no. 2 (2012): 90–92.

McDermott, William C. "Cato the Younger: *loquax* or *eloquens?*" *Classical Bulletin* 46 (1970): 65–75.

McInerney, Joseph J. *The Greatness of Humility: St Augustine on Moral Excellence.* Cambridge: James Clarke & Co., 2016.

McNamara, Peter, ed. *The Noblest Minds: Fame, Honor, and the American Founding.* Lanham, MD: Rowman & Littlefield, 1999.

Meens, Rob. *Penance in Medieval Europe, 600–1200.* Cambridge: Cambridge University Press, 2014.

Milbank, John. *Theology and Social Theory: Beyond Secular Reason.* 2nd ed. Malden, MA: Wiley-Blackwell, 2006.

Millar, Fergus. *The Roman Republic in Political Thought.* Lebanon, NH: University Press of New England, 2002.

Miller, David, ed. *Liberty.* Oxford: Oxford University Press, 1991.

Miller, Perry, ed. *The American Puritans: Their Prose and Poetry.* New York: Columbia University Press, 1956.

Miroff, Bruce. "Alexander Hamilton: The Aristocrat as Visionary," *International Political Science Review* 9, no. 1 (1988): 43–54.

Mommsen, Theodor E. "St. Augustine and the Christian Idea of Progress: The Background of the City of God," *Journal of the History of Ideas* 12, no. 3 (1951): 346–74.

Montaigne, Michel de. *The Complete Essays.* Translated by E. A. Screech. New York: Penguin, 1993.

Moore, Wayne D. *Constitutional Rights and Powers of the People.* Princeton, NJ: Princeton University Press, 1996.

Morgan, Edmund S. *Inventing the People: The Rise of Popular Sovereignty in England and America.* New York: Norton, 1988.

Morrison, Jeffry H. *The Political Philosophy of George Washington.* Baltimore, MD: Johns Hopkins University Press, 2009.

Morton, Keith and John Saltmarsh. "Addams, Day, and Dewey: The Emergence of Community Service in American Culture," *Michigan Journal of Community Service Learning* 4, no. 1 (1997): 137–49.

Moskop, Wynne Walker. "Jane Addams and Possibilities for Transnational Political Friendship," *American Political Thought* 7, no. 3 (2018): 400–31.

Mouritsen, Henrik. *Politics in the Roman Republic.* New York: Cambridge University Press, 2017.

Mughan, Anthony and S. C. Patterson, eds. *Political Leadership in Democratic Societies.* Chicago: Nelson-Hall, 1992.

Mumford, Michael D. and Judy R. Van Doom. "The Leadership of Pragmatism: Reconsidering Franklin in the Age of Charisma," *Leadership Quarterly* 12, no. 3 (2001): 279–309.

Mumford, Michael D., Jazmine Espejo, Samuel T. Hunter, Katrina Bedell-Avers, Dawn L. Eubanks, and Shane Connelly. "The Sources of Leader Violence: A Comparison of Ideological and Non-ideological Leaders," *Leadership Quarterly* 18, no. 3 (2007): 217–35.

Murphy, Cullen. *Are We Rome? The Fall of an Empire and the Fate of America.* New York: Houghton Mifflin Harcourt, 2007.

Nahmod, Sheldom. "Constitutional Education for *The People Themselves*," *Chicago-Kent Law Review* 81, no. 3 (2006): 1091–1107.

Nelson, Haviland. "Cato the Younger as a Stoic Orator," *The Classical Weekly* 44, no. 5 (1950): 65–69.

Nettels, Curtis. "The Washington Theme in American History," *Proceedings of the Massachusetts Historical Society* 68 (1952): 171–98.

Neuhaus, Richard John, ed. *Augustine Today.* Grand Rapids, MI: William B. Eerdmans, 1993.

Newell, Terry. *Statesmanship, Character, and Leadership in America*. New York: Palgrave Macmillan, 2012.

Newmyer, R. Kent. *John Marshall and the Heroic Age of the Supreme Court*. Baton Rouge, LA: Louisiana State University Press, 2007.

Nicgorski, Walter. "Cicero's Focus: From the Best Regime to the Model Statesman," *Political Theory* 19, no. 2 (1991): 230–51.

Niebuhr, Reinhold. *Christian Realism and Political Problems: Essays on Political, Social, Ethical, and Theological Problems*. Fairfield, NJ: Augustus M. Kelley Publishers, 1977.

Nietzsche, Friedrich. *Beyond Good and Evil: Prelude to a Philosophy of the Future*. Translated by Helen Zimmern. New York: Macmillan, 1907.

———. *Untimely Meditations*. Translated by R. J. Hollingdale. New York: Cambridge University Press, 1997.

Norton, David L. *Democracy and Moral Development: A Politics of Virtue*. Berkeley and Los Angeles: University of California Press, 1991.

Nozick, Robert. *Anarchy, State, and Utopia*. New York: Basic Books, 1974.

Nussbaum, Martha C. *The Fragility of Goodness: Luck and Ethics in Greek Tragedy and Philosophy*. Revised edition. New York: Cambridge University Press, 2001.

O'Daly, Gerard. *Augustine's City of God: A Reader's Guide*. Oxford: Clarendon, 1999.

O'Donnell, James J. *Augustine: A New Biography*. New York: Ecco, 2005.

O'Donovan, Oliver. *The Problem of Self-Love in St. Augustine*. Eugene, OR: Wipf and Stock, 1980.

———. "Augustine's *City of God* XIX and Western Political Thought," *Dionysius* 11 (1987): 89–110.

O'Gorman, Ned. "Stoic Rhetoric: Prospects of a Problematic," *Advances in the History of Rhetoric* 14, no. 1 (2011): 1–13.

Oman, Charles. *Seven Roman Statesmen of the Late Republic*. London: Edward Arnold, 1910.

Opdycke, Sandra. *Jane Addams and Her Vision for America*. Upper Saddle River, NJ: Prentice Hall, 2012.

Oslington, Paul, ed. *Adam Smith as Theologian*. New York: Routledge, 2011.

Ostwald, Martin. *From Popular Sovereignty to the Sovereignty of Law: Law, Society, and Politics in Fifth-Century Athens*. Berkeley, CA: University of California Press, 1986.

Overeem, Patrick and Femke E. Bakker. "Statesmanship Beyond the Modern State," *Perspectives on Political Science* (2016): 1–10.

Padover, Saul K. "The Political Ideas of John Marshall," *Social Research* 26, no. 1 (1959): 47–70.

Paffenroth, Kim and Kevin L. Hughes, eds. *Augustine and Liberal Education*. Burlington, VT: Ashgate, 2000.

Palmer, David R. *The Way of the Fox: American Strategy in the War for America*. Westport, CT: Greenwood Press, 1975.

Palmer, Michael. *Love of Glory and the Common Good: Aspects of the Political Thought of Thucydides*. Lanham, MD: Rowman & Littlefield, 1992.

Paolucci, Henry, ed. *The Political Writings of St. Augustine*. Washington, DC: Regnery, 1962.

Parker, Richard D. *"Here, the People Rule": A Constitutional Populist Manifesto*. Cambridge, MA: Harvard University Press, 1994.

Parrish, John M. *Paradoxes of Political Ethics: From Dirty Hands to the Invisible Hand*. Cambridge: Cambridge University Press, 2007.

Paterculus, Marcus Velleius. *Res Gestae Divi Augusti*. Translated by Frederick W. Shipley. London and New York: William Heinemann, 1924.

Paul, Joel Richard. *Without Precedent: Chief Justice John Marshall and His Times*. New York: Random House, 2018.

Pelling, Christopher. *Plutarch and History: Eighteen Studies*. London: Gerald Duckworth & Co., 2002.

———. "Greek Lives," *Ploutarchos* 2 (2004/2005): 71–88.

Perrin, Andrew J. *Citizen Speak: The Democratic Imagination in American Life*. Chicago: University of Chicago Press, 2006.

Plato. *Statesman*. Translated by Christopher J. Rowe. Indianapolis, IN: Hackett, 1999.

————. *Symposium*. Translated by M. C. Howatson. New York: Cambridge University Press, 2008.

————. *The Republic of Plato*. Translated by Allan Bloom. 3rd ed. Philadelphia: Perseus, 2016.

Plutarch. *Plutarch's Lives*. Translated by John Dryden and revised by Arthur Hugh Clough. 5 vols. Boston: Little, Brown, and Co., 1906.

Pocock, J. G. A. *The Machiavellian Moment: Florentine Political Thought and the Atlantic Republican Tradition*. Princeton, NJ: Princeton University Press, 1975.

Prasad, Anirudh. "Imprints of Marshallian Judicial Statesmanship," *Journal of Indian Law Institute* 22, no. 2 (1980): 240–58.

Primoratz, Igor, ed. *Politics and Morality*. New York: Palgrave Macmillan, 2007.

Raeder, Linda C. "Augustine and the Case for Limited Government," *Humanitas* 16, no. 2 (2003): 94–106.

Rawls, John. *Political Liberalism*. Expanded edition. New York: Columbia University Press, 2005.

————. *The Law of Peoples*. Cambridge, MA: Harvard University Press, 2003.

Ray, Clyde H. *John Marshall's Constitutionalism*. Albany, NY: State University of New York Press, 2019.

Rees, James and Stephen J. Spignesi. *George Washington's Leadership Lessons: What the Father of Our Country Can Teach Us About Effective Leadership and Character*. Hoboken, NJ: Wiley, 2007.

Rehfeld, Andrew. "Offensive Political Theory," *Perspectives on Politics* 8, no. 2 (2010): 465–86.

Reinhold, Meyer. *Classica Americana: The Greek and Roman Heritage in the United States*. Detroit, MI: Wayne State University Press, 1984.

Reno, R. R. "Getting Augustine Wrong," *First Things* 272 (2017): 3–4.

Reydams-Schils, Gretchen. *The Roman Stoics: Self, Responsibility, and Affection*. Chicago: University of Chicago Press, 2005.

Ridgely, C. V. "The Life of George Washington, by John Marshall," *Indiana Law Journal* 6, no. 4 (1931): 277–88.

Rist, John M. "Plutarch's *Amatorius*: A Commentary on Plato's Theories of Love," *Classical Quarterly* 51, no. 2 (2001): 557–75.

Romance, Joseph and Neil Reimer, eds. *Democracy and Excellence: Concord or Conflict?* Westport, CT: Praeger, 2005.

Roosevelt, Franklin Delano. *The Public Papers and Addresses of Franklin D. Roosevelt*. Edited by Samuel I. Rosenman. 13 vols. New York: Macmillan, 1938–50.

Roosevelt, Theodore. *The Strenuous Life: Essays and Addresses*. New York: Century, 1906.

Rorty, Richard. *Contingency, Irony, and Solidarity*. New York: Cambridge University Press, 1989.

Rorty, Richard, J. B. Schneewind, and Quentin Skinner, eds. *Philosophy in History: Essays on the Historiography of Philosophy*. Cambridge: Cambridge University Press, 1984.

Rosenau, James, ed. *In Search of Global Patterns*. New York: Free Press, 1976.

Rousseau, Jean-Jacques. *The Collected Writings of Rousseau*. Translated by Judith R. Bush, Roger D. Masters, and Christopher Kelly. 14 vols. Hanover, NH: University Press of New England, 1990–2010.

Rowe, Christopher and Malcolm Schofield, eds. *The Cambridge History of Greek and Roman Political Thought*. Cambridge: Cambridge University Press, 2000.

Ruderman, Richard S. "Democracy and the Problem of Statesmanship," *Review of Politics* 59, no. 4 (1997): 759–87.

————. "Statesmanship Reconsidered," *Perspectives on Political Science* 41, no. 2 (2012): 86–89.

Russell, Donald A. "On Reading Plutarch's *Lives*," *Greece & Rome* 13, no. 2 (1966): 139–54.

————. *Plutarch*. London: Longwood, 1973.

————. "Plutarch and the Antique Hero," *The Yearbook of English Studies* 12 (1982), 24–34: 34.

Ryn, Claes. "Remarks at the Center for the Study of Statesmanship Launch Event." September 13, 2017. Washington, DC.

Saïd, Suzanne. "Plutarch's Deterrent Lives: Lessons in Statesmanship." PhD diss., Columbia University, 2011.

Salisbury, John of. *Policraticus*. Edited and translated by Cary J. Nederman. New York: Cambridge University Press, 1990.

Sallust. *The Jugurthine War/The Conspiracy of Cataline*. Translated by S. A. Handford. New York: Penguin, 1963.

Sanders, Ed, Chiara Thumiger, Chris Carey, and Nick J. Lowe, eds. *Erôs in Ancient Greece*. Oxford: Oxford University Press, 2013.

Sartre, Jean-Paul. *No Exit and Three Other Plays*. Translated by Lionel Abel. New York: Vintage, 1989.

Schaar, John H. *Legitimacy in the Modern State*. New Brunswick, NJ: Transaction Publishers, 1989.

Schaff, Philip, ed. *A Select Library of Nicene and Post-Nicene Fathers of the Christian Church*. 14 vols. Grand Rapids, MI: Wm. B. Eerdman's, 1956.

Schall, James V. *The Politics of Heaven and Hell*. Lanham, MD: University Press of America, 1984.

Schlesinger, Joseph. *Ambition and Politics: Political Careers in the United States*. Chicago, IL: Rand McNally and Co., 1966.

Scott, John T., ed. *Jean-Jacques Rousseau: Critical Assessments of Leading Political Philosophers*. 4 vols. New York: Routledge, 2006.

Sears, Matthew A. *Athens, Thrace, and the Shaping of Athenian Leadership*. New York: Cambridge University Press, 2013.

Seigfried, Charlene Haddock. *Feminism and Pragmatism: Reweaving the Social Fabric*. Chicago: University of Chicago Press, 1996.

Shakespeare, William. *Julius Caesar*. Ed. Louis B. Wright. New York: Washington Square Press, 1969.

Shapiro, Ian and Judith Wagner Decew, eds. *Theory and Practice: NOMOS XXXVII*. New York: New York University Press, 1995.

Shevory, Thomas C., ed. *John Marshall's Achievement: Law, Politics, and Constitutional Interpretations*. New York: Greenwood Press, 1989.

Shields, Patricia M. "Building the Fabric of Peace: Jane Addams and Peaceweaving," *Global Virtue Ethics Review* 7, no. 3 (2016): 21–33.

Siegel, Neil S. "The Virtue of Judicial Statesmanship," *Texas Law Review* 86, no. 5 (2008): 959–1032.

Singer, Peter, ed. *A Companion to Ethics*. Oxford: Wiley-Blackwell, 1993.

Skinner, Quentin. *The Foundations of Modern Political Thought: The Renaissance*. Cambridge: Cambridge University Press, 1978.

Sleat, Matt, ed. *Politics Recovered: Realist Thought in Theory and Practice*. New York: Columbia University Press, 2018.

Slote, Michael. *The Ethics of Care and Empathy*. New York: Routledge, 2007.

Smil, Vaclav. *Why America Is Not a New Rome*. Cambridge, MA: MIT Press, 2010.

Smith, Jean Edward. *John Marshall: Definer of a Nation*. New York: Henry Holt and Co., 1996.

Smith, William Raymond. *History as Argument: Three Patriot Historians of the American Revolution*. The Hague: Mouton & Co., 1966.

Sparks, Jared, ed. *The Writings of George Washington: Life of Washington*. New York: Harper & Brothers, 1852.

Spears, Larry C. and Michele Lawrence, eds. *Focus on Leadership: Servant-Leadership for the Twenty-First Century*. New York: John Wiley & Sons, 2002.

Stadter, Philip. *Plutarch and His Roman Readers*. New York: Oxford University Press, 2014.

Stengel, Richard. *Mandela's Way: Lessons for an Uncertain Age*. New York: Random House, 2018.

Stern, Rex. "The First Eloquent Stoic: Cicero on Cato the Younger," *The Classical Journal* 101, no. 1 (2005): 37–49.

Stockt, L. Van Der, ed. *Rhetorical Theory and Practice in Plutarch*. Louvain: Peeters, 2000.

Storing, Herbert. *Toward a More Perfect Union: Writings of Herbert J. Storing*. Edited by Joseph M. Bessette. Washington, DC: American Enterprise Institute Press, 1995.

Straumann, Benjamin. *Crisis and Constitutionalism: Roman Political Thought from the Fall of the Republic to the Age of Revolution*. New York: Oxford University Press, 2016.

Strauss, Barry. *Fathers and Sons in Athens: Ideology and Society in the Era of the Peloponnesian War*. Princeton, NJ: Princeton University Press, 1993.

Strauss, Barry. *The Spartacus War*. New York: Simon & Schuster, 2009.

Strauss, Leo. *The City and Man*. Chicago: University of Chicago Press, 1964.

Strauss, Leo and Joseph Cropsey, eds. *History of Political Philosophy*. 3rd ed. Chicago: University of Chicago Press, 1987.

Stokes, S. V. "M. Porcius Cato Uticensis," *Ancient Society* 16 (1986): 19–51.

Stump, Eleonore and Norman Kretzmann, eds. *The Cambridge Companion to Augustine*. Cambridge: Cambridge University Press, 2001.

Sunstein, Cass R. *The Partial Constitution*. Cambridge, MA: Harvard University Press, 1998.

———. *Going to Extremes: How Like Minds Unite and Divide*. New York: Oxford University Press, 2009.

Swain, Simon. "Character Change in Plutarch," *Phoenix* 43, no. 1 (1989): 62–8.

———. "Plutarch, Hadrian, and Delphi," *Historia* 40 (1991): 318–30.

———. *Hellenism and Empire: Language, Classicism, and Power in the Greek World, AD 50 250*. Oxford: Clarendon Press, 1996.

Tatum, W. Jeffrey. "The Regal Image in Plutarch's *Lives*," *The Journal of Hellenic Studies* 116 (1996): 135–51.

Taylor, Lily Ross. *Party Politics in the Age of Caesar*. Berkeley, CA: University of California Press, 1949.

Thayer, Kate. "Hull House closing Friday," *The Chicago Tribune*, January 25, 2012. https://www.chicagotribune.com/news/ct-xpm-2012-01-25-ct-met-hull-house-20120126-story.html.

Thomas, George. *The Founders and the Idea of a National University: Constituting the American Mind*. New York: Cambridge University Press, 2015.

Thompson, Dennis F. *Political Ethics and Public Office*. Cambridge, MA: Harvard University Press, 1987.

Thornton, John F. and Susan B. Varenne, eds. *Late Have I Loved Thee: Selected Writings of Saint Augustine on Love*. New York: Random House, 2006.

Thornton, Margaret. "Plutarch and Athenian Democracy," *Ancient Society* 1, no. 4 (1971): 3–22.

Thucydides. *The Peloponnesian War*. Translated by Thomas Hobbes. Chicago: University of Chicago Press, 1989.

Tims, Margaret. *Jane Addams of Hull-House, 1860–1935*. London: George Allen & Unwin, 1961.

Tocqueville, Alexis de. *Democracy in America*. Translated by George Lawrence. New York: Perennial Classics, 2000.

Tronto, Joan. *Moral Boundaries: A Political Argument for an Ethic of Care*. New York: Routledge, 1993.

Tulis, Jeffrey K. and Stephen Macedo, eds. *The Limits of Constitutional Democracy*. Princeton, NJ: Princeton University Press, 2010.

Tushnet, Mark. *Taking the Constitution Away from the Courts*. Princeton, NJ: Princeton University Press, 1999.

Usher, Stephen. "Alcibiades and the Lost Empire," *History Today* 21, no. 2 (1971): 116–22.

Verdegem, Simon. *Plutarch's Life of Alcibiades: Story, Text and Moralism*. Leuven: Leuven University Press, 2010.

Vessey, Mark, ed. *A Companion to Augustine*. Malden, MA: Wiley-Blackwell, 2012.

Vessey, Mark, Karla Pollmann, and Allan D. Fitzgerald, eds. *History, Apocalypse and the Secular Imagination*. Bowling Green, OH: Bowling Green State University Press, 1999.

Waldron, Jeremy. *Law and Disagreement*. New York: Oxford University Press, 1999.

———. *Political Political Theory: Essays on Institutions*. Cambridge, MA: Harvard University Press, 2016.

Walzer, Michael. "Political Action: The Problem of Dirty Hands," *Philosophy & Public Affairs* 2, no. 2 (1973): 160–80.

———. *Just and Unjust Wars: A Moral Argument with Historical Illustrations*. 5th edition. New York: Basic Books, 2015.

Ward, Ann and Lee Ward, eds. *Natural Right and Political Philosophy: Essays in Honor of Catherine Zuckert and Michael Zuckert*. Notre Dame, IN: University of Notre Dame Press, 2013.

Weaver, David R. "Leadership, Locke, and The Federalist," *American Journal of Political Science* 41, no. 2 (1997): 420–46.

Weber, Max. *From Max Weber: Essays in Sociology*. Translated by Hans Heinrich Gerth and C. Wright Mills. New York: Oxford University Press, 1977.

———. *The Vocation Lectures: Science as a Vocation, Politics as a Vocation*. Edited by Tracy B. Strong, David Owen, and Rodney Livingstone. Indianapolis, IN: Hackett, 2004.

Weiner, Greg. *American Burke: The Uncommon Liberalism of Daniel Patrick Moynihan*. Lawrence, KS: University Press of Kansas, 2016.

Weithman, Paul J. "Augustine and Aquinas on Original Sin and the Function of Political Authority," *Journal of the History of Philosophy* 30, no. 3 (1992): 353–76.

White, Michael J. "Pluralism and Secularism in the Political Order," *University of Dayton Review* 22, no. 3 (1994): 137–53.

Will, George F. *Statecraft as Soulcraft: What Government Does*. New York: Simon & Schuster, 1983.

Wills, Garry. *Confessions of a Conservative*. Garden City, NY: Doubleday, 1979.

———. *Cincinnatus: George Washington and the Enlightenment*. Garden City, NY: Doubleday, 1984.

———. *Saint Augustine*. New York: Penguin, 1999.

Winkelman, Joel. "A Working Democracy: Jane Addams on the Meaning of Work," *Review of Politics* 75, no. 3 (2013): 357–82.

Wolin, Sheldon S. *Politics and Vision: Continuity and Innovation in Western Political Thought*. Boston: Little, Brown, and Company, 1960.

Wolloch, Nathaniel. "Cato the Younger in the Enlightenment," *Modern Philology* 106, no. 1 (2008): 60–82.

Woo, B. Hoon. "Pilgrim's Progress in Society: Augustine's Political Thought in *The City of God*," *Political Theology* 16, no. 5 (2015): 421–41.

Wood, Gordon S. *Empire of Liberty: A History of the Early Republic, 1789–1815*. New York: Oxford, 2009.

Wren, J. Thomas, ed. *The Leader's Companion: Insights on Leadership Through the Ages*. New York: Free Press, 1995.

Wright, Esmond, ed. *The Fire of Liberty*. London: Folio Society, 1983.

Wyke, Maria. *Caesar in the USA*. Oakland, CA: University of California Press, 2012.

Yukl, Gary. "How Leaders Influence Organizational Effectiveness," *The Leadership Quarterly* 19, no. 6 (2008): 708–22.

Yukl, Gary and Ribina Mahsud, "Why Flexible and Adaptive Leadership is Essential," *Consulting Psychology Journal: Practice and Research* 62, no. 2 (2010): 81–93.

Zadorojnyi, Alexei V. "Cato's Suicide in Plutarch," *The Classical Quarterly* 57, no. 1 (2007): 216–30.

Index

About the Author

Clyde Ray is a scholar of political theory, constitutional law, and American politics. His previous book, *John Marshall's Constitutionalism*, was published by State University of New York Press in 2019. He earned his PhD in political science from the University of North Carolina, Chapel Hill. He and his wife, Gladys, have two sons and reside in Asheville, North Carolina.